**1993
EDITION**

THE

OFFICIAL

BASEBALL

ATLAS

A SPORTS
TRAVEL
GUIDE

RAND McNALLY

Photo Credits

Cover: Brian Drake/Sports Chrome West and Ed Nagel.

HistoMap: Page 144 *Cartwright, Card* National Baseball Library, Cooperstown, NY, *Memorabilia* Susan J. Friedman; 145 *1869 Reds, Cummings, Hulbert* National Baseball Library; 146 *Kelly, Anson* National Baseball Library, *Bottle* Susan J. Friedman; 147 *Keefe, Young, Wagner, Duffy* National Baseball Library, *Spalding Ad* Susan J. Friedman; 148 *Lajoie, Mathewson, Evans, Cubs* National Baseball Library, *Glove* Susan J. Friedman; 149 *Johnson, Cobb, Fenwick* National Baseball Library; 150 *Gehrig, Ruth, Bell* National Baseball Library; 151 *Dean, VanderMeer, Foxx, Gehrig, Hartnett* National Baseball Library; 152 *Doby, Williams, Musial, Robinson, Kamenshek* National Baseball Library; 153 *Berra, Mays, Spahn, Banks* National Baseball Library; 154 *Mantle, Clemente* National Baseball Library, *Alou Brothers* Associated Press Photo; 155 *Bench* UPI, *Aaron* National Baseball Library; 156 *Brett, Jenkins* National Baseball Library; *Hershiser* TV Sports Mailbag, *Ryan* UPI.

Photos of baseball memorabilia and equipment throughout, unless otherwise noted: Susan J. Friedman.

"Take Me Out to the Ballgame" Words by Jack Norworth, Music by Albert Von Tilzer, copyright 1987 Hal Leonard Publishing Corporation. International Copyright Secured. All Rights Reserved. Used with permission.

Appreciation

Special thanks to Jeff Szynal, manager White Sox Hall of Fame, for the use of the memorabilia and equipment for photography.

Contents

Major League Stadiums, Teams, & Cities

Information on Major League stadiums and teams includes a history of each park; stadium seating diagrams; directions; parking, public transportation and ticket information; and team statistics. Information on Major League host cities includes local sports-activity spots, restaurants, accommodations, and major attractions.

Stadium & Vicinity Maps

HistoMap of Baseball

Baseball & Travel

Team Schedules

Map Legend

🛡90	National Interstate Highways
(6)	U.S. Highways
[2]	State and Provincial Highways
◄ ►	One-Way Streets
	Parks
—	Subway Stops

A tlanta-Fulton County Stadium will never be the same after the 1991 season.

The 52,000-seat stadium is home to the Atlanta Braves, whose Cinderella climb from last place in 1990 to the National League Championship and a trip to the World Series in 1991, is an inspiration to fans everywhere. Fan support helped lift the Braves to dazzling heights and a chance at their first World Championship since 1957, when the franchise played in Milwaukee.

Atlanta's success showcased the determination of both the team and the enthusiastic fans who rocked the three-tiered stadium, built in 1965. Not since Hammerin' Hank Aaron belted his 715th home run here on April 8, 1974, had the stadium hosted such excitement.

Knuckleballer Phil Niekro hurled a no-hitter here in 1973, and Braves pitchers Larry McWilliams and Gene Garber combined to stop Pete Rose's hitting streak at 44 games in 1978.

But ask someone about 1991. And listen to them start cheering.

Atlanta Braves

Atlanta C & VB

Atlanta-Fulton County Stadium.

■ Dugout & Club Levels
■ Field Level
□ Lower Pavilion
■ Upper Level
■ General Admission

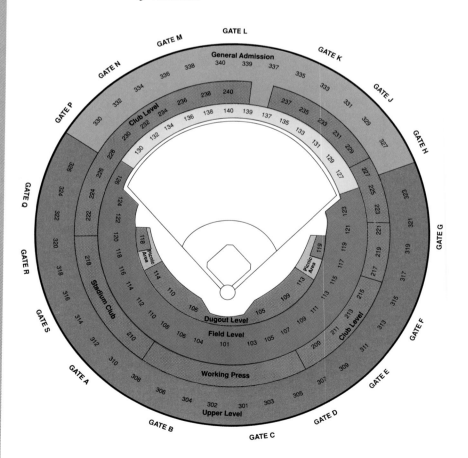

Purchasing Tickets

By mail:
Atlanta-Fulton County Stadium
Ticket Office
P.O. Box 4064
Atlanta, GA 30302
Include the game dates desired,
number of tickets, price,
and $3 handling charge.

In person:
Advance Ticket Office
Gate G on the stadium's south side
521 Capitol Ave. S.W.
Ticket Office hours: Monday - Saturday,
8:30 a.m. - 5:30 p.m.; Sunday, 1 p.m. - 5 p.m.
and until the seventh inning on game days.

By phone:
TicketMaster
800/326-4000
TicketMaster accepts American Express, Visa, and
MasterCard. Phone orders are subject to convenience
charge.

Directions to the Stadium

- I-20 Westbound: Take Exit #24 (Capitol Avenue).
  Turn left onto Capitol. Stadium is on right.

- I-20 Eastbound: Take Exit #22 (Windsor Street-
  Stadium). Turn right on Windsor; left on Fulton.
  Stadium ahead on the right.

- I-75/85 Northbound: Take Exit #90 (Georgia Avenue-
  Stadium). Turn left at stop sign on Washington, turn
  right on Georgia. Stadium on the left.

- I-75/85 Southbound: Take Exit #91 (Fulton Street-
  Stadium). Turn left on Fulton. Stadium is on right.

Public Transportation

Shuttle bus service to the stadium is provided by
MARTA (Metropolitan Atlanta Rapid Transit Authority).
For information, call 404/848-3456.

Parking

Parking is available in lots operated by the Stadium
Authority on Capitol Avenue and on both sides of
Georgia Avenue.

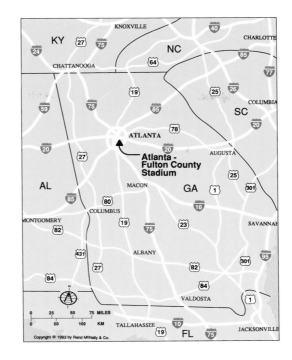

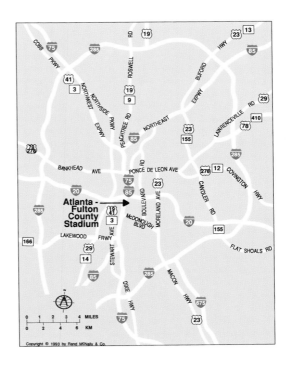

Profile

Team Address
Atlanta Braves
Atlanta-Fulton County Stadium
521 Capitol Ave. S.W.
Atlanta, GA 30302
404/522-7630

Franchise History
Boston Braves 1876 - 1952
Milwaukee Braves 1953 - 1965
Atlanta Braves 1966 -

World Series Titles
1914 vs. Philadelphia Athletics
1957 vs. New York Yankees

National League Pennants
1877, 1878, 1883, 1891, 1892, 1893,
1897, 1898, 1914, 1948, 1957, 1958,
1991, 1992

West Division Titles
1969, 1982, 1991, 1992

Hall of Fame Inductees
Babe Ruth, 1936
George Wright, 1937
Cy Young, 1937
Charles Radbourn, 1939
George Sisler, 1939
Rogers Hornsby, 1942
Dan Brouthers, 1945
James J. Collins, 1945
Hugh Duffy, 1945
Mike "King" Kelly, 1945
Jim O'Rourke 1945
Johnny Evers, 1946
Thomas F. McCarthy, 1946
Ed Walsh, 1946
Kid Nichols, 1949
Paul Waner, 1952
Al Simmons, 1953
Harry Wright, 1953
Rabbit Maranville, 1954
Billy Hamilton, 1961
John Clarkson, 1963
Burleigh Grimes, 1964
Bill McKechnie, 1962
Casey Stengel, 1966
Lloyd Waner, 1967
Joe "Ducky" Medwick, 1968
Dave Bancroft, 1971
Joe Kelley, 1971
Rube Marquard, 1971
Warren Spahn, 1973
Earl Averill, 1975
Billy Herman, 1975
Al Lopez, 1977
Eddie Mathews, 1978
Henry Aaron, 1982
Enos Slaughter,1985
Hoyt Wilhelm, 1985
Ernie Lombardi, 1986
Red Schoendienst, 1989
Gaylord Perry, 1991

Award Winners
Cy Young Award
Warren Spahn, 1957
Tom Glavine, 1991

Most Valuable Player
Bob Elliott, 1947
Henry Aaron, 1957
Dale Murphy, 1982, 1983
Terry Pendleton, 1991

Rookie of the Year
Alvin Dark, 1948
Samuel Jethroe, 1950
Earl Williams, 1971
Bob Horner, 1978
Dave Justice, 1990

Retired Uniform Numbers
21 Warren Spahn
35 Phil Niekro
41 Eddie Mathews
44 Hank Aaron

Atlanta

Atlanta is an historic city with a modern flair. Atlanta-Fulton County Stadium is convenient to downtown Atlanta and a plentiful offering of hotels and restaurants.

Sports Spots

Champions
Marriott Marquis Hotel
265 Peachtree Center Ave.
404/521-0000
Sports bar.

Dirty Al's Saloon
1402 Northside Drive
404/351-9504
6600 Roswell Road
404/843-1260
Sports bar/restaurants ($)

Grandstands
3069 Peachtree Road
404/262-7908
Sports bar/restaurant ($)

Jocks 'n' Jills
Corner of 10th and Peachtree
404/873-5405
Sports bar/restaurant ($)

Parkaire Olympic Ice
4880 Lower Roswell Road
404/973-0753
Year-round ice-skating rink.

White Water Park
I-75 North, Exit 113, North
Marietta Parkway, Marietta
404/424-WAVE
Water rides in 35-acre park.

Underground Atlanta.

Restaurants

Aunt Fanny's Cabin
2155 Campbell Road
404/436-9026
Southern cuisine ($$)

Brasserie
The Stouffer Waverly Hotel at the Galleria
404/953-4500
Seafood, light meals ($-$$)

City Grill
50 Hurt Plaza
404/524-2489
Modern American cuisine ($$$)

Kafe Kobenhavn
Hyatt Regency Atlanta
265 Peachtree St.
404/577-1234
Sidewalk cafe serves light fare ($-$$)

Manuel's
602 N. Highland Ave.
404/525-3447
Bar with sandwiches ($)

Morton's of Chicago/Atlanta
245 Peachtree Center Ave.
404/577-4366
Steak, lobster, veal ($$$)

Pano and Paul's
1232 West Paces Ferry Road
404/261-3662
American, Continental cuisine ($$$)

Pittypat's Porch
25 International Blvd.
404/525-8228
Traditional Southern cuisine ($$)

The Pleasant Peasant
555 Peachtree St. N.E.
404/874-3223
American, Continental cuisine ($$)

Sports Spots & Restaurants (Dinner for two without beverage or tip):
$ Under $20
$$ $20-$40
$$$ More than $40

Accommodations

Atlanta Hilton Hotel and Towers
255 Cortland St. N.E.
404/659-2000 ($$$)

Best Western American Hotel
160 Spring St. N.W.
404/688-8600, 800/621-7885 ($$)

Comfort Inn
101 International Blvd. N.W.
404/524-5555 ($$)

Days Inn Downtown
300 Spring St.
404/523-1144 ($$)

Hyatt Regency
265 Peachtree St. N.E.
404/577-1234 ($$$)

Marriott Marquis
265 Peachtree Center Ave.
404/521-0000, 800/228-9290 ($$$)

Radisson Hotel Atlanta
Courtland at International Boulevard
404/659-6500, 800/333-3333 ($$-$$$)

Westin Peachtree Plaza Hotel
Peachtree Street and International Boulevard
404/659-1400, 800/228-3000 ($$$)

Price ranges: Double room during the week (lower rates often available on weekends)
$ Under $75
$$ $75-$125
$$$ More than $125

Attractions

CNN Studio Tours
1 CNN Center
Marietta Street at Techwood Drive
404/827-2300
A 45-minute walking tours of Cable News Network.

The High Museum of Art.

High Museum of Art
1280 Peachtree St. N.E.
404/892-3600
American and European fine arts.

Jimmy Carter Library and Museum
North Highland and Cleburne
404/331-3942
Photos, documents, and memorabilia of the Carter presidency.

Martin Luther King Jr. Historic District
Auburn Avenue between Jackson and Randolph
404/331-3920
Includes his birthplace and church where he preached.

Six Flags Over Georgia.

Six Flags Over Georgia
Off I-20
404/739-3400
Rides, live entertainment.

Stone Mountain Park
Off U.S. 78 East, Stone Mountain
404/498-5600
Theme park with an 825-foot granite monolith carved with images of Confederate heroes.

Underground Atlanta
Peachtree Street at Alabama
404/523-2311
Historic city blocks below the streets with restaurants, nightclubs, shops.

World of Coca-Cola
55 Martin Luther King Drive
404/676-5151
Museum traces the history of the famous soft drink.

Zoo Atlanta
Grant Park
800 Cherokee Ave. S.E.
404/624-5678
Animal park with natural habitats.

For More Information

Atlanta Convention & Visitors Bureau

233 Peachtree St. N.E., Suite 2000
Atlanta, GA 30303
404/521-6600

O riole Park at Camden Yards is everything a ballpark should be.

The stadium presents all the elements of a baseball trendsetter—a modern facility with a wonderful aura of nostalgia. Just a 12-minute walk from Baltimore's attraction-rich Inner Harbor and two blocks from the Babe Ruth Birthplace/Orioles Museum, the team's fancy new nest opened in 1992.

The new stadium, with a capacity of 48,041, is a tribute to the game. The asymmetrical playing field, which recalls early 20th-century stadium design, is natural grass. The seats are wide, with lots of leg room. The structure is traditional brick and steel, not concrete. Even the scoreboard advertisements blend into the park-like atmosphere.

The field is situated 16 feet below street level, which keeps the ballpark in excellent scale with downtown buildings and the landmark Baltimore & Ohio Railroad warehouse, visible beyond right field. The warehouse's brick facade offers an inviting target for American League sluggers. But it will take a prodigious drive—more than 460 feet—to hit the bricks.

For a glimpse into the past, check the aisle seats. They are decorated with the old logo used by the Orioles of the 1890s, a National League team that won consecutive pennants in 1894, '95, and '96. It's an appropriate touch at a park that encourages baseball nostalgia while providing up-to-date fan comfort and convenience.

Baltimore Orioles

Club Seats
Lower Boxes
Terrace Boxes
Upper Boxes
Upper Reserved
Lower Reserved
General Admission
Bleacher Seats

Erik Kvalsvik

Oriole Park at Camden Yards.

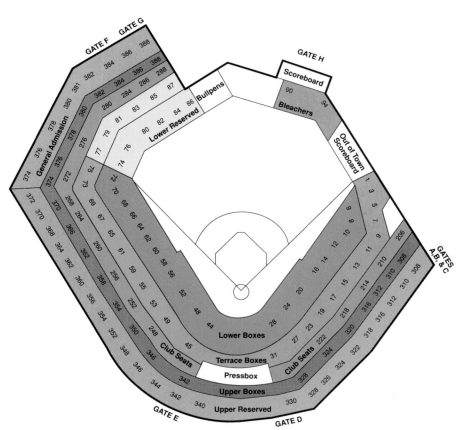

Purchasing Tickets

In person:

Oriole Park at Camden Yards Ticket Office
Bounded by Russell, Camden, and Howard streets and
Martin Luther King Boulevard
Ticket Office hours/information: Monday - Saturday,
9 a.m. - 6 p.m., during night games until 8:30 p.m.;
Sundays (when the club is at home), 12 noon - 6 p.m.
For information, call 410/685-9800.

By phone:

TicketMaster PhoneCharge
Baltimore area—410/481-SEAT
Washington, D.C. area—202/432-SEAT
PhoneCharge hours: Daily 10 a.m. - 9 p.m.

Directions to the Stadium

- From the north: Take I-83 and use southbound city
  streets (Maryland Avenue, St. Paul Street).
  Park downtown, north or west of the ballpark.

- From the west: Take I-70 to I-695 and U.S. 40.
  Park downtown, north or west of the ballpark.

- From the east: Take U.S. 40 or Eastern Avenue.
  Park downtown, north or east of the ballpark.

- From the south: Take I-395 (from I-95) or Russell
  Street (from Baltimore Washington Parkway or I-95).
  Park south of the ballpark in Lots D-H.

Public Transportation

The Charles Center and Lexington Market stations on
the Baltimore Metro rapid transit system are within a
10-minute walk of the stadium. Metro stations at various locations offer more than 8,000 free parking spots
near the stations. Fans who live in northwest Baltimore, Carroll County, and southern Pennsylvania may
find the Metro and its direct access to I-795 a good
alternative to driving downtown.

Take Light Rail Service, Baltimore's newest form of
mass transit, directly to Oriole Park at Camden Yards.
More than 1,100 free parking spaces are available at
the rail stations. Trains run every 15 minutes, and
service extends up to an hour after the game.

Additionally, the Mass Transit Administration operates
more than 20 bus lines that pass within several blocks
of the stadium. The MTA also provides direct bus
service from outlying communities to a bus staging
terminal located east of the Camden Warehouse.

Train service is available from Washington, D.C. and
points in between via the Maryland MARC commuter
rail lines to the Baltimore terminal at the Camden
Stadium Complex.

Parking

Parking lots on the stadium grounds accommodate
5,000 cars; more than 20,000 additional parking spaces
in adjacent areas surround the stadium.

An off-ramp from northbound I-395 leads directly into
the stadium parking lots.

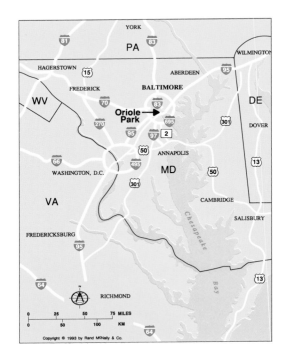

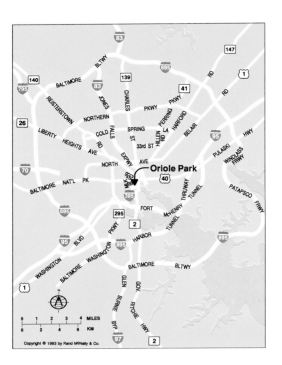

Baltimore

Baltimore is a classic American seaport with a rich and eclectic mix of attractions. Hotels and restaurants listed are in the Inner Harbor area or near the ballpark.

Sports Spots

Balls All-American Sports Bar
200 W. Pratt St.
410/659-5844
Sports bar/restaurant ($)

Lacrosse Foundation Hall of Fame Museum
113 W. University Parkway
410/235-6882
Historical displays and memorabilia dating to 1800s.

Sports
10 Halesworth Road, Cockeysville
410/666-2227
Sports complex with batting cages, miniature golf, air hockey, and basketball.

Restaurants

Chiapparelli's Restaurant
237 S. High St., Little Italy
410/837-0309
Neapolitan Italian ($$)

World-renowned collections are housed in the Walters Art Gallery.

City Lights
Harborplace
Light Street Pavilion
301 Light St.
410/244-8811
Seafood, steak ($$)

Obrycki's Crab House and Seafood Restaurant
1727 E. Pratt St.
410/732-6399
Seafood ($$$)

Phillips Harborplace
Harborplace
Light Street Pavilion
301 Light St.
410/685-6600
Seafood ($$)

Pier 500
Harborview Marina
500 Harborview Drive
410/625-0500
Seafood ($$)

Pizzeria Uno
Harborplace
Pratt Street Pavilion
201 E. Pratt St.
410/625-5900
All types of pizza ($)

Prime Rib
1101 N. Calvert St.
410/539-1804
Prime rib, seafood ($$$)

Rusty Scupper
Inner Harbor Marina
402 Key Highway
410/727-3678
Seafood, pasta, chicken ($$)

Sabatino's
901 Fawn St., Little Italy
410/727-9414
Pasta, veal, shrimp ($$)

Tio Pepe
10 E. Franklin
410/539-4675
Spanish cuisine ($$)

Velleggia's
829 E. Pratt St., Little Italy
410/685-2620
Italian cuisine ($$$)

Sports Spots & Restaurants (Dinner for two without beverage or tip):
$ Under $20
$$ $20-$40
$$$ More than $40

Accommodations

Baltimore Marriott Inner Harbor
110 S. Eutaw St.
410/962-0202 ($$$)

Clarion Inn—Inner Harbor
Harrison's Pier 5
711 Eastern Ave.
410/783-5553 ($$$)

Harbor Court Hotel
550 Light St.
410/234-0550 ($$$)

Holiday Inn—Inner Harbor
410 W. Lombard St.
410/685-3500 ($$)

Hyatt Regency Baltimore Inner Harbor
300 Light St.
410/528-1234 ($$$)

The Inner Harbor skyline.

Omni Hotel
101 W. Fayette St.
410/752-1100 ($$$)

Radisson Plaza Lord Baltimore Hotel
20-30 W. Baltimore St.
410/539-8400 ($$$)

Sheraton Inner Harbor Hotel
300 S. Charles St.
410/962-8300 ($$$)

Stouffer Harborplace Hotel
202 E. Pratt St.
410/547-1200, 800/HOTELS-1 ($$$)

Price ranges: Double room during the week (lower rates are often available on weekends)
$ Under $75
$$ $75-$125
$$$ More than $125

Attractions

Baltimore Museum of Art
Art Museum Drive between Charles and 31st streets
410/396-7101
Collections of 20th-century art.

Fells Point
Broadway, south of Eastern Avenue to the harbor
Historic port-side neighborhood with shops, pubs, and restaurants.

Fort McHenry National Monument
Foot of East Fort Avenue
410/962-4299
Site of the defeat of the British in the War of 1812.

Harborplace
Pratt and Calvert streets
410/332-4191
Glass-enclosed pavilions at Inner Harbor feature cafes, restaurants, markets, and specialty shops.

Maryland Science Center
601 Light St.
410/685-5225
Hands-on science exhibits, a theater, and a planetarium.

National Aquarium in Baltimore.

National Aquarium in Baltimore
Pier 3
501 E. Pratt St.
410/576-3810
More than 5,000 aquatic animals.

U.S.S. Constellation
Inner Harbor Constellation Dock
410/539-1797
The first commissioned U.S. Navy ship, launched in 1797.

For More Information

Baltimore Area Convention & Visitors Center
300 W. Pratt St.
Baltimore, MD 21201
410/837-4636
800/282-6632

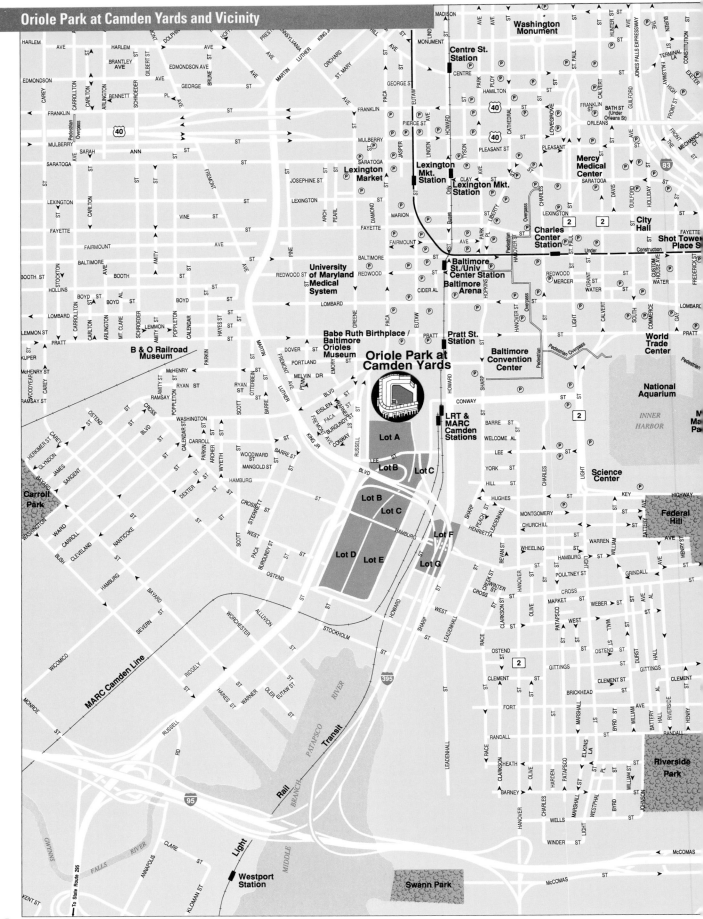

Johns Hopkins
Hospital Station

Johns
Hopkins
Hospital

Church
Hospital
Corporation

Shot
Tower

Patterson   Park

Marine
Mammal
Pavilion   Pier 5

Pier 6

Bridges

Fells Point

NORTHWEST   BRANCH

PATAPSCO

Locust Point

RIVER

N

Latrobe
Park

0   1/2

MILE

Copyright © 1993 by Rand McNally & Co.

If you want to immerse yourself in baseball, go to a game at Fenway Park.

Tucked into what was known as the Fens section of Boston, the 33,000-plus seat baseball park has put time on hold.

Smell the Italian sausage and other goodies cooking at pushcarts outside the park and at the concession stands inside. (The food here is some of the best in Major League baseball!) Glare at the 37-foot high "Green Monster" in leftfield—its proximity to home plate has broken many a pitcher's heart and added points to many a right-handed hitter's batting and slugging average. Just sit back and let this historic park embrace you.

The legends, the great moments, are very much alive here. Joe Cronin. Jimmie Foxx. Ted Williams. Walt Dropo. Jim Piersall. Rico Petrocelli. Carl Yastrzemski. Jim Rice. Fred Lynn. Carlton Fisk. The stars and their legends ricochet through history like baseballs ricochet off the Green Monster.

The Boston Red Sox, Fenway's only tenants since it opened in 1912, respect their heritage. Fenway shares the title (with Tiger Stadium in Detroit) as the oldest major league ballpark still in use.

In recent years, although the club added amenities, the modernizations did not blemish the park's historic presence. Fenway retains its place on the short list of every baseball fan's dream trip.

American League East

Boston Red Sox

Fenway Park.

Travers/Boston Red Sox

☐ Field Box Seats
☐ Upper Box Seats
☐ Reserved Grandstand
☐ 600 Club Private Suites
☐ Roof Box Seats
☐ Bleachers

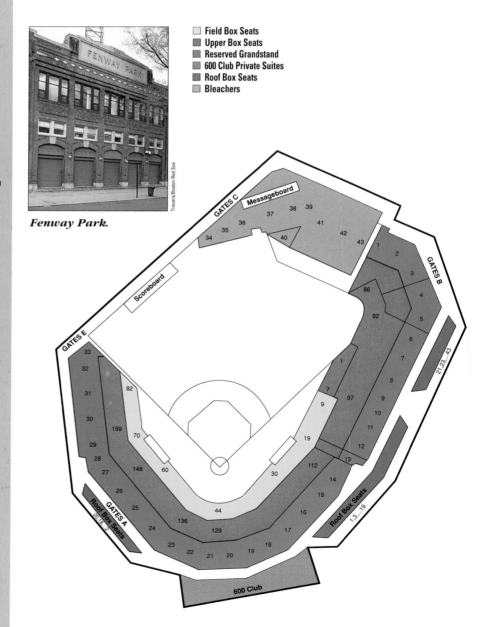

Purchasing Tickets

By mail (individual and season ticket orders):
Red Sox Tickets
Fenway Park
4 Yawkey Way
Boston, MA 02215

By phone:
Ticket information - 617/267-8661
Credit card sales - 617/267-1700
Group sales - 617/262-1915

Directions to the Stadium

- From Rhode Island: Take I-95 North; follow the Dedham, Maine, New Hampshire split. Take Exit 20A-Route 9 East. Follow Route 9 East approximately 10 to 12 miles. Go past the Chestnut Hill Reservoir; sign for Kenmore Square is on the left. Turn left onto Brookline Avenue; ballpark is straight ahead.

- From Cape Cod: Take Route 3 to the Boston split; continue to Storrow Drive. Take Storrow to the Fenway-Kenmore Square exit. At the top of the exit ramp, bear right onto Boylston Street. Go through two sets of lights and turn right onto Yawkey Way. The ballpark is on the right.

- From Coastal New Hampshire and Maine: Take I-95 South to Route 1 South to Boston. Cross the Mystic Tobin Bridge (toll). At split, follow signs for Boston/Cape Cod. Where road intersects Route 93 South, merge right and follow signs to Storrow Drive. Take Storrow to the Fenway-Kenmore Square exit. At the top of the exit ramp, bear right onto Boylston Street. Go through two sets of lights and take a right onto Yawkey Way. The ballpark is on the right.

- From Central New Hampshire and Vermont: Follow Route 93 South to Boston. Once on lower deck of bridge, stay right and follow signs for Storrow Drive. Take Storrow to the Fenway-Kenmore Square exit. At the top of the exit ramp, bear right onto Boylston Street. Go through two sets of lights and turn right onto Yawkey Way. The ballpark is on the right.

- From the Mass Pike: Take the Mass Pike to the Prudential exit. Take a sharp right. At the Sheraton Boston, turn right onto Dalton Street. Turn left at the light onto Boylston Street. At the second set of lights, turn right onto Ipswich Street. Ballpark is straight ahead.

Public Transportation

The Red Sox encourage patrons to use public transportation whenever possible. Shuttle buses stop at the Park Street, Government Center, and North and South Stations on the Massachusetts Bay Transportation Authority (MBTA) subway lines. Take the Green Line Riverside Car to the Kenmore Square or Fenway Park exit. For information, call 617/722-3200 or 800/392-6100.

Parking

Public parking, although limited, is available within a few blocks of the park at the Prudential Center Garage at 400 Commonwealth Ave. or the Riverside MBTA Station. Several private lots in the Kenmore Square area offer public parking on game days.

Boston University also operates lots in Kenmore Square at Newbury Street and Kenmore Street, 30 Deerfield St., and Granby Street at Commonwealth Avenue.

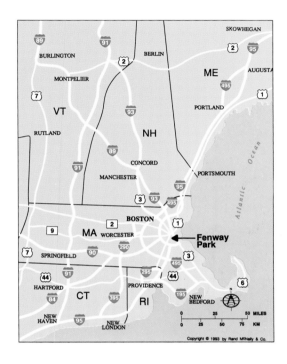

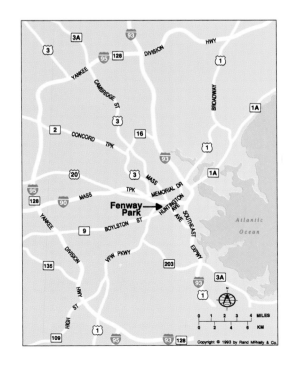

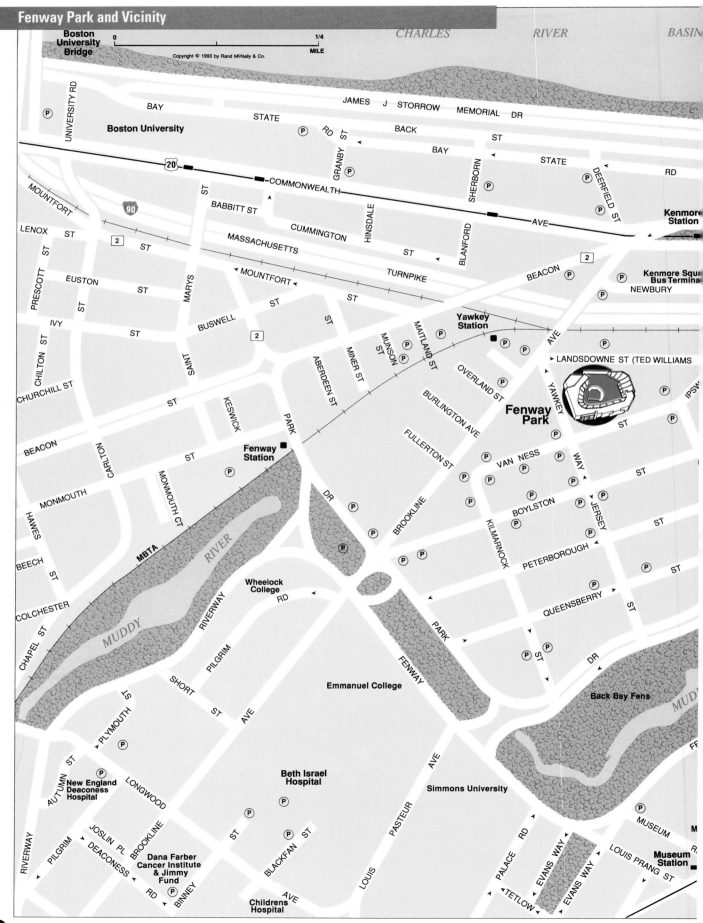

CHARLES   RIVER   BASIN

Boston
University
Bridge

0   1/4
MILE
Copyright © 1993 by Rand McNally & Co.

UNIVERSITY RD

BAY
STATE   JAMES   J   STORROW   MEMORIAL   DR

Boston University   RD   ST   BACK
ST

BAY   STATE

20   COMMONWEALTH   SHERBORN   ST   RD   DEERFIELD ST   Kenmore
Station

MOUNTFORT   BABBITT ST   AVE

90   HINSDALE   BLANFORD

LENOX   ST   CUMMINGTON   Kenmore Squa
Bus Termina

2   ST   MASSACHUSETTS   BEACON   NEWBURY

PRESCOTT   EUSTON   ST   MOUNTFORT   TURNPIKE   ST   2

IVY   ST   BUSWELL   2   MAITLAND ST   AVE   Yawkey
Station

CHILTON ST   MARYS   SAINT   MINER ST   MUNSON ST   OVERLAND ST   LANDSDOWNE ST (TED WILLIAMS

CHURCHILL ST   ABERDEEN ST   BURLINGTON AVE   Fenway
Park   YAWKEY   IPSW

BEACON   KESWICK   ST   FULLERTON ST   ST

CARLTON   PARK   Fenway
Station   VAN   NESS   WAY   ST

MONMOUTH   DR   BROOKLINE   BOYLSTON   JERSEY

HAWES   MONMOUTH CT   RIVER   KILMARNOCK   PETERBOROUGH   ST

BEECH   ST   MBTA   ST

COLCHESTER   RIVERWAY   Wheelock
College   RD   PARK   QUEENSBERRY   ST

CHAPEL ST   MUDDY   ST   Back Bay Fens   MUDD

PILGRIM   FENWAY   DR

SHORT
ST   AVE   Emmanuel College   PARK

PLYMOUTH   ST

AUTUMN   ST   New England
Deaconess
Hospital   Beth Israel
Hospital   PASTEUR   AVE   Simmons University   MUSEUM

RIVERWAY   LONGWOOD   JOSLIN PL   BROOKLINE   Dana Farber
Cancer Institute
& Jimmy
Fund   BLACKFAN   ST   LOUIS   PALACE RD   EVANS WAY   LOUIS PRANG ST   Museum
Station

PILGRIM   DEACONESS   RD   BINNEY   Childrens
Hospital   AVE   TETLOW   EVANS WAY   FR

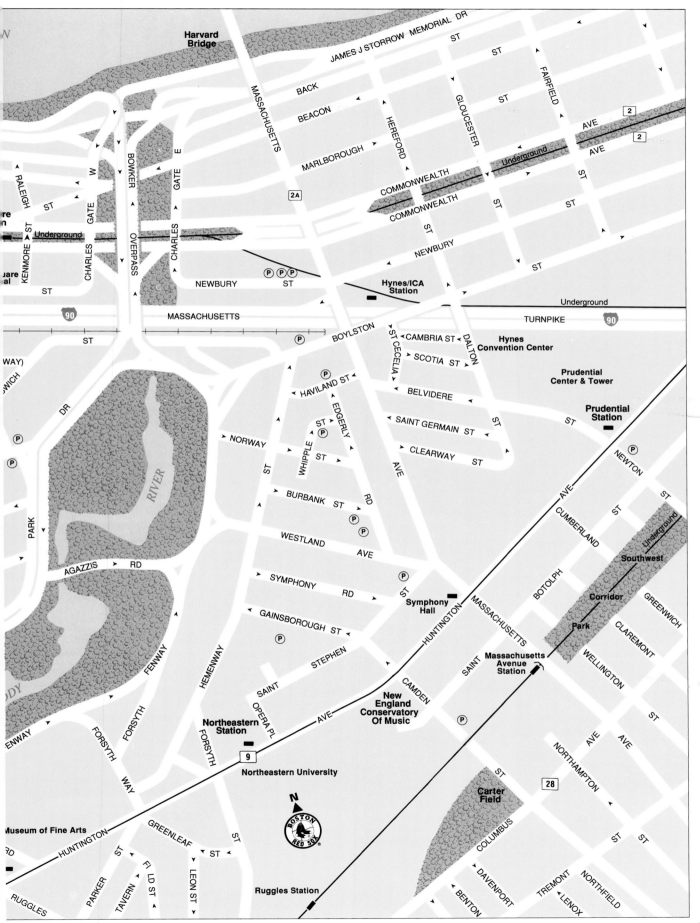

Harvard
Bridge

JAMES J STORROW MEMORIAL DR

ST

ST

FAIRFIELD

BACK

BEACON

GLOUCESTER

AVE

2

MARLBOROUGH

HEREFORD

AVE

2

Underground

MASSACHUSETTS

BOWKER

GATE E

COMMONWEALTH

ST

ST

RALEIGH

ST

GATE W

CHARLES

COMMONWEALTH

CHARLES

ST

OVERPASS

KENMORE

Underground

NEWBURY

ST

ST

re

al

uare

al

NEWBURY

ST

P P P

ST

Hynes/ICA
Station

Underground

ST

MASSACHUSETTS

Underground

90

ST

TURNPIKE

90

P

BOYLSTON

ST

CAMBRIA ST

DALTON

Hynes
Convention Center

ST CECELIA

SCOTIA ST

P

Prudential
Center & Tower

HAVILAND ST

BELVIDERE

ST

Prudential
Station

DR

ST

EDGERLY

SAINT GERMAIN ST

ST

NEWTON

WAY)

NORWAY

P

ST

CLEARWAY

ST

AVE

P

WICH

WHIPPLE

RD

AVE

ST

CUMBERLAND

P

PARK

RIVER

BURBANK ST

P

Underground

P

Southwest

WESTLAND

AVE

BOTOLPH

GREENWICH

AGAZZIS

RD

Corridor

SYMPHONY

RD

ST

CLAREMONT

Symphony
Hall

Park

GAINSBOROUGH ST

HUNTINGTON

MASSACHUSETTS

WELLINGTON

FENWAY

HEMENWAY

ST

STEPHEN

Massachusetts
Avenue
Station

FORSYTH

CAMDEN

SAINT

AVE

AVE

ODY

New
England
Conservatory
Of Music

NORTHAMPTON

FORSYTH

OPERA PL

AVE

P

FORSYTH WAY

Northeastern
Station

28

FORSYTH

9

Carter
Field

Northeastern University

ST

N

Museum of Fine Arts

HUNTINGTON

GREENLEAF

ST

COLUMBUS

ST

ST

RD

PARKER

ST

LEON ST

DAVENPORT

TREMONT

NORTHFIELD

RUGGLES

TAVERN

FI LD ST

Ruggles Station

BENTON

LENOX

17

Boston

Boston offers a bountiful selection of sports activities and historic sites. Hotels and restaurants listed are near Fenway Park, in the downtown area, or on the waterfront.

Sports Spots

Bull & Finch Pub
84 Beacon St.
617/227-9600
Sports-motif pub that inspired the TV series "Cheers." Sandwiches, memento shop.

Champions Bar
In Boston Marriott Hotel
Copley Plaza
110 Huntington Ave.
617/236-5800
Sports bar/restaurant ($)

Eliot Lounge
370 Commonwealth Ave.
617/262-1078
Sports bar/restaurant ($)

Red Sox Clubhouse Shop
Mall at Middlesex Road & Route 128, Burlington
617/273-0883
Official Sox memorabilia shop.

Sports Saloon
In Copley Square Hotel
47 Huntington Ave.
617/536-9000
Sports bar/restaurant ($$)

Who's On First
19 Yawkey Way, across from
Fenway Park
617/247-3353
Sports bar/restaurant.
Baseball memorabilia ($)

Restaurants

Anthony's Pier 4
140 Northern Ave.
617/423-6363
Seafood and New England specialties; overlooking Boston Harbor ($$$)

The Cactus Club
939 Boylston St.
617/236-0200
Southwestern cuisine ($-$$)

Casa Romero
30 Gloucester St.
617/536-4341
Mexico City cuisine ($$)

The Chart House
60 Long Wharf
617/227-1576
Fresh fish, prime rib ($$$)

Cafe Budapest
90 Exeter St.
617/266-1979, 617/734-3388
Hungarian, Continental cuisine ($$$)

Historic Boston Harbor.

J.C. Hillary's
793 Boylston St.
617/536-6300
Steak, seafood, chicken ($$)

Jimmy's Harborside
242 Northern Ave.
617/423-1000
Seafood; overlooking Boston Harbor ($$)

Skipjack's Seafood Emporium
500 Boylston St.
617/536-3500
Seafood ($$)

Statue of Paul Revere.

Ye Olde Union Oyster House
41 Union St.
617/227-2750
Boston's oldest restaurant -1826
($$)

Sports Spots & Restaurants (Dinner for two without beverage or tip):
$ Under $20
$$ $20-$40
$$$ More than $40

Accommodations

Boston Marriott Hotel Copley Plaza
110 Huntington Ave.
617/236-5800, 800/228-9290 ($$$)

Boston Bay Bay Hilton
40 Dalton St.
617/236-1100, 800/874-0663 ($$$)

Colonnade Hotel
120 Huntington Ave.
617/424-7000 ($$$)

Copley Square Hotel
47 Huntington Ave.
617/536-9000 ($$)

Fenway Park Howard Johnson Lodge
1271 Boylston St.
617/267-8300, 800/654-2000 ($$)

Hyatt Regency Alicante
100 Plaza Alicante
Garden Grove
714/750-1234 ($$$)

Westin Hotel, Copley Place
10 Huntington Ave.
617/262-9600, 800/228-3000 ($$$)

Price ranges: double room during the week (lower rates often available on weekends)
$ Under $75
$$ $75-$125
$$$ More than $125

Attractions

Faneuil Hall Marketplace
Congress Street/Quincy Market
617/523-3886
Shops and restaurants housed in 19th-century warehouses.

Downtown & Faneuil Hall Marketplace.

Filene's Basement
426 Washington St.
617/542-2011
The oldest bargain store in the U.S., founded in 1908.

The Freedom Trail
Starts at Boston Common Visitor Information Center
Tremont Street side of Boston Common
617/242-5642
A three-mile walking tour of 16 historic sites from the Colonial and Revolutionary eras.

John Hancock Observatory
200 Clarendon St.
617/247-1977
Observatory offers a bird's-eye view of Boston and the surrounding area.

John F. Kennedy Library and Museum
Columbia Point on Dorchester Bay
617/929-4567
Documents, films, photographs and memorabilia.

Museum of Fine Arts
465 Huntington Ave.
617/267-9300
Comprehensive collection of fine art.

Museum of Science and the Charles Hayden Planetarium
Science Park on the Charles River Dam
617/723-2500
Exhibits highlight medicine, technology, and space.

New England Aquarium
Central Wharf
617/973-5200
Four-story glass ocean tank, sea lion shows.

U.S.S. Constitution Museum
Charlestown Navy Yard, Boston Harbor
617/242-0543
Exhibits, prints, paintings, memorabilia, and information on "Old Ironsides."

For More Information

Greater Boston Convention & Visitors Bureau
Prudential Tower, Suite 400
P.O. Box 490
Boston, MA 02199
617/536-4100

Baseball and sushi? Well, why not? It's a baseball tradition in the making at the "Big A," the California Angels' Anaheim Stadium.

In 1960, former cowboy star, singer, and broadcaster Gene Autry attended the Major League winter meetings in St. Louis to secure rights to broadcast a baseball team's games. Instead, he returned home the owner of the fledgling Los Angeles Angels, one of the new expansion teams of the American League.

The road from radio broadcast executive to baseball mogul has been a happy one for Autry and his fellow Southern California baseball fans.

From 1961 through 1965, the Angels played in other ballparks, including Dodger Stadium. In 1966, they landed at their permanent home: Anaheim Stadium in Orange County, 27 miles south of Los Angeles and close to another popular Southern California attraction— Disneyland.

With the move, the team was rechristened the California Angels, and the new $24 million, 43,250-seat stadium was immediately dubbed the "Big A" because of the giant A-frame supporting the scoreboard in the outfield, which was topped by the Angels' signature halo.

In 1979, the park was enlarged to accommodate 65,000 fans for baseball and 70,000 for football. The "Big A" scoreboard was moved to its new location in the stadium parking lot.

American League West

California Angels

Anaheim Stadium.

California Office of Tourism

- ■ Field and Club Level
- ■ Terrace Boxes
- □ Center Field Boxes
     Club and Terrace
- ■ Centerfield Field
- ■ View Level Reserved
- ■ General Admission
- ■ Group Seating Area

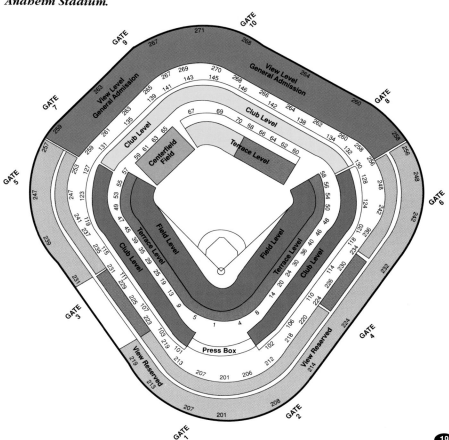

Purchasing Tickets

By mail:
Angels Tickets
P.O. Box 2000
Anaheim, CA 92803

Mail orders must be received at least seven days prior to the game. Make check or money order payable to the California Angels and add $4 for postage and handling. Specify the date of the game or games, number of tickets, and price.

In person:
Anaheim Stadium
2000 Gene Autry Way

Tickets are available in the spring at the advance ticket window at Gate 1, which is located behind home plate on the field level. Hours: Monday - Saturday, 9 a.m. - 5:30 p.m. For information: 800/6-ANGELS. Tickets may also be purchased at TicketMaster outlets in Tower Records, Music Plus, May Co., and Smith's stores. For information, call 800/6-ANGELS

By phone:
TicketMaster
213/480-3232, 805/583-8700, 714/740-2000,
619/278-TIXS

TicketMaster accepts Visa, MasterCard, American Express, and Discover. Tickets ordered 10 days prior to the game will be mailed to buyer; tickets ordered less than 10 days prior to game will be available on the day of the game at the Will Call window at Gate 1 in Anaheim Stadium. Order by phone, seven days a week, 8 a.m. - 9 p.m.

Directions to the Stadium

- From Los Angeles (via I-5): Travel south on I-5 to Anaheim, exit on Katella Avenue. Turn left on Katella. Follow Katella to State College Boulevard. Turn right on State College to the stadium.

- From Long Beach (via Highway 22—Garden Grove Freeway): Travel east on Highway 22 to City Centre Drive. Turn left on City Centre, which becomes State College Boulevard, and go north to stadium entrance six blocks on the right side.

- From South County (via I-5): Travel north on I-5 to Anaheim, exit to Highway 57 (Orange Freeway) North. Exit at Orangewood; turn left onto Orangewood and travel one block to the stadium entrance on the right.

- From Diamond Bar, Brea, and Covina (via Highway 57—Orange Freeway): Travel south on Highway 57, exit at Orangewood, turn right on Orangewood and travel one block to the stadium entrance on the right.

Public Transportation

Orange County Transit District, 714/636-7433
Yellow Cab of Anaheim, 714/535-2211

Parking

Anaheim Stadium lots accommodate more than 60,000 cars. Handicapped individuals should request from the parking attendants a space in the reserved parking lot closest to the gate that corresponds to the gate designation on their ticket.

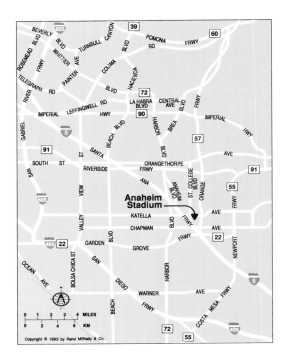

Anaheim

Anaheim is a major hub in Southern California. The restaurants and hotels listed here are all located in Anaheim or close to the stadium in Orange County, California.

Sports Spots

Anaheim Hills Public Country Club
6501 E. Nohl Ranch Road
714/637-7311
18-hole golf course in the Santa Ana Canyons.

"Dad" Miller Golf Course
430 N. Gilbert St.
714/991-5530
18-hole public golf course.

Dana Wharf Sportfishing
34675 Golden Lantern
Dana Point
714/496-5794
Marinas, boat rentals, para-sailing, and fishing.

Davey's Locker Sportfishing
Balboa Pavilion
400 Main St., Balboa
714/673-1434
Deep-sea fishing, rentals.

Golf N' Stuff
1656 S. Harbor Blvd.
714/778-4100
Two miniature golf courses.

Disney's Tennisland Racquet Club
1330 S. Walnut St.
714/535-4851
Ten championship courts open day and night, teaching pro, practice court.

Wild Rivers
8770 Irvine Center Drive, Irvine
714/768-WILD
Water park with more than 40 rides and attractions.

Restaurants

Beef Rigger
105 N. State College Blvd.
Orange
714/634-9288
Beef, seafood, chicken ($$)

Benihana of Tokyo
2100 E. Ball Road
714/774-4940
Japanese cuisine ($$-$$$)

Casa Maria
1801 E. Katella Ave.
714/634-1888
Mexican cuisine ($)

The Catch
1929 S. State College Blvd.
714/634-1829
Fish, prime rib, pasta ($$)

Cattleman's Wharf
1160 W. Ball Road
714/535-1622
Steak, seafood ($$-$$$)

El Torito
2020 E. Ball Road
714/956-4880
Mexican cuisine ($)

Jolly Roger Inn Restaurant
640 W. Katella Ave.
714/772-7621
Steak, seafood, sandwiches ($)

Mr. Stox
1105 E. Katella Ave.
714/634-2994
Duck, fish, lamb ($$-$$$)

T.G.I. Friday's
3339 City Parkway East
714/978-3308
Oriental and Southwestern cuisine ($-$$)

Sports Spots & Restaurants (Dinner for two without beverage or tip):
$ Under $20
$$ $20-$40
$$$ More than $40

Accommodations

The Anaheim Hilton and Towers
777 Convention Way
714/750-4321, 800/HILTONS ($$$)

The Anaheim Ramada Inn
1331 E. Katella Ave.
714/978-8088, 800/228-0586 ($)

Castle Inn and Suites
1734 S. Harbor Blvd.
714/774-8111, 800/521-5653 ($$)

Disneyland Hotel
1150 W. Cerritos Ave.
714/956-6400 ($$$)

Doubletree Hotel
100 The City Drive, Orange
714/634-4500 ($$)

Grand Hotel
7 Freedman Way
714/772-7777, 800/421-6662 ($$)

The Pan Pacific Hotel
1717 S. West St.
714/999-0990, 800/821-8976 ($$$)

Quality Inn & Conference Center
616 Convention Way
714/750-3131, 800/228-5151 ($-$$)

Price ranges: Double room during the week (lower rates are often available on weekends)
$ Under $75
$$ $75-$125
$$$ More than $125

Attractions

Crystal Cathedral
12141 Lewis St., Garden Grove
714/971-4000
Designed by architect Philip Johnson, cathedral features more than 10,000 panes of glass. Tours.

The Crystal Cathedral in Garden Grove.

Disneyland
1313 S. Harbor Blvd.
714/999-4000
Probably the most famous theme park in the world.

Knott's Berry Farm
8039 Beach Blvd., Buena Park
714/220-5200
Features 165 rides and attractions.

Medieval Times
7662 Beach Blvd., Buena Park
714/523-1100
The days and knights of the Middle Ages come to life in this re-creation of an 11th-century European castle.

Mission San Juan Capistrano
31882 Camino Capistrano, San Juan Capistrano
714/248-2048
The oldest historical landmark in Southern California.

Movieland Wax Museum
7711 Beach Blvd., Buena Park
714/522-1154
Wax figures of movie and TV stars.

Richard Nixon Presidential Library & Birthplace
18001 Yorba Linda Blvd., Yorba Linda
714/993-3393
Memorabilia (including baseballs from opening days), historical films, exhibits, and interactive video displays.

Ripley's Believe It or Not
7850 Beach Blvd., Buena Park
714/522-1155
An eight-legged pig, a man with four eyes, a painting of the Last Supper made from 240 pieces of toast.

South Costa Plaza
3333 Bristol St., Mesa
714/241-1700
More than 200 specialty stores rival those on Rodeo Drive. Across the street, in Crystal Court, are 75 more shops and boutiques.

Wild Bill's
7600 Beach Blvd., Buena Park
714/522-6414, 800/827-1546
Entertainment in a Wild West Saloon and Music Hall.

For More Information

Anaheim Visitor & Convention Bureau
P.O. Box 4270
Anaheim, CA 92803
714/999-8999

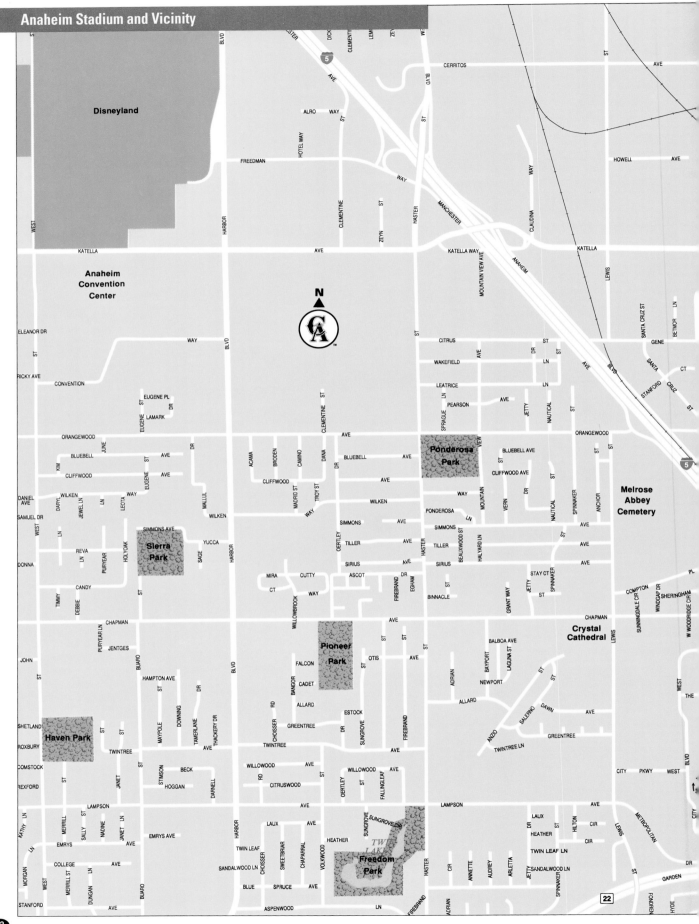

Disneyland

Anaheim
Convention
Center

Ponderosa
Park

Melrose
Abbey
Cemetery

Sierra
Park

Pioneer
Park

Crystal
Cathedral

Haven Park

Freedom
Park

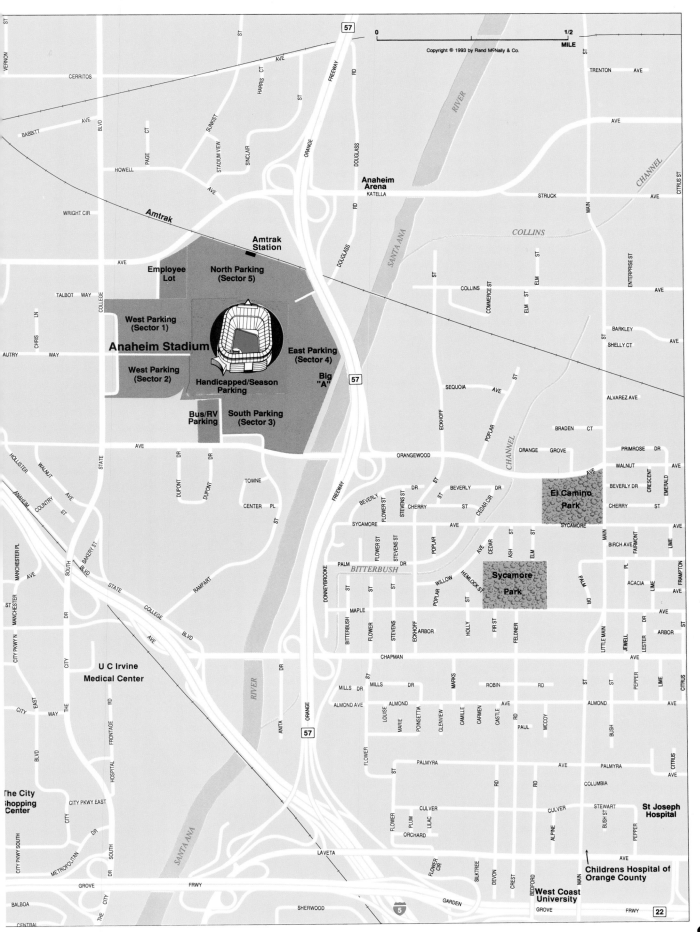

Welcome to Wrigley Field, the "friendly confines" of the Chicago Cubs. On a warm sunny day, there is no better place to be.

Even with the addition of modern touches like plush boxes and lights for night games, Wrigley Field and its ivy-covered outfield walls recall the game as it was played earlier this century.

The club, formed in 1876, was a charter member of the National League. In 1919, the Wrigley family, of chewing-gum fame, bought the club from Charles H. Weeghman, a wealthy restaurant-chain proprietor. The history of the Wrigley family and the Cubs was intertwined until 1981 when the family sold the Cubs to another Chicago institution, the Tribune Company, which publishes the *Chicago Tribune* and owns the superstation WGN, among other holdings.

Red-brick Wrigley Field dates from 1914, when it was called Weeghman Park, and offers plenty of baseball traditions: It was the last park in the majors to add lights, installing them in 1988. The scoreboard is still hand-operated. And Hall of Fame announcer Harry Caray still sings "Take Me Out to the Ballgame" for the seventh-inning stretch.

It can be difficult to get tickets to many games, especially if the arch-rival St. Louis Cardinals are in town. And no wonder. The sun shines brightly on a summer afternoon. Cool breezes waft in from nearby Lake Michigan. The grass is green; ivy covers the brick walls. The people are some of the friendliest in town. With a stadium and a setting like this, any day is a good day for a ballgame.

National League East

Chicago Cubs

Wrigley Field.

Connie Blaze

- ■ Club Boxes
- ▢ Field Boxes
- ■ Terrace Boxes
- ■ Terrace Reserved
- ▢ Upper Deck Boxes
- ■ Upper Deck Reserved
- ▢ Bleachers
- ■ Family Section
- ▢ Group Section

GATE N

249-246

Bleachers

150 146

152 144

153 143

Family Section

Group Sec.

GATE K

GATE D

142 242

202 102 140 240

204 104 5 38 138 239

35 136 237 438 528

205 106 6 33 134 236 436 536

206 108 8 31 132 235 434 534

503 208 110 10 27 130 233 433

504 403 209 112 12 Club Boxes 25 128 231 431

506 406 211 114 15 23 Field Boxes 126 229 429

409 213 116 17 21 124 227 427 527

Upper Deck Reserved 412 215 118 19 Club Boxes 122 226 425 526

512 415 216 219 Field Boxes 224 427 527

516 417 218 Terrace Boxes 223 425 523

517 418 419 Terrace Reserved 422 423 523

518 519 Upper Deck Boxes 422 523

Press Box

GATE F

Purchasing Tickets

By mail or in person:
Cubs' Ticket Office
Wrigley Field
1060 W. Addison St.
Chicago, IL 60613
312/404-CUBS

By phone:
TicketMaster
312/831-CUBS in Illinois
800/347-CUBS outside Illinois

Phone orders will be taken at the Wrigley Field ticket office only for groups of 25 or more. Call 312-404-CUBS for group sales or for more information.

Directions to the Stadium

The stadium is located on the block bounded west and east by Clark Street and Sheffield Avenue and the north and south by Waveland Avenue and Addison Street on the north side of Chicago.

Public Transportation

The Howard-Englewood/Jackson Park north/south rapid transit line stops next to the ballpark at the Addison Street station. Both "A" and "B" trains stop there beginning 90 minutes before Cubs games and ending 90 minutes after the games. On non-game days and at other times during the day, Addison is a "B" train stop only.

Bus service to Wrigley Field is provided on the #152 Addison Street bus and the #22 Clark Street bus. The #152 Addison bus links Wrigley Field with the O'Hare-Congress-Douglas rapid transit line west of the ballpark at the Addison Street station (an "A" stop). Call CTA at 312/836-7000 for more information.

Cab service is available to and from the park; cabs can be hailed along most busy streets.

Parking

Because parking is very limited in the neighborhood around Wrigley Field, the easiest way to get to the park is to park at outlying lots and shuttle via Chicago Transit Authority (CTA) elevated trains and buses.

The #154 Wrigley Field Express bus runs to and from Wrigley Field and a 1,200-car parking area near Lane Technical High School and DeVry Institute. The buses run from two hours prior to night home games until one hour after the games. The parking lots are located south of Addison Street between Western Avenue and Rockwell Street. Call CTA at 312/836-7000 for more information.

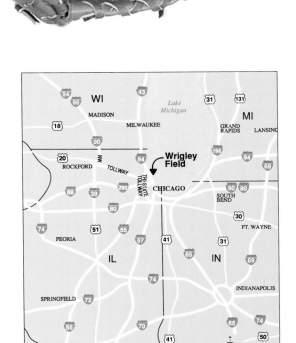

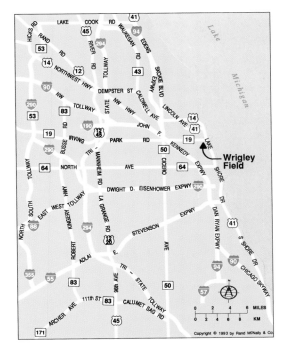

0   1/4
MILE

Copyright © 1993 by Rand McNally & Co

WARNER   AVE

BELLE PLAINE   AVE   BELLE   PLAINE   AVE

CUYLER   AVE

IRVING   PARK   RD   19   CLARK

LARCHMONT   AVE

RAVENSWOOD PKWY

BYRON   ST   BYRON   ST   ST

BERENICE   AVE

LINCOLN

GRACE   ST   GRACE   ST   GRACE   ST

BRADLEY   PL

WAVELAND   AVE   WAVELAND   AVE

AVE

PATTERSON   AVE

ADDISON   ST   ADDISON   ST

EDDY   ST   EDDY   EDDY

CORNELIA   AVE   CORNELIA   AVE

NEWPORT   AVE   Ravensw

PKWY

RAVENSWOOD

ROSCOE   ST   ROSCOE   ST

HENDERSON   ST   LINCOLN   HENDERSON   ST

SCHOOL   ST   SCHOOL   ST

MELROSE   ST   MELROSE   ST   MELROSE   ST

BELMONT   AVE   BELMONT   AVE

AVE

FLETCHER   ST   AVE   FLETCHER   ST

HERMITAGE PAULINA AVE AVE AVE GREENVIEW SOUTHPORT GRACE

RAVENSWOOD AVE ST AVE ASHLAND

HERMITAGE PAULINA AVE AVE WAYNE LAKEWOOD MAGNOLIA

MARSHFIELD AVE BOSWORTH AVE JANSSEN AVE

ASHLAND GREENVIEW SOUTHPORT AVE

LAKEWOOD

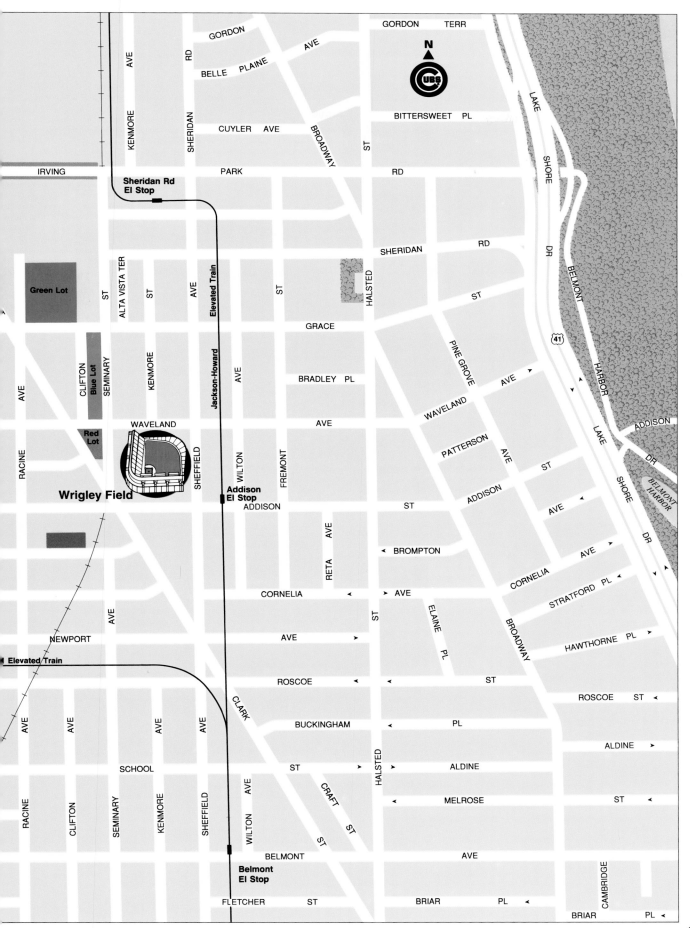

Chicago

Wrigley Field is located in a densely populated, North Side city neighborhood. The hotels and restaurants listed are mostly in the Near North and downtown areas.

Sports Spots

America's Bar
219 W. Erie St.
312/915-5986
This Walter Payton-owned spot rocks to the tunes of Top-40.

Chicago Beaches
Lakefront
312/294-2333
21 bathing beaches.

The Wrigley Building, along the Chicago River.

Chicago Park District Lakefront Path
Lakefront
312/294-2493
More than 20 miles of bicycling and jogging paths.

Cubby Bear Lounge
1059 W. Addison St.
312/327-1662
Sports bar/restaurant across from Wrigley Field ($)

Golf Courses
Chicago Park District
312/753-8670
Nine- and 18-hole golf courses in various parks.

Harry Caray's
33 W. Kinzie St.
312/465-9269
Cubs' legendary announcer operates his own restaurant with a Hall of Fame display. Italian cuisine ($$-$$$)

Sluggers World Class Sports Bar & Grill
3540 N. Clark St.
312/248-0055, 312/472-9696
Batting cages on one level, sports bar with food below.

Sports Wall of Fame
MC Mages Sporting Goods
620 N. LaSalle St.
312/337-6151
Compare your handprints to former Chicago greats on plaques outside the store.

Restaurants

The Berghoff
17 W. Adams St.
312/427-3170
German; a Loop institution since 1898 ($$)

Buckingham Fountain in Grant Park.

Cafe Ba Ba Reeba!
2024 N. Halsted St.
312/935-5000
Spanish cuisine features tapas, appetizer-size selections ($$)

Ed Debevic's
640 N. Wells St.
312/664-1707
Popular '50s diner theme ($)

El Jardin
3335 N. Clark St.
312/528-6775
Mexican cuisine; near Wrigley Field ($)

Gene & Georgetti
500 N. Franklin St.
312/527-3718
Steak, chops, fish ($$$)

Leona's
3215 N. Sheffield Ave.
312/327-8861
Italian; near Wrigley Field ($).

A survivor of the 1871 fire, the Water Tower.

Pizzeria Uno
29 E. Ohio St.
312/321-1000
Chicago-style deep-dish pizza was invented here ($)

Red Tomato
3417 N. Southport Ave.
312/472-5300
Italian menu; near the Wrigleyville neighborhood ($$)

Sports Spots & Restaurants (Dinner for two without beverage or tip):
$ Under $20
$$ 20-$40
$$$ More than $40

Accommodations

Days Inn Near North
644 W. Diversey Parkway
312/525-7010 ($$)

Drake Hotel
140 E. Walton Place
312/787-2200, 800/55-DRAKE ($$$)

Holiday Inn Chicago City Centre Hotel and Sports Center
300 E. Ohio St.
312/787-6100, 800-HOLIDAY ($$$)

Hyatt Regency
151 E. Wacker
312/565-1234 ($$$)

Price ranges: Double room during the week (lower rates are often available on weekends)
$ Under $75
$$ $75-$125
$$$ More than $125

Attractions

Adler Planetarium
1300 S. Lake Shore Drive
312/322-0300, 312/322-0304
Multi-media sky shows.

The Art Institute of Chicago
Michigan Avenue at Adams Street
312/443-3600
Features French Impressionist and Post-Impressionist art.

Chicago Historical Society
Clark Street at North Avenue
312/642-4600
Highlights the Great Chicago Fire of 1871 and American history.

Field Museum of Natural History
Roosevelt Road and South Lake Shore Drive
312/922-9410
Displays from anthropology, geology, botany, and zoology.

Lincoln Park Zoo
2200 N. Cannon Drive
312/294-4660
Famous in-city free zoo.

Museum of Science and Industry
57th Street and Lake Shore Drive
312/684-1414
Some 2,000 exhibits, including a space center and a 16-foot walk-through heart.

Sears Tower Skydeck
233 S. Wacker Drive
312/875-9696
Sweeping views from the top of the world's tallest building.

John G. Shedd Aquarium & Oceanarium
1200 S. Lake Shore Drive
312/939-2438
World's largest indoor aquarium with more than 6,600 aquatic animals.

For More Information

Chicago Convention & Tourism Bureau
2301 S. Lake Shore Drive
Chicago, IL 60616
312/567-8500

In 1991, the Chicago White Sox took a giant step into the 21st century and they only went across the street. They moved from old Comiskey Park, where the team had played since 1910, to the new Comiskey Park.

The 44,000-seat state-of-the-art stadium has a concourse wide enough to land a jet plane. In a more practical application, the concourse—indeed the whole park—is fan-friendly: you can take a break, visit the concession areas, or just stroll around the park and never lose sight of the game.

Several excellent Comiskey Park traditions have moved across the street along with the team: The scoreboard still announces home runs with major fireworks; the fans still annoy the opposing team by singing "Nah Nah Hey Hey Goodbye;" and there's still a picnic area.

Founding father Charles Comiskey would be proud of the team's new home. The carved arches on the rose-colored concrete exterior of the new stadium reflect the old stadium's configuration, and a Hall of Fame, located on the concourse, honors former White Sox greats like Minnie Minoso and Luis Aparicio.

Bleacher seats, complete with back supports, are a real bargain. And the pillars, necessary for support at the old park, are gone. As the saying goes, there's not a bad seat in the house.

American League West

Chicago White Sox

Lower Deck Boxes
Club Boxes
Upper Deck Boxes
Upper Deck Reserved
Lower Deck Reserved
Bleachers

Comiskey Park.

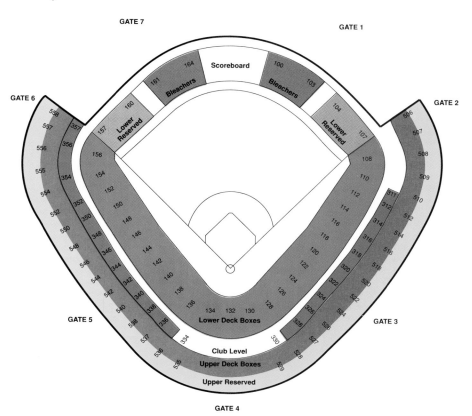

Purchasing Tickets

By mail:

Chicago White Sox Ticket Office
Comiskey Park
333 W. 35th St.
Chicago, IL 60616
312/924-1000

In person:

The White Sox box office accepts cash, credit cards, and personal checks with proper identification. Ticket office hours when the team is out of town: Monday - Friday, 10 a.m. - 6 p.m.; Saturday and Sunday, 10 a.m. - 4 p.m; when the team is in town: Monday - Saturday, 9 a.m. - 9 p.m.; Sunday, 9 a.m. - 4 p.m.

By phone:

TicketMaster
312/831-1769
Visa, MasterCard, and American Express are accepted.
For season tickets or group sales, call 312/924-1000.

Directions to the Stadium

• From the north: Take Lake Shore Drive south to the 31st Street exit.

• From the northwest: Take the Kennedy Expressway (I-90/94) east to the Dan Ryan Expressway (I-94) east to the 31st Street exit.

• From the west: Take the Eisenhower Expressway (I-290) east to the Dan Ryan Expressway (I-94) east to the 31st Street exit.

• From the south: Take the Dan Ryan Expressway (I-94) west to the 35th Street exit.

• From northern Indiana: Take the Indiana Toll Road (I-90) to the Dan Ryan Expressway (I-94) west to the 35th Street exit.

Public Transportation

By elevated trains ("el") and subways: Take the Dan Ryan "el" to 35th Street. From the Evanston "el" or the Ravenswood "el," transfer at the Clark/Lake station. Exit the O'Hare-Congress-Douglas subway at the Lake transfer station to access the Dan Ryan "el" at the Clark/Lake station. Call Chicago Transit Authority Travel Information Center, 312/836-7000.

By bus: Take Route 24 (Wentworth) or Route 44 (Wallace/Racine) north or south to Comiskey Park, or Route 35 (35th Street) east or west to Comiskey Park. Call CTA information: 312/836-7000.

Parking

More than 7,000 parking spaces are available in lots surrounding Comiskey Park, accessed from the Dan Ryan Expressway. When lots are full, free shuttle-bus service is available to and from remote lots located at the Illinois Institute of Technology, two blocks east of the park. The drop-off and pick-up point for the shuttle service is at 35th Street and Wentworth Avenue. Call 312/924-1000 to confirm shuttle availability.

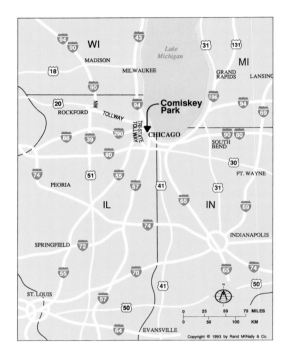

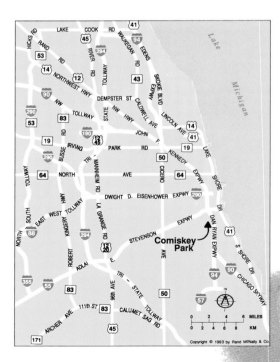

Chicago

Chicago is a world-class metropolis and a town of many small neighborhoods. Hotels listed are all in the downtown area, but restaurants cover downtown and the Near South Side.

Sports Spots

America's Bar
219 W. Erie St.
312/915-5986
This Walter Payton-owned spot rocks to the tunes of Top-40. Large happy-hour spread.

Chicago's Gold Coast and Magnificent Mile.

Chicago Beaches
Lakefront
312/294-2333
Chicago's lakefront offers 21 bathing beaches.

Chicago Park District Lakefront Path
Lakefront
312/294-2493
More than 20 miles of bicycling and jogging paths.

Chicago White Sox Clubhouse Shop
520 Oakbrook Center, Oak Brook
708/990-0459
Official licensed memorabilia shop.

Golf Courses
Chicago Park District
312/753-8670
Nine- and 18-hole golf courses in various parks. Also a miniature golf course and driving range at Diversey Parkway in Lincoln Park and a driving range in Jackson Park.

Marina City Bowl
300 N. State St.
312/527-0747
Bowling in the heart of downtown, 38 lanes.

Sport Fishing
Lake Michigan and Cook County Forest Preserves
Lake Michigan abounds with salmon, perch, and trout. Salmon fishing requires a license and stamps (312/814-2070 for license information). The Cook County Forest Preserves are the place for crappie, northern pike, bass, bullheads, and bluegills (708/366-9420). Charter boats are also available from the Chicago Sportfishing Association (312/922-1100).

Restaurants

Carson's, The Place for Ribs
612 N. Wells St.
312/280-9200
Barbecued rib and chicken ($$)

Ed Debevic's
640 N. Wells St.
312/664-1707
Popular '50s diner theme ($)

Leona's
1419 W. Taylor St.
312/850-2222 and
1936 W. Augusta Blvd.
312/292-4300
Two locations in proximity to Sox park. Italian pasta, pizza, great sandwiches ($-$$)

Pizzeria Uno
29 E. Ohio St.
312/321-1000
Chicago-style deep-dish pizza was invented here ($)

Rosebud Cafe
1500 W. Taylor St.
312/942-1117
Classic southern Italian preparations at a popular Little Italy restaurant. Huge portions of pasta, chicken, seafood ($$)

Taylor Street Bistro
1400 W. Taylor St.
312/829-2828
Classic French bistro food ($-$$)

Sports Spots & Restaurants (Dinner for two without beverage or tip):
$ **Under $20**
$$ **$20-$40**
$$$ **More than $40**

Accommodations

Best Western River North Hotel
125 W. Ohio St.
312/467-0800, 800/727-0800 ($$)

Chicago Hilton and Towers
720 S. Michigan Ave.
312/922-4400, 800/HILTONS ($$$)

Congress Hotel
520 S. Michigan Ave.
312/427-3800, 800/635-1666 ($$)

Days Inn Lake Shore Drive
644 N. Lake Shore Drive
312/943-9200, 800/942-7543 ($$)

Essex Inn
800 S. Michigan Ave.
312/939-2800, 800/621-6909 ($$)

Hyatt Regency
151 E. Wacker Dr.
312/565-1234 ($$$)

Price ranges: Double room during the week (lower rates are often available on weekends)
$ **Under $75**
$$ **$75-$125**
$$$ **More than $125**

Attractions

Adler Planetarium
1300 S. Lake Shore Drive
312/322-0300, 312/322-0304
Multi-media sky shows.

The Art Institute of Chicago
Michigan Avenue at Adams Street
312/443-3600
One of the finest collections of French Impressionist and Post-Impressionist art outside of France.

Picasso sculpture in Daley Center.

Field Museum of Natural History
Roosevelt Road and South Lake Shore Drive
312/922-9410
Collections from the fields of anthropology, geology, botany, and zoology.

Museum of Science and Industry
57th Street and Lake Shore Drive
312/684-1414
This museum offers about 2,000 exhibits, including the Apollo 8 spacecraft, a captured German U-505 submarine, and a 16-foot walk-through heart.

John G. Shedd Aquarium & Oceanarium
1200 S. Lake Shore Drive
312/939-2438
Indoor aquarium presents more than 6,000 aquatic animals.

Sightseeing Boats
The Chicago River at Michigan Avenue and Wacker Drive; and at Navy Pier, Grand Avenue, and Lake Michigan
Choice of guided boat rides on Chicago River and Lake Michigan or lunch and dinner cruises with entertainment.

For More Information

Chicago Convention & Tourism Bureau
2301 S. Lake Shore Drive
Chicago, IL 60616
312/567-8500

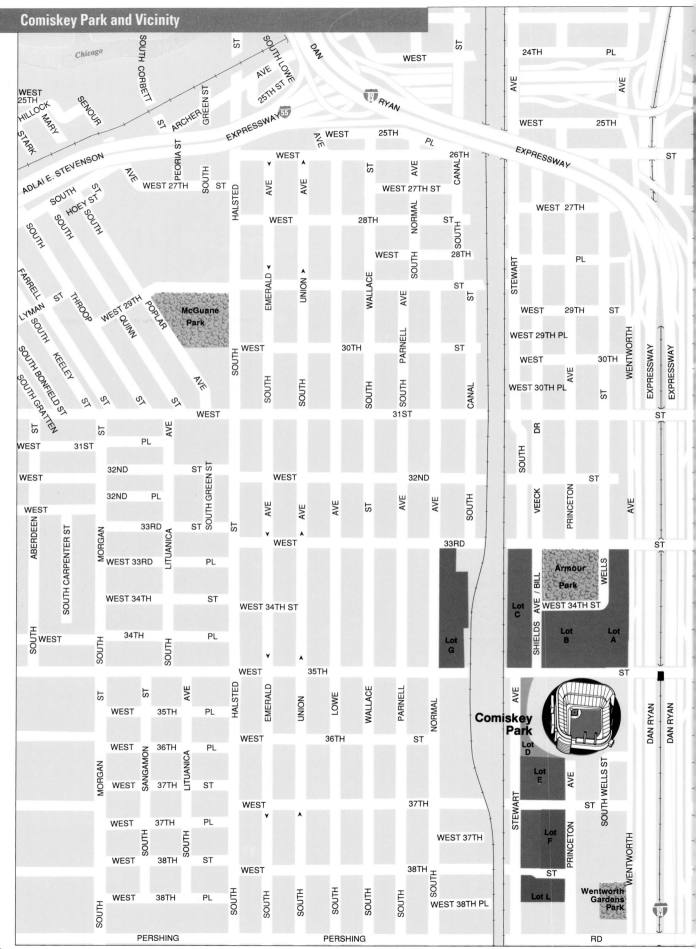

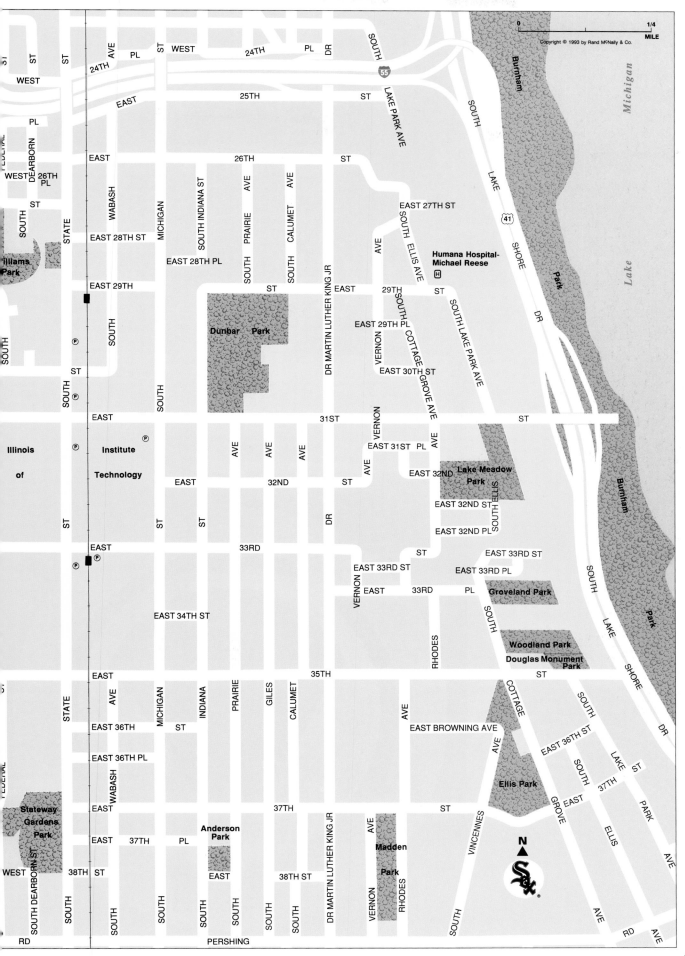

0   1/4
MILE

AVE PL ST WEST 24TH PL DR SOUTH

24TH AVE

WEST

EAST 25TH ST LAKE PARK AVE

55

PL

WEST DEARBORN

WEST 26TH PL 26TH ST

ST EAST WABASH

SOUTH MICHIGAN

SOUTH INDIANA ST

PRAIRIE AVE

CALUMET AVE

EAST 27TH ST

SOUTH

STATE EAST 28TH ST

SOUTH ELLIS AVE

Humana Hospital-
Michael Reese
H

illams Park

SOUTH

ST EAST 28TH PL

SOUTH

SOUTH

DR MARTIN LUTHER KING JR

EAST

29TH

SOUTH

SOUTH LAKE PARK AVE

ST

LAKE

SHORE

Burnham

Park

41

Michigan

Lake

EAST 29TH ST

ST EAST 29TH PL

SOUTH COTTAGE GROVE AVE

VERNON

EAST 30TH ST

Dunbar Park

SOUTH ST

SOUTH

DR

EAST 31ST ST

31ST ST

VERNON AVE

EAST 31ST PL

AVE

Illinois

of

P P Institute

Technology

P

AVE AVE AVE

EAST 32ND ST

AVE

EAST 32ND

Lake Meadow
Park

SOUTH ELLIS

ST

Burnham

ST EAST 32ND ST

ST ST ST DR

EAST 32ND PL

P P EAST 33RD

ST

EAST 33RD ST

EAST 33RD ST

EAST 33RD PL

VERNON

EAST 33RD PL

Groveland Park

SOUTH

SHORE

Park

EAST 34TH ST

RHODES

Woodland Park

Douglas Monument
Park

LAKE

EAST 35TH ST

STATE AVE MICHIGAN INDIANA PRAIRIE GILES CALUMET

ST

AVE

ST

COTTAGE

SOUTH

EAST 36TH ST

EAST 36TH

ST

EAST BROWNING AVE

AVE

GROVE

EAST

LAKE

ST

37TH

EAST 36TH PL

WABASH

Ellis Park

SOUTH

ELLIS

Stateway
Gardens
Park

EAST

EAST 37TH ST

ST

Anderson
Park

DR MARTIN LUTHER KING JR

AVE

VINCENNES

PARK

SOUTH DEARBORN ST

EAST 37TH PL

EAST

Madden
Park

N

VERNON

AVE

RD

WEST 38TH ST

SOUTH

SOUTH

SOUTH

SOUTH PRAIRIE

SOUTH 38TH ST

SOUTH

DR MARTIN LUTHER KING JR

VERNON

RHODES

SOUTH

AVE

RD RD PERSHING

33

Cincinnati loves Riverfront Stadium and the Cincinnati Reds for good reasons.

The "Big Red Machine" powered its way to four pennants in the 1970s. Johnny Bench, Pete Rose, Tony Perez, and Joe Morgan became household names in cities throughout America.

Successful baseball in Cincinnati started long before Riverfront Stadium existed. The winning tradition was launched in 1869, when the Cincinnati Red Stockings went undefeated in their first season. The Red Stockings played in parks constructed of wood—one actually looked like an ancient palace with pillars and columns—until 1912. Then the team, renamed the Reds, moved into Crosley Field. On May 24, 1935, this park was the site of the first night game in baseball history.

In 1970, the Reds left Crosley Field for Riverfront Stadium, a 56,000-seat, multi-purpose field of play. In a nod to their long baseball history, the Reds brought a piece of their past with them: home plate from Crosley Field.

Inside the new park, the upper deck offers a great view of the Cincinnati downtown area. The best seats for catching home-run balls are in left field. Taste the "Mett," a specialty sausage sandwich served here.

Professional baseball has been played in Cincinnati since 1869. The Reds and their generations of fans remember well the traditions of baseball. Riverfront Stadium is a late-20th-century addition to the team's long and distinguished history.

Cincinnati Reds

Riverfront Stadium.

- ■ Blue Level Box Seats
- ■ Green Level Box Seats
- ☐ Yellow Level Box Seats
- ■ Red Level Box Seats
- ☐ Green Level Reserved
- ■ Red Level Reserved

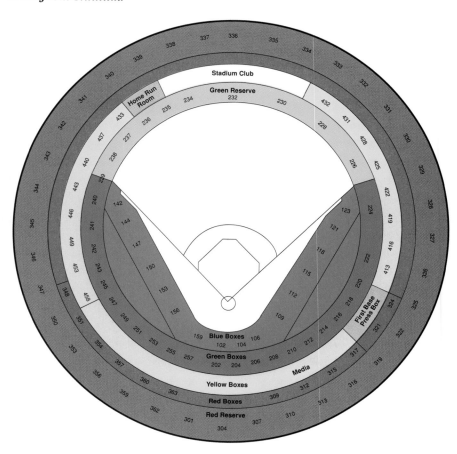

Purchasing Tickets

By mail:
Cincinnati Reds
100 Riverfront Stadium
Cincinnati, OH 45202
513/421-4510

Make check or money order payable to the Cincinnati Reds and specify the date, number, and price of tickets desired. Add $2 per order for postage and handling.

In person:
Ticket Office
Riverfront Stadium, northwest corner on the plaza level
513/421-4510, ext. 300/301/302
Ticket office hours: Monday - Friday, 9 a.m. - 5:30 p.m. and on home game days from 9 a.m. until bottom of the fifth inning. The ticket office accepts cash, Visa, MasterCard, and personal checks with ID and one of the two credit cards.

Cincinnati Reds Gift Shop
Hyatt Regency Hotel
Fifth and Elm streets
513/651-7200
Ticket Sales Hours: Monday - Saturday,
9 a.m. - 5:30 p.m.

By phone:
TicketMaster
513/421-REDS or 513/749-4949 in Cincinnati;
800/829-5353 outside Cincinnati

Directions to the Stadium

- From the north: Take I-75 South, follow Downtown signs and exit on Pete Rose Way. Or connect to I-71 South, pass through the tunnel and take the 3rd Street exit. Turn right on 3rd, right on Broadway, and right on Pete Rose Way.

- From Kentucky: Take I-75 North, follow north I-71 sign to Pete Rose Way exit. Or take I-471 to the 6th Street exit, turn left on Sycamore, left on 3rd Street, right on Broadway, and right on Pete Rose Way.

- From Indiana: Take I-74 East to I-75 South, follow Downtown signs to Pete Rose Way exit.

Public Transportation

Take the Number 28 or 49 bus to 4th and Broadway. From there, it's a short walk to the stadium. For information, call 513/621-4455.

Parking

About 5,100 parking spaces are available in the Riverfront Stadium garage and lots. Spaces are reserved for handicapped individuals on the plaza level of the stadium. Bus and RV parking is also available on the plaza level. The city operates underground parking garages located between Sixth Street and the stadium; private parking lots are available east and west of the stadium.

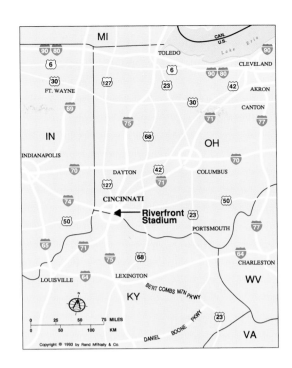

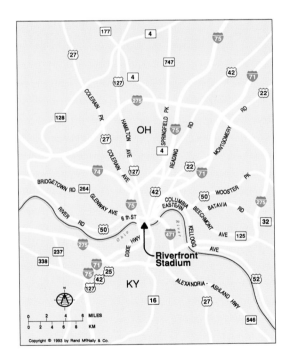

Union Station

LINCOLN PARK DR

HOPKINS ST

GEST ST

NINTH ST

EIGHTH ST

SEVENTH ST

BUDD ST

DALTON

SIXTH ST EXPRESSWAY

FRONT

SARGENT

CARR

FRONT

WESTERN AVE

MILL CREEK

FREEMAN AVE

LINN

EXPRESSWAY

EZZARD ST

CHARLES ST

CLARK ST

COURT ST

CUTTER

RICHMOND

NOTRE DAME PL

MOUND ST

GEST ST

EXPRESSWAY

SIXTH ST

LINN ST

MEHRING

FIFTH ST

THIRD ST

BAYMILLER

GEST ST

SECOND WAY

OHIO
KENTUCKY

JOHN ST

FOURTEENTH DR

CENTRAL

ANN ST

HOPKINS ST

CLARK ST

CHESTNUT

ELIZABETH

GENESSEE ST

RICHMOND

NINTH ST

EIGHTH

SEVENTH

CENTRAL

GEORGE ST

SIXTH

PLUM AVE

GRANT ST

TWELFTH PARKWAY

CHARLES ST

ELM ST

RACE

CENTRAL

COURT ST

City Hall

27 **52** **127**

27

27 **52** **127**

27
42
52
127

264

42

GARF

3

264

22

Cincinnati
Convention
Center

22
27
52
127 FIFTH

3 PERRY ST

42
52
127 FOURTH

42

264

27
42

MCFARLAND

FORT

42 FORT

THIRD

27

JOHN ST

CORRIGAN AL

AUGUSTA

PRODUCE

SMITH

WATER ST

MEHRING

P
P
P
P

Amtrak

ROSE ST

RIVER RD

LIVINGSTON

WEST

FREEMAN ST

ALTAMONT

BOND

AUDREY AVE

MONCLAIRE

MASON CT

ALBERTA ST

LUDLOW

HAZEN

WEST

WEST

LEXINGTON

HILL ST

BELLVUE ST

HILLCREST AVE

ALTAMONT AVE

ALBERTA ST

REID ST

HIGHWAY

HIGH ST

WEST SPRING ST

PARKWAY

CONE ST

SWAIN

VIEW ST

HILLCREST CT

PARKWAY

CLARK ST

LUDLOW ST

FOREST

HATHAWAY CT HIGHWAY

SPRING PARKWAY

WILSON ST

JOHN ST

SECOND ST

SPRING ST

RIDGE ST

WRIGHT ST

WESTERN AVE

HIDDEN HILLS RD

HILL AVE

DR
RIDGEWAY DR
RIVER RD

SUNSET RD
PANORAMA
EDGE HILL RD

WAYNE

8

8

8

Brent Spence Bridge

Clay Wade Bailey Bridge

42
127

THIRD ST

8

BEECH CT

PHILADELPHIA

FOURTH

BAKEWELL

ELM ST

FIFTH

71
75

Goebel
Park

SIXTH

8

MAIN

25
42

Deveu Park

0   1/4

Copyright © 1993 by Rand McNally & Co.

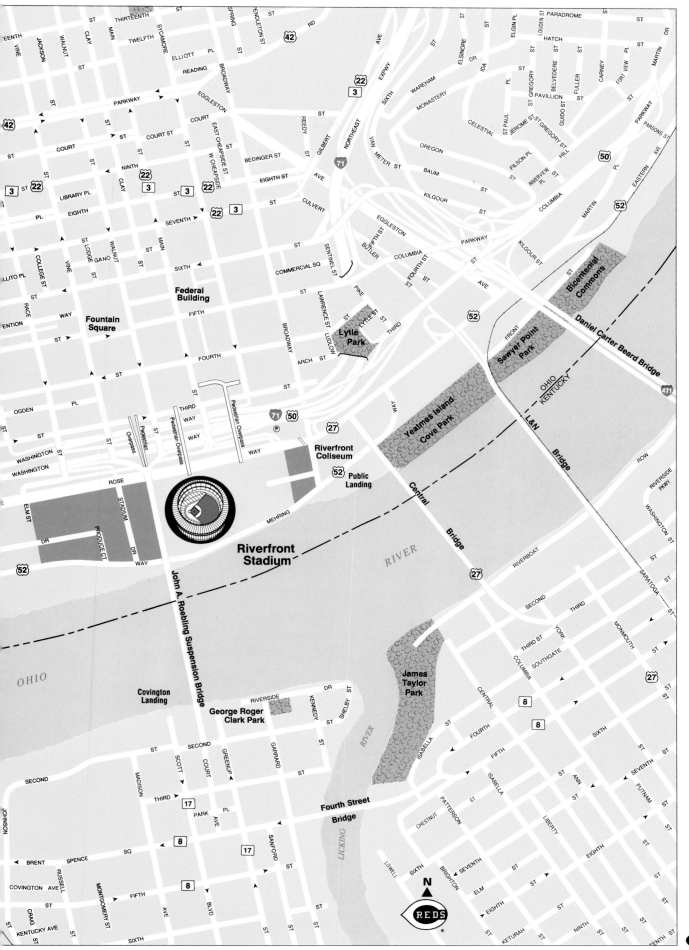

Cincinnati

Riverfront Stadium is, indeed, right on the river, as are many attractions. Hotels and restaurants listed are downtown or directly across the river in northern Kentucky.

Sports Spots

Barleycorn's
124 E. 6th St.
513/621-5511
Sports bar/restaurant ($)

The Beach Waterpark
2590 Waterpark Drive, Mason
513/398-4356
Waves, rides, volleyball.

Coney Island
6201 Kellogg Ave.
513/232-8230
Swimming, water slides.

Along the Ohio River with a view of downtown.

Flanagan's Landing
212 W. Pete Rose Way
513/421-4055
Irish pub/sports hangout ($)

Jack Nicklaus Sports Center
6042 Fairway Drive, Mason
513/398-5200
Golf courses, tennis courts.

La Boom
14 Pete Rose Pier, Covington, KY
606/581-1414
Sports bar partly owned by Bengal quarterback Boomer Esiason.

Surf Cincinnati Waterpark
11460 Sebring Drive
513/742-0620
Wave pool, slides.

Willie's Bar and Grill
8740 Montgomery Road
513/891-2204
Sports bar/restaurant ($)

Restaurants

Campanello's Italian Restaurant
414 Central Ave.
513/721-9833
Italian cuisine ($$)

Dining and entertainment at Oldenberg Brewery.

Crockett's River Cafe
1 Riverboat Road, Newport, KY
606/581-2800
Steak, seafood, raw bar ($$)

El Greco
2440 Alexandria Pike
Southgate, KY
606/441-6600
Continental cuisine ($$)

La Normandie Grill
118 E. 6th St.
513/721-2761
Steak, fish, chops ($$)

Maisonette
114 E. 6th St.
513/721-2260
French cuisine ($$$)

Mike Fink's Restaurant
Foot of Greenup Street
Covington, KY
606/261-4212
Riverboat restaurant, American cuisine ($$)

Montgomery Inn Boathouse
925 Eastern Ave.
513/721-RIBS
Ribs, chicken, shrimp ($$)

The Precinct
311 Delta Ave.
513/321-5454
Chicken, seafood ($$$)

Skyline Chili
212 Pete Rose Way
513/651-4400
Chili, burritos ($)

The Waterfront
14 Pete Rose Pier, Covington, KY
606/581-1414
Seafood, pasta ($$-$$$)

*Sports Spots & Restaurants
(Dinner for two without beverage or tip)*
$ Under $20
$$ $20-$40
$$$ More than $40

Accommodations

Cincinnatian Hotel
601 Vine St.
513/381-3000 ($$$)

Clarion Hotel
141 6th St.
513/352-2100 ($$)

Embassy Suites Hotel
10 E. RiverCenter Blvd.
Covington, KY
606/261-8400 ($$$)

Holiday Inn—Riverfront
3rd and Philadelphia
Covington, KY
606/291-4300, 800/HOLIDAY ($$)

Howard Johnson's Erlanger
630 Commonwealth Ave.
Erlanger, KY
606/727-3400, 800/446-4656 ($)

Hyatt Regency
151 W. 5th St.
513/579-1234 ($$$)

Quality Hotel Riverview
666 5th St., Covington, KY
606/491-1200 ($)

Terrace Hilton
15 W. 6th St.
513/381-4000 ($$$)

Price ranges: Double room during the week (lower rates are often available on weekends)
$ Under $75
$$ $75-$125
$$$ More than $125

Outdoor events at the Procter & Gamble Pavilion.

Attractions

Cincinnati Zoo
3400 Vine St.
513/281-4700
Zoo and botanical gardens.

Covington Landing at RiverCenter
Foot of Madison Avenue,
Covington, KY
606/291-9992
Boat cruises, restaurants, night-clubs, shops, theater.

Kings Island Theme Park
Off I-71, 24 miles north of Cincinnati
513/398-5600
Thrill rides, water activities.

Museum Center at Union Terminal
1301 Western Ave.
513/287-7000
Contains the Cincinnati Historical Society Museum and Library, Cincinnati Museum of Natural History, Omnimax Theater, shops.

Oldenberg Brewery
I-75 at Buttermilk Pike
Ft. Mitchell, KY
606/341-2800
Micro-brewery tours.

Riverboat Cruises
Covington Landing
Covington, KY
606/261-8500 (BB Riverboats),
606/292-8687 (Queen City Riverboats)
Sightseeing, breakfast, lunch, and dinner cruises.

For More Information

*Greater Cincinnati Convention and Visitors Bureau
300 W. 6th St.
Cincinnati, OH 45202
513/621-2142*

Cleveland Stadium has been the site of several baseball firsts.

The first Native American to play in the big leagues, Louis Sockalexis, played for Cleveland from 1897 to 1899.

In 1948, Larry Doby broke the color barrier in the American League, a year after Jackie Robinson did the same in the National.

Cleveland Stadium pioneered the concept of publicly financed downtown ballparks in an era when other parks like Wrigley Field, Crosley Field, and Yankee Stadium were built by (and often named for) their owners. For most of its existence, Cleveland Stadium was the biggest park in baseball, seating more than 70,000.

Cleveland also hosted big crowds in 1920 and 1948 when the Indians brought home the world's championship, and in 1954 when the team reached the Series. That team posted an amazing 111-43 regular-season record but lost the Series in four games to the New York Giants and the glove of the dazzling Willie Mays, who made "The Catch" that broke the heart of every Indians fan.

The Cleveland Indians plan to move out of their giant-sized (74,483) home and into a baseball-only park for the 1994 season. To be built by the same architects who designed Oriole Park at Camden Yards, the new 42,000-seat stadium will be located on the south side of downtown at Carnegie and Ontario streets.

The Indians plan to move their history with them and perhaps even add some "firsts" in the new stadium.

Cleveland Indians

Field Boxes
Lower Boxes
Upper Boxes
Lower Reserved
Upper Reserved
General Admission
Bleachers

Cleveland Indians

Cleveland Stadium.

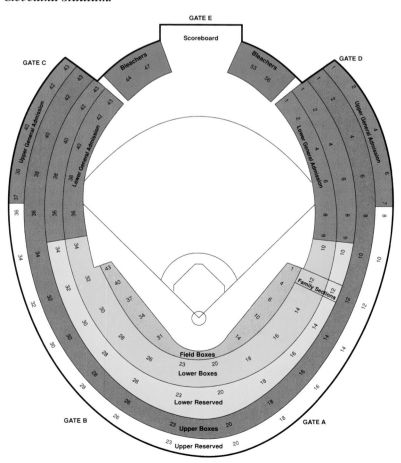

GATE E

Scoreboard

GATE C

Bleachers
44 47

Bleachers
53 56

GATE D

Upper General Admission

Lower General Admission

Upper General Admission

Lower General Admission

Family Section

Field Boxes

Lower Boxes

Lower Reserved

GATE B

Upper Boxes

Upper Reserved

GATE A

Purchasing Tickets

By mail:

Call 216/861-1200 to request a mail order form, or mail order with requested game, the number of tickets, and price. Add $3 for postage and handling. Send to:

Cleveland Stadium
Gate A
1805 W. Third St.
Cleveland, OH 44114

In person:

Cleveland Indians Ticket Office, Gate A
Cleveland Stadium
1805 W. Third St.
Ticket office hours: Monday - Friday, 9 a.m. - 5:30 p.m.; Saturday 10 a.m. - 4 p.m., and from 9 a.m. until the game ends on days when home games are played.

Cleveland Indians Gift Shop
The Galleria at Erieview, 2nd floor
Hours: Monday - Friday, 10 a.m. - 7:30 p.m.; Saturday, 10 a.m. - 7 p.m.; Sunday, noon - 5 p.m.

By phone:

TicketMaster
216/241-5555

Directions to the Stadium

- From the south: Take I-71 North to the East 9th Street exit; proceed north on East 9th Street to the lakefront. Or take I-71 North to the Ontario Street exit. Go north on Ontario through Public Square to Lakeside Avenue. Turn left onto Lakeside, then right onto West 3rd Street; proceed north to the stadium.

- From the east: Take I-90 West to Ohio Route 2 West to the 9th Street exit. Proceed north on East 9th Street to the lakefront. Or take I-480 West to I-77 North to the East 9th Street exit. Proceed North on East 9th to the lakefront.

- From the west: Take I-90 East to I-71 North to East 9th Street exit; proceed north on East 9th to lakefront. Or take I-480 East to I-71 North to East 9th Street exit. Proceed north on East 9th to lakefront. Or take Ohio Route 2 to Detroit Avenue exit. Go east over Veterans-Memorial (Detroit-Superior) Bridge onto Superior Avenue. Turn left at West 3rd Street; proceed north to stadium.

Public Transportation

No public transportation serves Cleveland Stadium directly. However, several Regional Transit Authority bus and rail routes stop at Terminal Tower downtown. The stadium is about a 10-minute walk from Terminal Tower. For bus and rail routes, contact the Regional Transit Authority, 216/621-9500.

Parking

Extensive public parking surrounds Cleveland Stadium. Parking for handicapped persons is available on a first-come, first-served basis on West 3rd Street inside the yellow poles between Gates A and B and on Erieside Avenue adjacent to Gate D. When the West 3rd Street lot is full, vehicles may park temporarily on West 3rd Street along the yellow poles between Gates A and B to drop off handicapped persons before going on to the public lot across the street. For information, call the Indians Operations Department at 216/861-1200.

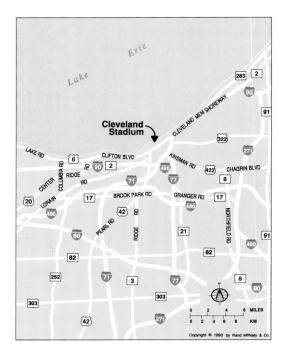

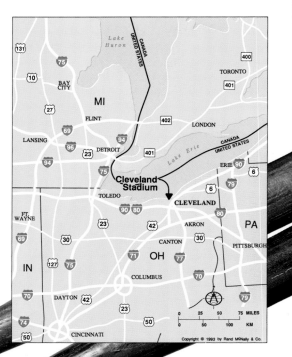

Cleveland

Cleveland has been dubbed a "comeback city" thanks to extensive urban renewal. Hotels and restaurants listed are convenient to downtown, the ballpark, and the airport.

Sports Spots

Alvies Stadium Cafe
Cleveland Stadium, Gate A,
Fourth Floor
216/861-5055
Snacks, light fare ($$)

Bat-A-Rama
15330 Broadway, Maple Heights
216/662-7668
Batting cages, refreshments($)

Celebrities
6901 Rockside Road
Independence
216/642-STAR
Burgers, pasta, ribs ($)

Family Sports Center
6699 Eastland Road
216/234-5221
Driving range, game room, pool
tables, pizza ($)

**Grand Slam Grille &
Power Play**
The Powerhouse
2000 Sycamore St.
216/696-4884, 696-7664
Sports bar/restaurant, game
room and more ($)

Pro Football Hall of Fame
2121 George Halas Drive N.W.,
Canton
216/456-7762
Football history, nostalgia, and
memorabilia.

Sports World
2083 E. 21st St.
216/781-7403
Restaurant and sports entertain-
ment complex with Playoffs Bar
and Grill, and outdoor volleyball
courts ($-$$)

Skyline view of Cleveland.

Restaurants

Jim's Steak House
1800 Scranton Road
216/241-6343
Steak, seafood ($$)

John Q's Public Bar & Grill
55 Public Square
216/861-0900
Steak, seafood ($)

**Morton's of
Chicago/Cleveland**
Tower City Center
West 2nd Street and Prospect
216/621-6200
Beef, chops, seafood ($$$)

New York Spaghetti House
2173 E. 9th St.
216/696-6624
Northern Italian ($$)

Ninth Street Grill
The Galleria at Erieview
1301 E. 9th St.
216/579-9919
Steak, seafood, pasta ($$)

Sammy's
1400 W. 10th St.
216/523-5560
American cuisine ($$$)

Shooter's Waterfront Cafe
1148 Main
216/861-6900
Seafood, burgers, ribs; along the
Cuyahoga River ($$)

Sweetwater's Cafe Sausalito
The Galleria at Erieview
1301 E. 9th St.
216/696-CAFE
Seafood, pasta, regional cuisine
($$)

***Sports Spots & Restaurants
(Dinner for two without
beverage or tip):***
$ **Under $20**
$$ **$20-$40**
$$$ **More than $40**

Accommodations

Cleveland Airport Marriott
4277 W. 150th St.
216/252-5333 ($$)

Holiday Inn—Lakeside
1111 Lakeside Ave.
216/241-5100 ($$)

Marriott at Society Center
127 Public Square
216/696-9200 ($$$)

Playhouse Square, the restored theater area.

The Omni International
206 E. 96th St.
University Circle
216/791-1900 ($$)

Radisson Plaza Hotel
1701 E. 12th St.
216/523-8000 ($$)

Ritz-Carlton Cleveland
Tower City Center
1515 W. 3rd St.
216/623-1300 ($$$)

Sheraton City Centre
777 St. Clair Ave.
216/771-7600, 800/362-2727 (in
Ohio), 800/321-1090 (outside
Ohio) ($$)

**Stouffer Tower City Plaza
Hotel**
24 Public Square
216/696-5600 ($$$)

***Price ranges: Double room
during the week (lower rates
often available on weekends)***
$ **Under $75**
$$ **$75-$125**
$$$ **More than $125**

*Tower City Center on
Public Square.*

Attractions

Cleveland Metropark Zoo
3900 Brookside Park Drive
216/661-6500
The lions, tigers, bears and their
rainforest relatives.

Cleveland Museum of Art
11150 East Blvd.
216/421-7340
Works of art from all cultures
and periods.

**Cleveland Museum of Natural
History**
Wade Oval Drive
University Circle
216/231-4600
Dinosaur and human fossils,
planetarium, observatory.

The Flats
Historic warehouse district lo-
cated just west of downtown on
the Cuyahoga River.
Renovated area with galleries,
marinas, nightclubs, restaurants.

Playhouse Square Center
1519 Euclid Ave.
216/771-4444, 800/492-6048 (in
Ohio), 800/492-9696 (outside
Ohio),
Cleveland's restored theater dis-
trict offers musicals, ballet,
opera, and drama.

Sea World of Ohio
1100 Sea World Drive, Aurora
216/562-8101, 800/63-SHAMU
Marine life park features live
aquatic shows and exhibits.

Tower City Center
50 Public Square
216/623-4750
Renovated complex of specialty
shops, movie theaters, restau-
rants, and hotels.

For More Information

*Convention & Visitors Bureau of
Greater Cleveland
3100 Tower City Center
Cleveland, OH 44113
216/621-4110*

0   1/2
        MILE
Copyright © 1993 by Rand McNally & Co.

ERIE

EAST BASIN

LAKE

Burke Lakefront Airport

NORTH
COAST HARBOR

Stadium
Pier

North Lot

East Lot

West 3rd St
Pier

West 6th St
Pier

Cleveland
Stadium

West 9th St
Pier

City
Hall

Amtrak

Amtrak
Station

Galleria
& Tower at
Erieview

WEST BASIN

County
Court
House

Convention
Center

Public
Square

Whiskey

Island

Amtrak

CUYAHOGA

Tower
City Center

Rapid Transit
Station

Erie

Site of new
ballpark
scheduled
to open in
1994

Edgewater
Park

OLD   RIVER

RIVER   BED

Veterans

RIVER

CUYAHOGA

BREAKWATER

Hope Memorial Bridge

W 25th St Rapid
Transit Station

Lincoln
Park

Monroe
Cemetery

W 65th St Rapid
Transit Station

Tremont Valley
Playground

Mile High Stadium has seen a lot of great baseball games over the years, so it's no surprise that the Colorado Rockies will call it home for the next two years.

In fact, Denver and baseball go back a long way. Professional baseball found its way to Denver in 1947, when the Howsam family founded the Class AAA Denver Bears and built Bears Stadium.

The team was so popular that additional seating capacity was added in 1959. In 1968, a non-profit group expanded and rededicated the Bears' home as Mile High Stadium.

By 1985, a then-minor league affiliate of the Cincinnati Reds arrived onto the Denver scene. From this foundation, a proud baseball tradition grew, culminating in 1993 with the inaugural season of the Colorado Rockies at Mile High.

Mile High Stadium is also the home of the Denver Broncos. To convert the football field into a baseball diamond and back into a football field, the entire east stands (three tiers containing 21,000 seats) float out to left field on a cushion of water, transforming a 100-yard football field into an asymmetrical baseball field.

In 1995, the Rockies are scheduled to move into Coors Field, a traditional 43,000-seat, open-air, natural grass ballpark in lower downtown Denver at 20th and Blake streets. Until then, Mile High continues its proud heritage of great pro ball.

Colorado Rockies

Mile High Stadium.

☐ VIP Field Boxes
☐ Infield Plaza Boxes
☐ Outfield Plaza Boxes
☐ Private Loge Suites
☐ Infield Mezzanine Boxes
☐ Outfield Mezzanine Boxes
☐ Infield Terrace Boxes
☐ Outfield Terrace Boxes
☐ Infield View
☐ Outfield View
☐ Reserved Pavilion
☐ Reserved-General Admission
☐ Rockpile-Reserved

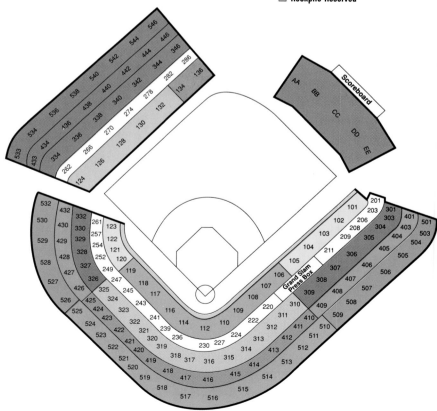

Purchasing Tickets

By mail or in person:
Colorado Rockies Baseball Club
1700 Broadway, Suite 2100
Denver, CO 80290
Attn: Ticket Operations

By phone:
303/ROCKIES (303/762-5437)
303/292-0200

Directions to the Stadium

Beginning 1-1/2 hours before a game, traffic cannot turn left from southbound Federal Boulevard between 20th and 17th avenues; no traffic from westbound Colfax Viaduct will be allowed onto northbound Federal.

• From the south on Federal or from Colfax: Use Holden Place or Howard Place to get to the parking lots.

• From the south on I-25: Exit at 8th Avenue (Exit 209C). Turn left on 8th, then right on Zuni Street to 13th Avenue or Lower Colfax.

You can get to the Auraria parking lots from 1-25, Speer Boulevard, or Colfax.

Public Transportation

The Regional Transit District (303/778-6000) provides shuttle service to the Auraria Campus, as well as shuttles from outlying areas.

Parking

Mile High Stadium is surrounded by 9,010 parking spaces. Access is possible from I-25 (Exit 210B), Federal Boulevard, 20th Avenue, Bryant Street, and 17th Avenue. Parking for baseball events at city-operated parking lots around the stadium is $3. On-street parking in the neighborhood around the stadium is for residents only and violators will be towed.

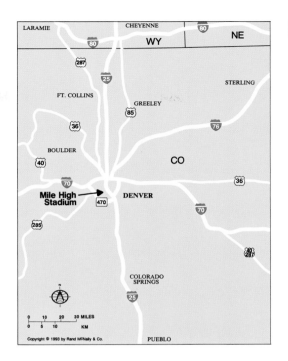

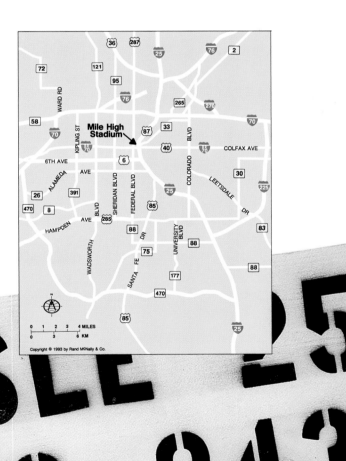

Profile

Team Address
Colorado Rockies
Mile High Stadium
1900 Eliot St.
Denver, CO 80204
303/292-0200

Franchise History
Colorado Rockies, 1993-

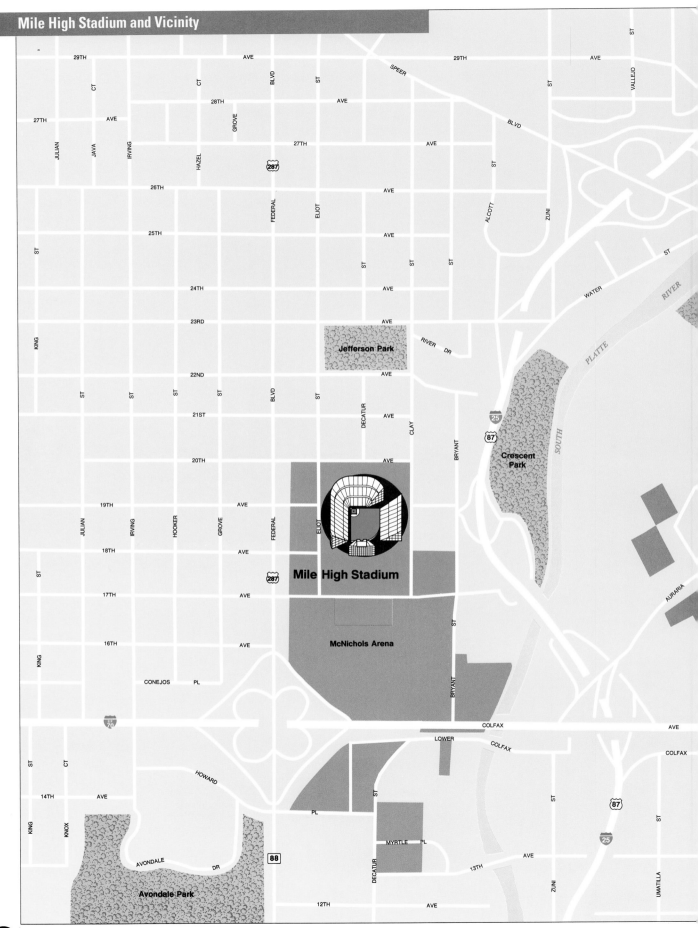

Mile High Stadium

McNichols Arena

Jefferson Park

Crescent Park

Avondale Park

0   1/4
MILE

Copyright © 1993 by Rand McNally & Co.

N

Union
Station

Centennial
Park

CENTRAL
16TH
15TH
PLATTE
ST
ST
19TH
20TH
ST
ST
ST
INCA ST
HURON ST
GALAPAGO ST
FOX ST
AV
29TH
23RD
24TH
ST
ST
22ND
21ST
20TH
19TH
18TH
17TH
ST
ST
ST
ST
ST
ST
ST
ST
ST
ST
ST
ST

DELAGANY
WYNKOOP
WAZEE
SPEER
CHERRY
BLVD
CREEK
BLAKE
16TH
15TH
MARKET
LARIMER
14TH
LARIMER
Square

33
33
33

Larimer
Square

LAWRENCE
ARAPAHOE
CURTIS
CHAMPA
STOUT
CALIFORNIA
WELTON
GLENARM
TREMONT
COURT
PL
PL
PL
13TH

WEWATTA
ST
11TH
ST
ST
12TH
WAZEE
PKWY
8TH
7TH
LARIMER
ST
ST
CURTIS
ST

Denver
Performing Arts
Complex

Convention
Center

Auraria
Campus

12TH
ST

40
287
70
COLFAX
AVE
AVE

SPEER
US
Mint

Civic Center
Park

AVE
LA
RIO
CT
OSAGE
ST
ST
14TH
ST
ST
KALAMATH
DR
ST
ST
AVE
ST
ST

SHOSHONE
QUIVAS
ST
Lincoln
Park
13TH
SANTA FE
12TH
BLVD
ELATI
DELAWARE
CHEROKEE
BANNOCK
ACOMA

Denver Art Museum
AVE
AVE
AVE
MARIPOSA
LIPAN

Denver

Denver was originally founded as a gold-mining camp and then a center for silver mining. Mile High Stadium is located just west of the downtown area.

Sports Spots

Adrenalin Adventures
P.O. Box 1667, Boulder
303/440-6292
Bungee jumping.

Arrowhead Golf Club
10850 W. Sundown Trail
Littleton
303/973-9614
Stunning setting 45 minutes from downtown Denver.

Bandimere Speedway
3051 S. Rooney Road, Morrison
303/697-6001, 303/697-4870
Drag-racing events April-October.

Boulder Creekpath
Downtown Boulder, along
Boulder Creek, Boulder
Jogging, biking, roller-skating trails. Kayak slalom course.

Celebrity Sports Center
888 S. Colorado Blvd.
303/757-3321
Pool, waterslides, bowling, arcades.

The Cloud Base, Inc.
5117 Independence Road
Boulder
303/530-2208
Gliding rides and instruction.

Platte River Rafting, Inc.
2200 Seventh St.
303/477-0379
River rafting and trolley rides.

ProRodeo Hall of Fame & American Cowboy Museum
I-25 at Rockrimmon Boulevard, Exit 147, Colorado Springs
719/528-4764
Museum of cowboys, the West, and Western art.

Two Wheel Tours
P.O. Box 2655, Littleton
303/798-4601, 800/343-8940
Down-hill bicycling tours of Mt. Evans, Vail, Summit County.

United States Olympic Complex
1750 E. Boulder, Colorado Springs
719/578-4618
Free one-hour tours of the nation's Olympic training center.

World Figure Skating Hall of Fame and Museum
20 First St., Colorado Springs
719/635-5200
Costumes of skiing champions, skating art.

Tabor Center.

Restaurants

Broker Restaurant
821 17th St.
303/292-5065
Steak, seafood in elegant surroundings; ask to dine in the bank vault ($$-$$$)

Marlowe's
511 16th St.
303/595-3700
Steaks, chops, seafood. Great place for locals and celebrities ($$)

Rock Bottom Brewery
1001 16th St.
303/534-7616
On-site micro brewery/restaurant ($$)

Rocky Mountain Diner
800 18th St.
303/293-8383
1900s Western diner ($)

Strings
1700 Humboldt
303/831-7310
Casual setting ($$-$$$)

Tante Louise
4900 E. Colfax Ave.
303/355-4488
French cuisine ($$$)

Sports Spots & Restaurants (Dinner for two without beverage or tip):
$ Under $20
$$ $20-$40
$$$ More than $40

Denver's active nightlife.

Accommodations

Brown Palace Hotel
321 17th St.
303/297-3111 ($$$)

Denver Marriott City Center
1701 California St.
303/297-1300 ($$$)

Hotel Denver Downtown
1450 Glenarm Place
303/573-1450, 800/423-5128 ($-$$)

Hyatt Regency Denver
1750 Welton St.
303/295-1234, 800/233-1234 ($$$)

Oxford Hotel
1600 17th St.
303/628-5400 ($$$)

Radisson Hotel Denver
1550 Court Place
303/893-3333 ($$)

Price ranges: Double room during the week (lower rates are often available on weekends)
$ Under $75
$$ $75-$125
$$$ More than $125

Attractions

Colorado Railroad Museum
17155 W. 44th Ave., Golden
303/279-4591
Locomotives, artifacts, model railroad.

Coors Brewing Company
13th and Ford, Golden
303/277-BEER
Free tours of brewing facility.

Denver Museum of Natural History
2001 Colorado Blvd.
303/370-6357
Dioramas, objects from Native Americans, gems, dinosaurs.

The Denver Zoo
E. 23rd and Steele, in City Park
303/331-4110
Exotic animals in spacious, barless enclosures.

Larimer Square, the city's oldest area.

Larimer Square
1400 block of Larimer Street
303/534-2367
Denver's oldest retail district. Victorian buildings, distinctive shops.

Mile High Flea Market
7007 E. 88th Ave., Henderson
303/289-4656
One of Denver's largest attractions.

Molly Brown House Museum
1340 Pennsylvania
303/832-4092
Restored Victorian home of Molly Brown, heroine of the *Titanic* disaster.

United States Mint
320 W. Colfax Ave.
303/844-3582
More than 5 billion coins are produced here each year.
Free tours.

For More Information

Denver Metro Convention & Visitor Bureau
2225 W. Colfax
Denver, CO 80202
303/892-1112

Since 1900, fans have come by foot, by horse-drawn carriage, and, appropriately, by motor car to Michigan and Trumbull streets, home of the Detroit Tigers.

Tiger Stadium is one of a vanishing breed of classic concrete and steel ballparks built in the early part of this century.

Tiger Stadium has seen its share of great baseball. Ty Cobb won 12 American League batting titles, posting a .367 lifetime average and 4,191 career hits. All-Star Al Kaline played here 22 years, winning 10 Gold Gloves. Charlie Gehringer, Harvey Kuenn, Hank Greenberg, Goose Goslin, Mickey Cochrane, and Harry Heilman all played on this field.

The original stadium for the "Tigers" was Bennett Park. Because the field was laid over a layer of cobblestones, infielders blamed their errors on the stones that pushed their way through the dirt. When the current stadium was constructed on the same site in 1912, the cobblestones were removed, the field was turned 90 degrees, and the ballpark was named Navin Field (for Frank Navin, a Tiger owner). In 1938, the name was changed to Briggs Stadium; in 1961, the park was renamed for the team. The seating capacity has grown from approximately 25,000 in 1912 to the current 52,416 seats.

This park has the only double-decked bleachers in the majors (the upper deck runs from left center to center, while the lower deck runs from center to right center). The short upper deck in the outfield has been the backdrop for some awesome home runs, including Reggie Jackson's blast that hit the light tower atop the roof in right center in the 1971 All-Star Game.

American League East

Detroit Tigers

Tiger Stadium.

Metropolitan Detroit C & VB

- ☐ Lower Deck Box
- ☐ Upper Deck Box
- ☐ Lower Deck Reserved
- ☐ Upper Deck Reserved
- ☐ General Admission
- ☐ Bleachers

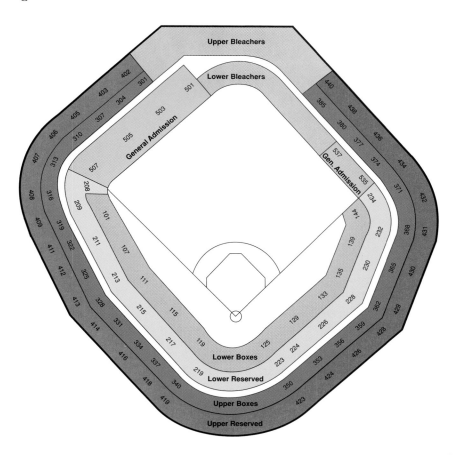

Purchasing Tickets

By mail:

Detroit Tigers
Ticket Department
P.O. Box 77322
Detroit, MI 48277

Send a check or money order payable to Detroit Baseball Club, or send credit card number and expiration date along with your signature. Specify the game date and the type and number of tickets.

In person:

The Advance Ticket Office, located at the corner of Michigan and Trumbull, opens every year about March 4 and remains open for the season daily from 9 a.m. - 6 p.m. Tickets are also available at all TicketMaster outlets throughout Michigan and Toledo, Ohio, and Windsor, Ontario.

By phone:

313/963-7300—credit card orders
313/963-2050—group and season ticket sales and ticket price information

Directions to the Stadium

- From U.S. 10 (Lodge Freeway) Southbound: Exit at I-75, Fisher Freeway, Flint-Toledo. Stay to the far right and immediately exit at Trumbull Avenue. Stadium is one block left.

- From I-75 (Chrysler Freeway) Southbound: Exit at Fisher Freeway, Toledo I-75 South (Exit 51 C). Drive 1.3 miles to Rosa Parks Boulevard (Exit 49 A). Stadium is one block left.

- From North Woodward Avenue: Take Woodward Avenue south to Michigan Avenue (one block past State Street). Turn right on Michigan Avenue. Stadium is ahead 1.5 miles.

- From I-94 (Ford Freeway) Westbound: Take I-94 West. Stay to the left and exit at U.S. 10 South (Lodge Freeway, Exit 215 A). Take U.S. 10 South (1.4 miles) to I-75 (Fisher Freeway, Flint-Toledo). Stay to the far right and immediately exit at Trumbull Avenue. Stadium is one block left.

- From I-94 (Ford Freeway) Eastbound: Take I-94 East. Exit at I-96 (Jeffries Freeway, Exit 213 B). Move to the second left lane (Lodge Freeway sign). Drive 1.3 miles to Lodge Freeway, Rosa Parks Boulevard, Civic Center exit. Take the first exit, Rosa Parks Boulevard/Tiger Stadium. Stadium is immediately ahead.

- From I-96 (Jeffries Freeway) Eastbound: Take I-96 East. Stay in the second left lane (Lodge Freeway sign). Exit at Lodge Freeway, Rosa Parks Boulevard, Civic Center exit (1.3 miles past I-94 Ford Freeway). Take the first exit, Rosa Parks Boulevard/Tiger Stadium. Stadium is immediately ahead.

Parking

The Tigers do not own any public parking facilities; however, numerous private lots are located near the stadium.

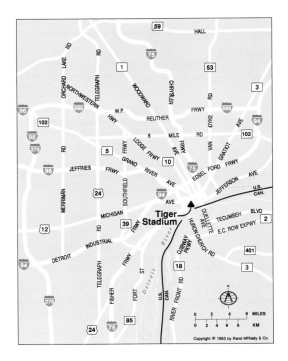

Profile

Team Address
Detroit Tigers
Tiger Stadium
2121 Trumbull
Detroit, MI 48216
313/962-4000

Franchise History
Detroit Tigers 1901-

World Series Titles
1935 vs. Chicago Cubs
1945 vs. Chicago Cubs
1968 vs. St. Louis Cardinals
1984 vs. San Diego Padres

American League Pennants
1907, 1908, 1909, 1934, 1935, 1940, 1945, 1968, 1984

East Division Titles
1972, 1984, 1987

Hall of Fame Inductees
Ty Cobb, 1936
Hugh Jennings, 1945
Mickey Cochrane, 1947
Charlie Gehringer, 1949
Harry Heilmann, 1952
Edward G. Barrow, 1953
Al Simmons, 1953
Hank Greenberg, 1956
Sam Crawford, 1957
Heinie Manush, 1964
Goose Goslin, 1968
Waite Hoyt, 1969
Sam Thompson, 1974
Earl Averill, 1975
Bucky Harris, 1975
Eddie Mathews, 1978
Al Kaline, 1980
George Kell, 1983
Hal Newhouser, 1992

Award Winners
Cy Young Award
Denny McLain, 1968, 1969
Willie Hernandez, 1984

Most Valuable Player
Mickey Cochrane, 1934
Hank Greenberg, 1935, 1940
Charlie Gehringer, 1937
Hal Newhouser, 1944, 1945
Denny McLain, 1968
Willie Hernandez, 1984

Rookie of the Year
Harvey Kuenn, 1953
Mark Fidrych, 1976
Lou Whitaker, 1978

Retired Uniform Numbers
2 Charlie Gehringer
5 Hank Greenberg
6 Al Kaline

Detroit

The Motor City began as a fur-trading center in 1701. Restaurants and hotels listed are downtown, near the stadium, or across the river in Windsor, Ontario.

Sports Spots

Belle Isle Park
Island in Detroit River
313/267-7115
Museums, sports, wildlife.

Chandler Park Golf Course
1281 Chandler Park Drive
313/331-7755
Public 18-hole course.

Hoot Robinson's
2114 Trumbull
313/965-7772
Sports bar near ballpark ($)

Lindell A C (Athletic Club)
1310 Cass St.
313/964-1122
Sports bar, memorabilia ($)

Reedy's Saloon
1846 Michigan Ave.
313/961-1722
Sports bar, memorabilia ($)

Restaurants

Carl's Chop House
3020 Grand River Ave.
313/833-0700
Prime rib, fish ($$$)

Fishbone's River Kitchen Cafe
400 Monroe
313/965-4600
Gulf Coast cuisine ($$)

Mario's Restaurant
4222 Second Ave.
313/832-1616
Northern Italian cuisine ($$)

Joe Muer's Restaurant
2000 Gratiot Ave.
313/567-1088
Seafood ($$$)

Nemo's Bar and Grill
300 Renaissance Center
313/259-1525
1384 Michigan
313/965-3180
American cuisine ($)

New Hellas Cafe
583 Monroe St.
313/961-5544
Greek cuisine and seafood ($)

Opus I
565 E. Larned
313/961-7766
French cuisine ($$$)

Pegasus
558 Monroe
313/964-6800
Greek cuisine ($)

Roma Cafe
3401 Riopelle
313/831-5940
Italian cuisine ($$)

The Whitney
4421 Woodward
313/832-5700
French, American cuisine ($$$)

Xochimilco
3409 Bagley
313/843-0179
Mexican cuisine ($)

Sports Spots & Restaurants (Dinner for two without beverage or tip):
$ Under $20
$$ $20-$40
$$$ More than $40

Accommodations

Compri Windsor Riverside
333 Riverside Drive West
Windsor, Ontario
519/977-9777, 800/4-COMPRI ($)

Monorail is a convenient people mover.

Holiday Inn Windsor
480 Riverside Drive West
Windsor, Ontario
313/963-7590, 519/253-4411 ($$)

Hyatt Regency Dearborn
Fairlane Town Center
313/593-1510 ($$$)

Omni International Hotel
333 E. Jefferson Ave.
313/222-7700, 800/THE OMNI
($$$)

Radisson Hotel Ponchartrain
Two Washington Blvd.
313/965-0200, 800/333-3333 ($$$)

Relax Plaza Hotel Windsor
33 Riverside Drive East
Windsor, Ontario
519/258-7774, 800/66-RELAX ($)

Westin Hotel Renaissance Center
Renaissance Center
313/568-8200 ($$$)

Windsor Hilton
277 Riverside Drive West
Windsor, Ontario
313/962-3834, 519/973-5555 ($$)

Price ranges: Double room during the week (lower rates are often available on weekends)
$ Under $75
$$ $75-$125
$$$ More than $125

Attractions

Detroit Institute of Arts
5200 Woodward Ave.
313/833-7900
Art treasures.

Evening in downtown.

Detroit Zoological Park
8450 W. Ten Mile Rd., Royal Oak
313/398-0903
1,200 animals.

Edsel & Eleanor Ford House
1100 Lake Shore Drive, Grosse Pointe Shores
313/884-4222, 313/884-3400
Cotswold-style house set on 87 acres along Lake St. Clair.

Fisher Mansion/ Behaktivedanta Cultural Center
383 Lenox
313/331-6740
Moorish mansion features art from Asia and India.

Henry Ford Estate
University of Michigan, Dearborn Campus
4901 Evergreen, Dearborn
313/593-5590
Home of Henry and Clara Ford, national landmark.

Henry Ford Museum and Greenfield Village
20900 Oakwood Blvd., Dearborn
313/271-1620
Shows evolution of industrial society.

Greektown
Monroe Street
Restaurants, nightspots.

Motown Museum celebrates Hittsville U.S.A.

Motown Museum
2648 W. Grand Blvd.
313/875-2264
Original home of Motown studios.

Trapper's Alley
Monroe Street, Greektown
Shopping plaza.

For More Information

Metropolitan Detroit Convention and Visitors Bureau
100 Renaissance Center
Suite 1950
Detroit, MI 48243-1056
313/259-4333

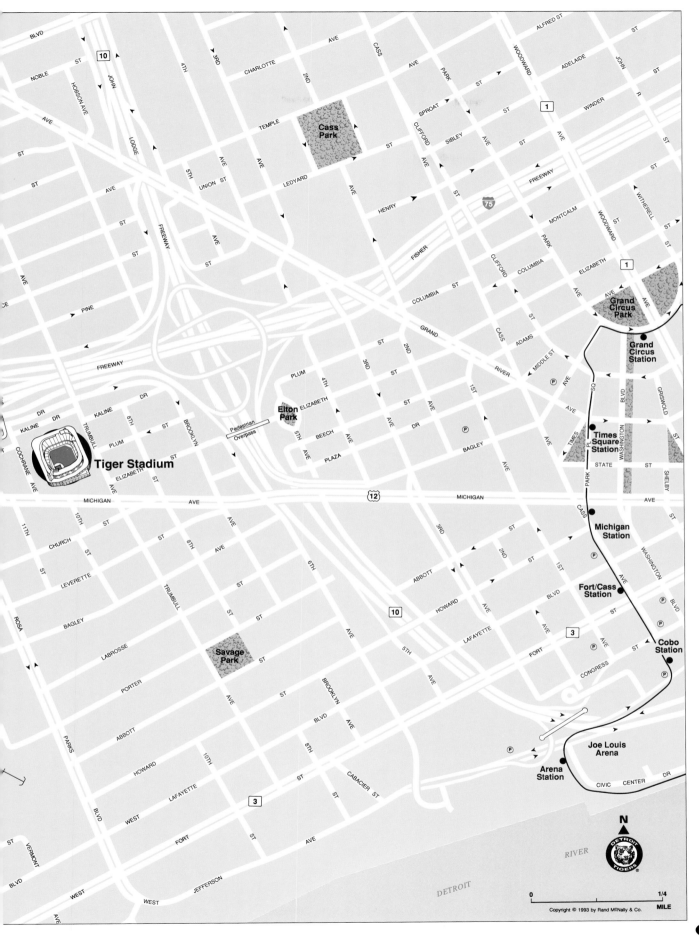

Tiger Stadium

Cass Park

Elton Park

Savage Park

Grand Circus Park

Grand Circus Station

Times Square Station

Michigan Station

Fort/Cass Station

Cobo Station

Joe Louis Arena

Arena Station

Pedestrian Overpass

DETROIT

RIVER

N

DETROIT TIGERS®

0 ─────── 1/4
MILE

Copyright © 1993 by Rand McNally & Co.

Joe Robbie Stadium is famous for hosting the Miami Dolphins, but this stadium is no stranger to baseball. When the Los Angeles Dodgers and Baltimore Orioles met for a spring training game at Joe Robbie Stadium in 1988, 24,247 spectators turned out for the first baseball game played at the new facility. It was the largest crowd ever to gather for a Major League game in the state.

In March 1991, the New York Yankees and the Orioles met for an exhibition game, attracting 67,654 fans to the stadium—the largest crowd in a non-Major League city. Clearly baseball and south Florida are a winning combination.

So it was no surprise when a new Major League franchise was awarded to south Florida in the summer of 1991. Generations of Floridian baseball fans who longed for a team of their own can now claim the Florida Marlins as their own.

Take sunscreen (after all, Florida is the sunshine state), and be prepared for afternoon showers. Weather changes quickly in south Florida.

The Marlins are the team of the Americas. They draw their enthusiastic fans from the United States and Canada, as well as Latin America, Puerto Rico, and South America. Concession stands at the park will even offer Cuban sandwiches, which are definitely worth a taste.

National League East

Florida Marlins

Joe Robbie Stadium.

Connie Blaze

- ☐ Infield Boxes
- ☐ Terrace Boxes
- ☐ Mezzanine Boxes
- ☐ Mezzanine Reserved
- ■ Club Zone A
- ☐ Club Zone B
- ☐ Club Zone C
- ☐ Outfield Reserved
- ☐ General Admission
- ■ Founder's Club Seats
- ■ Founder's Field Boxes

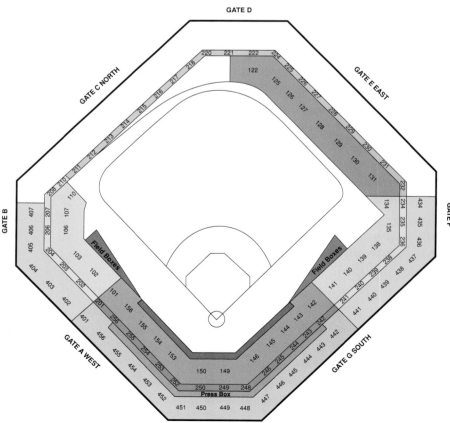

Purchasing Tickets

Not officially determined at presstime. Ticket office at stadium. Tickets will also be marketed internationally to Latin America, South America, and Puerto Rico. For information, call 305/779-7070, and ask for the ticket manager.

Directions to the Stadium

- Florida Turnpike northbound or southbound: Take the 199th Street exit. The ramp will run directly into the parking lot.

- I-95 northbound: Take I-95 to Ives Dairy Road, and go west for five miles. Stadium is on the right.

- Palmetto Expressway: Take the Northwest 27th Avenue exit. Make a left at the light, and go north to Northwest 199th Street. Make a right.

Public Transportation

Metro Dade Transportation offers service via the Tri-Rail, which stops at the stadium.

Parking

There are 14,970 parking spaces available. An off-ramp from the Florida Turnpike leads directly into lot.

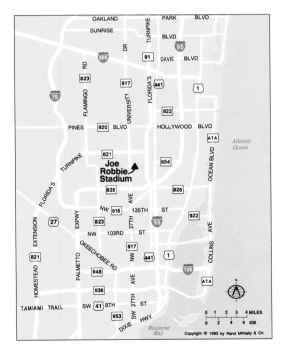

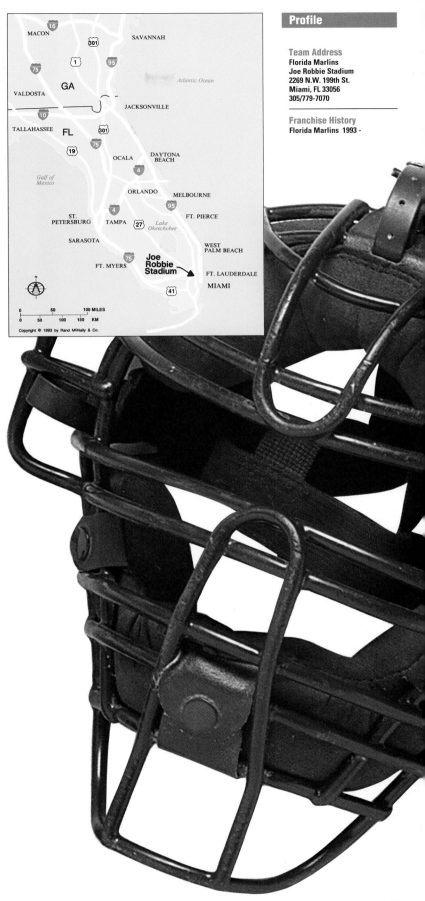

Profile

Team Address
Florida Marlins
Joe Robbie Stadium
2269 N.W. 199th St.
Miami, FL 33056
305/779-7070

Franchise History
Florida Marlins 1993 -

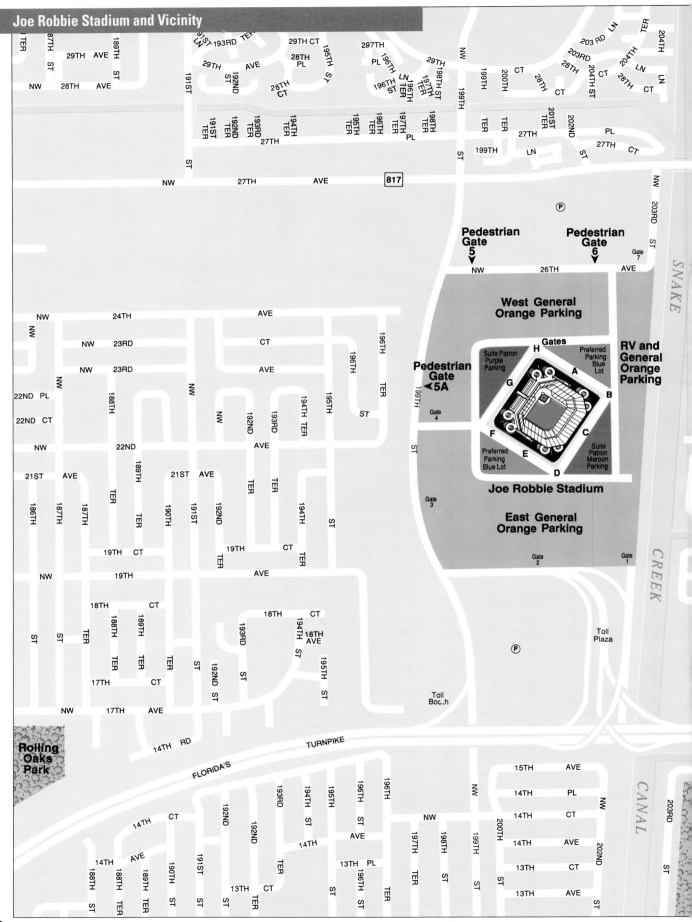

Pedestrian Gate 5

Pedestrian Gate 6

Gate 7

P

NW 26TH AVE

NW 203RD ST

SNAKE

West General Orange Parking

RV and General Orange Parking

Pedestrian Gate ◄5A

Gates

Gates

H

Suite Patron Purple Parking

Preferred Parking Blue Lot

A

G

B

Gate 4

F

C

E

D

Preferred Parking Blue Lot

Suite Patron Maroon Parking

Gate 3

Joe Robbie Stadium

East General Orange Parking

Gate 2

Gate 1

CREEK

P

Toll Plaza

Toll Boc.h

Rolling Oaks Park

TURNPIKE

FLORIDA'S

CANAL

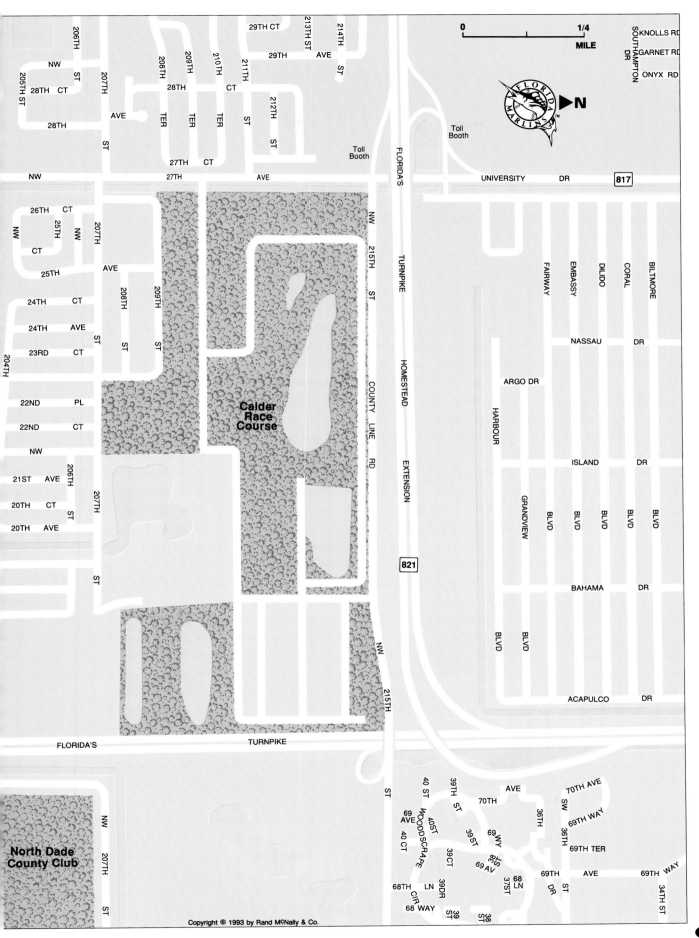

0 1/4
MILE

N

KNOLLS RD
SOUTHAMPTON DR
GARNET RD
ONYX RD

UNIVERSITY DR 817

206TH ST
205TH ST
NW 28TH CT
NW ST
28TH
27TH CT
27TH AVE
26TH CT
25TH NW
NW CT
25TH
24TH CT
24TH AVE
23RD CT
22ND PL
22ND CT
NW
21ST AVE
20TH CT
20TH AVE

207TH AVE
207TH ST
208TH TER
209TH
210TH TER
211TH TER
27TH CT
208TH ST
209TH ST
204TH
208TH ST
209TH ST
206TH ST
207TH ST

29TH CT
213TH ST
214TH ST
29TH AVE
208TH
209TH
210TH
211TH ST
212TH ST
212TH ST
29TH

Toll Booth
Toll Booth

FLORIDA'S TURNPIKE HOMESTEAD EXTENSION

NW 215TH ST
COUNTY LINE RD

Calder Race Course

821

FAIRWAY
EMBASSY
DLIDO
CORAL
BILTMORE
NASSAU DR
ARGO DR
HARBOUR
ISLAND DR
GRANDVIEW BLVD BLVD BLVD BLVD
BAHAMA DR
BLVD BLVD BLVD
ACAPULCO DR

FLORIDA'S TURNPIKE

NW 215TH ST

North Dade County Club

NW 207TH ST

40 ST
40ST
39TH ST
70TH AVE
70TH
AVE
SW
36TH
36TH
70TH AVE
69TH WAY
69TH TER
69 AVE
40 CT
WOODDSCRAPE
39ST
39CT
39 WY
69 WY
69 AV
68 LN
37ST
68TH
39DR
69TH AVE
69TH DR
69TH ST
69TH WAY
68TH CIR
68 WAY
39 WAY
39 ST
38 ST
34TH ST

Miami

South Florida–especially Miami–is the new American melting pot. Whether you stay in the Miami or Ft. Lauderdale area, you'll be close to great things to see and do.

Sports Spots

Miami

Five Star Rodeo
S.W. 65th Avenue and Orange Drive, Davie
305/437-8800
Professionals compete in bronco riding, steer wrestling, and calf roping.

Fun Watersports
Miami Airport Hilton Marina
5101 Blue Lagoon Drive
305/261-7687
Water-ski and jet-ski rentals and instruction.

Malibu Grand Prix
7775 N.W. 8th St.
305/266-2100
Miniature golf, batting cages, formula and sprint car racing.

Metro-Dade Artificial Reef Program
10 offshore and 12 Biscayne Bay sites
305/375-4180
For divers and fishermen.

Miami Jai Alai
3500 N.W. 37th Ave.
305/633-9661
World's fastest game.

Tour Wings of America
220 Sunny Isles Blvd., North Miami Beach
305/956-9906
Rents cruising and touring motorcycles.

Ft. Lauderdale

Bahia Mar Marina
801 Seabreeze Blvd.
305/764-2233
Charter boats.

International Swimming Hall of Fame
1 Hall of Fame Drive
305/462-6536
The history of swimming.

Lauderdale Diver
1334 S.E. 17th St.
305/467-2822
Diving excursions.

Ski Rixen
South of Hillsboro Boulevard on Powerline Road in Quiet Waters Park, Deerfield Beach
305/429-0215
Ski slalom, trick ski, ski barefoot, and hydroslide.

Miami: Hotels and ocean beachfront.

Restaurants

Miami

Cafe Chauveron
9561 E. Bay Harbor Drive
305/866-8779
French cuisine ($$$)

Joe's Stone Crab Restaurant
227 Biscayne St., South Miami Beach
305/673-0365
Seafood, 80-year-old institution, and worth the wait ($$-$$$)

Attractions include nature up close.

Ft. Lauderdale

Cap's Place
Cap's Dock
2765 N.E. 28 Court, Lighthouse Point
305/941-0418
TV celebrity hangout, fresh seafood ($$-$$$)

Don Arturo
1198 S.W. 27th Ave.
305/584-7966
Cuban cuisine ($)

Hotz Bar-b-que Shanty
4261 Griffin Road
305/581-9085
Cajun cooking ($-$$)

Old Florida Seafood House
1414 N.E. 26th St., Wilton Manors
305/566-1044
Raw bar and fresh seafood ($$)

*Sports Spots & Restaurants
(Dinner for two without beverage or tip):*
$ *Under $20*
$$ *$20-$40*
$$$ *More than $40*

Accommodations

Miami

Biscayne Bay Marriott
1633 N. Bayshore Drive
305/374-3900 ($$$)

Holiday Inn, Civic Center
1170 N.W. 11th St.
305/324-0800 ($)

Hyatt Regency Miami
400 S.E. 2nd Ave.
305/358-1234 ($$$)

Ft. Lauderdale

Best Western Oceanside Inn
1180 Seabreeze Blvd.
305/525-8115, 800/367-1007 ($)

Guest Quarters Suite Hotel
2670 E. Sunrise Blvd.
305/565-3800, 800/424-2900 ($$-$$$)

Sunrise Hilton
3003 N. University Drive, Sunrise
305/748-7000, 800/533-9555 ($$)

Westin Hotel Cypress Creek
I-95 at Cypress Creek
400 Corporate Drive
305/772-1331, 800/228-3000 ($$$)

Outdoor sports draw enthusiasts.

Price ranges: Double room for two on weekdays (lower rates may be available on weekends)
$ *Under $75*
$$$ *75-$125*
$$$ *More than $125*

Attractions

Miami

Miami Museum of Science & Space Transit Planetarium
3280 S. Miami Ave.
305/854-4247
Hands-on exhibits and demonstrations.

Miami Seaquarium
4400 Rickenbacker Causeway
305/361-5705
Home to TV's Flipper and a 10,000-pound killer whale.

Vizcaya Museum and Gardens
3251 S. Miami Ave.
305/579-2708
Italian-Renaissance-style villa with formal gardens.

Ft. Lauderdale

Everglades Holiday Park
21940 Griffin Road
305/434-8111
Unspoiled wilderness area.

Flamingo Gardens
3750 Flamingo Road, Davie
305/473-2955
Citrus groves, subtropical forest, botanical gardens.

Jungle Queen Cruises
Bahia Mar Yacht Basin
801 Seabreeze Blvd.
305/462-5596
Cruise up the New River.

For More Information

Miami Convention & Visitors Bureau
701 Brickell Ave., Suite 2700
Miami, FL 33131
305/539-3000

Ft. Lauderdale Convention & Visitors Bureau
200 E. Las Olas Blvd., Suite 1500
Ft. Lauderdale, FL 33301
305/765-4466

The Houston Astrodome was the very first air-conditioned, all-weather, multi-purpose domed sports arena—the model for all those that followed.

Opened in 1965, the Dome was conceived as an antidote to the heat, humidity, and rain of South Texas. The Colt .45s, the original name for the Astros, launched its life as an expansion team in 1962.

Grab some nachos—they were first introduced here,— then gaze at the expanse...it really is a wonder. The Astrodome's outside diameter measures 710 feet, and the dome itself rises 208 feet from the floor.

At first, a specially developed grass grew indoors. But portions of the original transparent dome had to be painted because outfielders couldn't pick up the ball against the clear panes of glass. Without sunlight, the grass died, and a synthetic "blade," called Astro Turf, was introduced to the game, changing the concept of "field of play"—indoors and out—for a generation.

Domed stadiums do have quirks, and the Astrodome is no exception. The bat meeting ball sounds different indoors. Rules are affected. For example, fly balls may hit speakers hanging from the roof. They are still in play, despite the funny caroms.

But when summer temperatures soar, air-conditioned comfort more than makes up for these small digressions from baseball traditions.

Houston Astros

Houston Astrodome.

- ■ Field Level
- ▨ Mezzanine
- ▨ Club Level
- ■ Loge Level
- □ Upper Box Terrace
- ▨ Skybox or Star Columbia Suite
- ▨ Pavilion

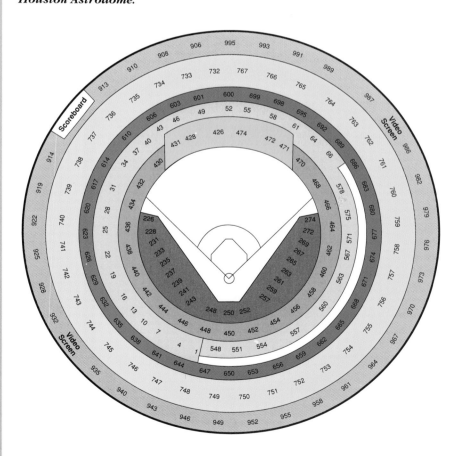

Purchasing Tickets

By mail:
Houston Astros
Ticket Department
P.O. Box 1691
Houston, TX 77001-1691

Send a check or money order payable to the Houston Astros. Specify the date or dates you want and the number and price of tickets. Add $4 for handling per order.

In person:
Houston Astrodome Ticket Office
8400 Kirby Drive

Ticket office hours: Daily, 9 a.m. - 5 p.m. For ticket information, call 713/799-9555.

By phone:
TicketMaster
713/629-3700 in Houston; 800/275-1000 outside the city.

Directions to the Stadium

- There is no entrance to the stadium from the South Loop, and traffic is usually heavy there.

- From Main Street: Approach the west entrances by way of McNee, Murworth, or Westridge.

- From Fannin Street side: There is usually less traffic on the Fannin Street side; approach the park by using Northeast Drive, Holly Hall, and Naomi.

- From Old Spanish Trail: Use the North Stadium Drive entrance.

Public Transportation

Metro buses from downtown. Take the number 18 Kirby or the Number 15 Hiram-Clark. Call 713/635-4000 for transit information.

Parking

Gates to the parking lots open 2-1/2 hours prior to the game, but Murworth Gate is always open. Note the aisle number on your tickets and use the entrance nearest your seat. Aisle numbers are in sequence. For aisles 738, 614, 527, and 432, enter at Northeast Drive. For aisles 740, 622, 531, 436, and 227, enter at North Stadium Drive. For aisles 745, 637, 539, 444 and 241, enter at McNee Street. For aisles 749, 649, 549, 449, and 249, enter at Murworth Street. For aisles 753, 662, 457, and 261, enter at Westridge. For aisles 761, 685, 468, and 274, enter at Naomi. For the bleachers, enter at Holly Hall.

Stadium gates open at the east and west entrances two hours before the first pitch; other entrances, 90 minutes before the first pitch.

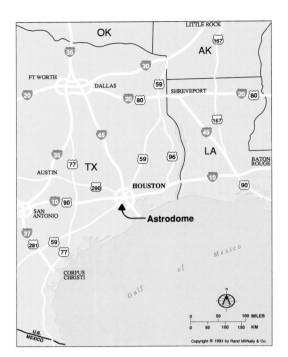

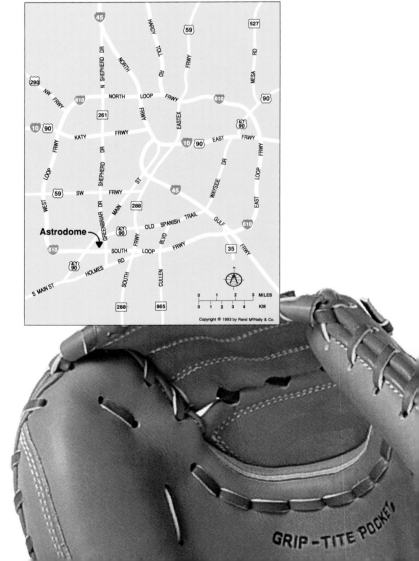

Houston

The Astrodome is in the midst of a complex that will make your visit both convenient and enjoyable. Hotels and restaurants listed are all close to the Astrodome.

Sports Spots

Action Charters/Deep Sea Fishing
429 Pompano, Surfside
409/265-0999, 800/456-6984
Charter boats for deep-sea fishing.

Alkek Velodrome
Cullen Park, 19008 Saums Road
713/578-0858
Track bikes for rent.

The Backroom
Hyatt Regency Houston
1200 Louisiana
713/654-1234
Tex-Mex sports bar/restaurant ($)

City Parks
Various locations
713/845-1000
Tennis courts, golf courses, hiking and biking trails.

Shucker's Sports Bar
The Westin Hotel
5011 Westheimer
713/960-8100
Sports bar/restaurant($$)

Water parks cool hot Texas days.

Splashtown
21300 I-45 North, Spring
713/355-3300
Water park with 17 major water rides and attractions.

WaterWorld
9001 Kirby Drive, adjacent to AstroWorld
713/799-1234
15-acre water park.

Restaurants

Brennan's of Houston
3300 Smith St.
713/522-9711
Creole cuisine with a Southwestern flair ($$$)

Carrabba's Italian Restaurant
3115 Kirby Drive
713/522-3131
Pasta, pizza, veal ($$)

Goode Company Texas Barbecue
5109 Kirby Drive
713/522-2530
Barbecued beef, ribs sausage, chicken, ham, and duck ($)

Hunan Restaurant
1800 Post Oak Blvd., Saks Center
713/965-0808
Hunan-Chinese cuisine ($$)

Little Pappas Seafood House
3001 S. Shepherd
713/522-4595
Seafood, oyster bar ($-$$)

Ninfas
3601 Kirby Drive
713/520-0203
Mexican food ($)

Pappadeaux Seafood Kitchen
2525 South Loop West
713/665-3155
Cajun seafood ($$)

Willie G's Seafood
1605 Post Oak Blvd.
713/840-7190
Seafood, gumbo ($$)

Sports Spots & Restaurants (Dinner for two without beverage or tip):
$ **Under $20**
$$ **$20-$40**
$$ **More than $40**

Accommodations

Days Inn Astrodome
8686 Kirby Drive
713/796-8383, 800/325-2525 ($$)

Gulf Freeway Inn
2391 S. Wayside
713/928-5321 ($)

Holiday Inn Astrodome
8111 Kirby Drive
713/790-1900, 800/465-4329 ($$)

La Quinta Astrodome
9911 Buffalo Speedway
713/668-8082, 800/531-5900 ($)

Premiere Inns
2929 Southwest Freeway
713/528-6161 ($)

Radisson Suites Hotel
1400 Old Spanish Trail
713/796-1000 ($$)

Sheraton Astrodome
8686 Kirby Drive
713/748-3221 ($$)

Wyndham Warwick
5701 Main St.
713/526-1991, 800/822-4200 ($$$)

Price ranges: Double room during the week (lower rates are often available on weekends)
$ **Under $75**
$$ **$75-$125**
$$$ **More than $125**

Attractions

AstroWorld
9001 Kirby Drive
713/799-1234
75-acre theme park with more than 100 rides and attractions.

A ride at AstroWorld.

FunPlex
13700 Beechnut
713/530-7777
Indoor amusement center features bowling, miniature golf, bumper cars, skating rink.

The Galleria
Westheimer at Post Oak
713/621-1907
Shopping center with 300 shops, plus restaurants and movies.

Houston Museum of Natural Science
1 Hermann Circle Drive
713/639-4600
Exhibits of gems and minerals, a dinosaur skeleton, seashells, and the Wortham Imax Theatre.

Activities include fun museums.

The Menil Collection
1515 Sul Ross
713/525-9400
Collection of art from prehistoric to modern times.

Museum of Fine Arts, Houston
1001 Bissonet
713/639-7300
Art from antiquity to present.

San Jacinto Museum of History
On Highway 134 off 225
713/479-2421
Monument to Texas history.

Space Center Houston
NASA Lyndon B. Johnson Space Center
2101 NASA Road, 1 mile off I-45 South
713/244-2100
Guided tours, tram rides, and hands-on space displays.

Zoological Gardens in Hermann Park
1513 N. MacGregor
713/525-3300
More than 2,500 animals.

For More Information

Houston Convention & Visitors Bureau
3300 Main St.
Houston, TX 77002
713/523-5050

Veterans Affairs
Medical Center

Copyright © 1993 by Rand McNally & Co.

Royals Stadium provides a remarkable backdrop for baseball.

The park blends beautiful landscaping with up-to-the-minute electronic wizardry. This is the only Major League stadium with waterfalls and dancing fountains on the embankment above and beyond centerfield. These touches of unexpected beauty are enhanced by a high-tech, 12-story electronic scoreboard and 30' x 40' Sony JumboTron color-video display board.

Royals Stadium and the team it hosts, the Kansas City Royals, are products of American League expansion. Between 1955 and 1967, the Athletics, formerly of Philadelphia, called Kansas City home. But in 1968, the team moved to Oakland, and Kansas City was a city without a Major League team.

One year later, in 1969, pharmaceutical businessman Ewing Kauffman brought a new team to his home town—the Kansas City Royals.

For the first four years, the Royals played in the Athletics' old park, Municipal Stadium. Then, in 1973, the Royals moved into a facility built just for baseball: Royals Stadium, part of the Harry S. Truman Sports Complex, which also includes Arrowhead Stadium, home of the National Football League Kansas City Chiefs.

Players see Royals Stadium as one of the best in the majors. For baseball fans, the view and the atmosphere are great. Royals Stadium is impeccable, immaculate, and immeasurable good fun.

American League West

Kansas City Royals

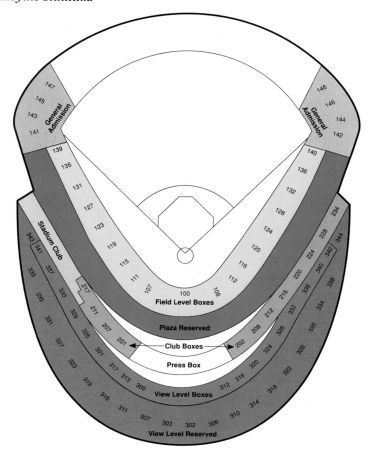

Royals Stadium.

Kansas City Royals Publicity Dept.

- ☐ Club Boxes
- ☐ Field Boxes
- ■ Plaza Reserved
- ■ View Level Boxes
- ■ View Level Reserved
- ☐ General Admission

Purchasing Tickets

By mail:

Mail Department
Kansas City Royals
P.O. Box 419969
Kansas City, MO 64141-6969

Specify dates of games, number of tickets desired, and preferred general location (home, first base, third base). Make checks payable to Kansas City Royals, or provide your charge-card number and expiration date.

In person:

Royals Advance Ticket Window is located on the south side of Royals Stadium. Ticket office hours: Daily, 9 a.m. - 6 p.m. VISA, MasterCard, American Express, and Discover credit cards are accepted. Ticket booths for day-of-game sales begin about 90 minutes prior to game time with sales on a cash basis.

By phone:

Charge Line hours are Monday - Saturday, 9 a.m. - 9 p.m.; Sundays, 9 a.m. - 6 p.m.
816/921-4400
800/422-1969
816/921-5434 (TDD-staffed for hearing- or speech-impaired)

Directions to the Stadium

- From the north or south: Take I-435 to the stadium exits.

- From the east or west: Take I-70 to the stadium exits.

Public Transportation

Call 816/921-8000 for the most up-to-date transportation information.

Parking

Extensive parking is available in lots surrounding Royals Stadium and throughout the Harry S. Truman Sports Complex.

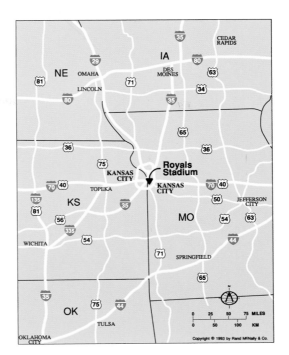

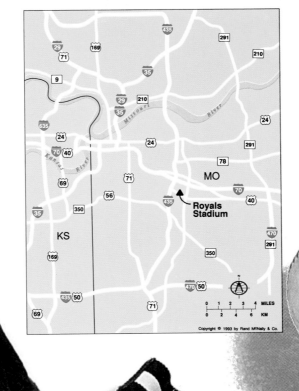

Profile

Team Address
Kansas City Royals
Royals Stadium
One Royal Way
Kansas City, MO 64129
816/921-2200

Franchise History
Kansas City Royals, 1969-

World Series Titles
1985 vs. St. Louis Cardinals

American League Pennants
1980, 1985

West Division Titles
1976, 1977, 1978, 1980, 1984, 1985

Hall of Fame Inductees
Bob Lemon, 1976
Harmon Killebrew, 1984
Gaylord Perry, 1991

Award Winners
Cy Young Award
Bret Saberhagen, 1985, 1989
Most Valuable Player
George Brett, 1980
Rookie of the Year
Lou Piniella, 1969
Retired Uniform Number
10 Dick Howser

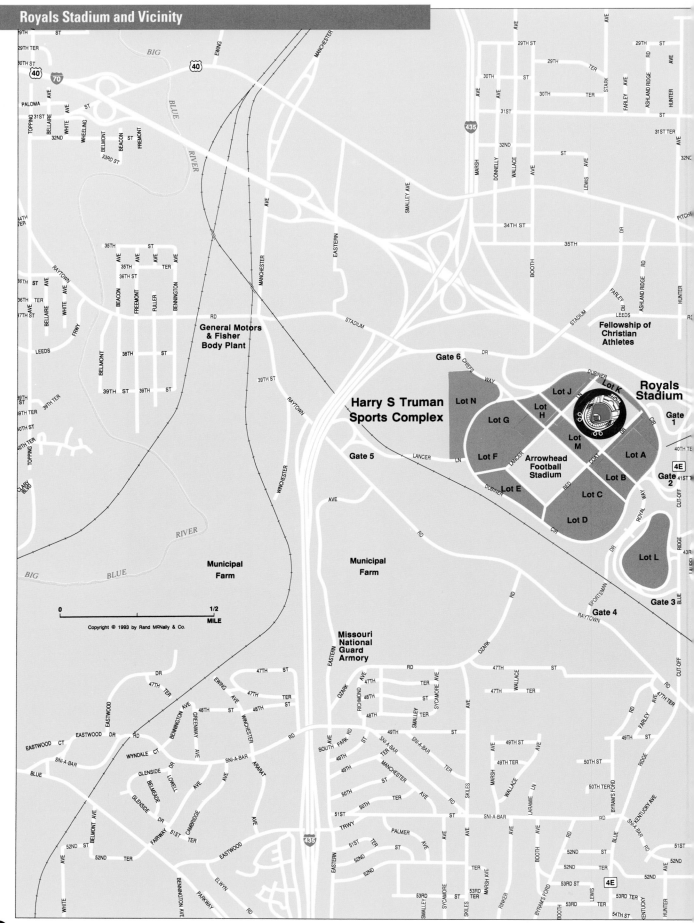

Copyright © 1993 by Rand McNally & Co.

Kansas City

Kansas City is one of the loveliest cities in the United States. Hotels and restaurants listed are either close to the stadium or in the downtown area.

Sports Spots

Fuzzy's Sports Bar and Grill
4113 Pennsylvania
816/561-9191
Sports bar/restaurant ($)

Hitters Bar and Grill
Radisson Suite Hotel
106 W. 12th
816/221-7000
Sports bar/restaurant ($-$$)

Lynn Dickey's Sports Cafe
535 Westport Road
816/756-1010
Sports bar/restaurant ($-$$)

Family activities abound in Kansas City.

Oceans of Fun Water Park
I-435, exit 54
816/454-4545
Water slides and adult and children's pools.

Quincy's
Adams Mark Hotel
I-70 at Sports Complex
816/737-0200
Sports hangout/bar/buffet ($)

Swope Park
5600 E. Gregory Blvd.
816/444-3113
City park with two 18-hole golf courses, swimming pool, and nature trails.

Restaurants

Bristol Bar and Grill
4740 Jefferson
816/756-0606
Seafood, steak, oyster bar ($$)

Cascone's Restaurant and Lounge
3733 N. Oak
816/454-7977
Southern, northern Italian cuisine ($-$$)

Golden Ox Restaurant and Lounge
1600 Genessee
816/842-2866
Steak, seafood, chicken ($$)

Plaza III Steakhouse
49th & Pennsylvania
816/753-0000
Steak, seafood, veal ($$-$$$)

S.A. Sanders
4111 Blue Ridge Cut-Off
816/924-6666
Chicken, steak, ham ($-$$)

Savoy Grill and Restaurant
9th and Central
816/842-3890
Seafood, steak ($$$)

Starker's Restaurant
200 Nichols Road
816/753-3565
Prime rib, steak, fish ($$-$$$)

Stephenson's Apple Farm Restaurant
16401 E. Highway 40
816/373-5400
Chicken, chops, fish, ham ($$)

Sports Spots & Restaurants (Dinner for two without beverage or tip):
$ Under $20
$$ $20-$40
$$$ More than $40

Accommodations

Best Western Seville Plaza
4309 Main St.
816/561-9600, 800/825-0197 ($)

Drury Inn—Stadium
3830 Blue Ridge Cut-Off
816/923-3000, 800/325-8300 ($)

Holiday Inn Sports Complex
4011 Blue Ridge Cut-Off
816/353-5300, 800/HOLIDAY ($$)

Hyatt Regency Crown Center
2345 McGee St.
816/421-1234, 800/233-1234 ($$$)

Park Place Hotel
1601 N. Universal Ave.
816/483-9900, 800/821-8532 ($$)

Ritz-Carlton Kansas City
401 Ward Parkway
816/756-1500, 800/241-3333 ($$$)

The Westin Crown Center
One Pershing Road
816/474-4400, 800/228-3000 ($$$)

Price ranges: Double room during the week (lower rates are often available on weekends)
$ Under $75
$$ $75-$125
$$$ More than $125

Attractions

Country Club Plaza
30 blocks south of downtown, near Broadway and 47th Street
816/753-0100
The first shopping center built in America; more than 185 specialty shops, theaters, restaurants.

Nichols Fountain at Country Club Plaza.

Crown Center
Grand Avenue and Pershing Road
816/274-8444
Entertainment and shopping center includes a retail center, two luxury hotels, restaurants, theaters, 10-acre square.

Crown Center, an entertainment and shopping complex.

Hallmark Visitors Center
In Crown Center complex, Grand Avenue and Pershing Road
816/274-5672
Exhibits tell the story of Hallmark cards.

Kansas City Museum
3218 Gladstone Blvd.
816/483-8300
Hands-on science exhibits, regional history exhibits, and a planetarium.

Liberty Memorial
100 W. 26th St.
816/221-1918
Tower with panoramic view of Kansas City; also, a World War I Museum.

Westport
On the western edge of Kansas City
Renovated historic district filled with specialty shops, a retail center, galleries, restaurants.

Worlds of Fun
I-435, exit 54
816/454-4545
Theme park with rides, shows, attractions.

For More Information

Kansas City Convention & Visitors Bureau
1100 Main, Suite 2550
Kansas City, MO 64105
816/221-5242

The beauty of Dodger Stadium has lived on through three decades.

The stadium, opened in 1962, is maintained in immaculate condition year-round. To the south is a breathtaking view of downtown Los Angeles; to the north and east are the green, tree-lined Elysian hills; beyond are the purple San Gabriel Mountains.

The only privately financed stadium since the 1923 construction of Yankee Stadium, Dodger Stadium comfortably seats 56,000 and offers parking for 16,000 cars.

More than 80 million fans have watched Dodger games at Dodger Stadium over the past 30 years. An average of more than 3 million fans visit each year. In 1978, Dodger Stadium became the first ballpark to host more than 3 million fans in a single season: 3,347,845 people attended Dodger games that year.

Dodger Stadium also recalls great baseball names from the latter half of the 20th century: Maury Wills, Duke Snider, Sandy Koufax, Steve Garvey, and Fernando Valenzuela all once played on this field.

Dodger Stadium has been the site of many memorable moments and record-setting performances, as well as the 1980 Major League Baseball All-Star Game, the 1984 Olympic Baseball Tournament, and eight World Series contests. There's also a variety of food to choose from, including the world-famous Dodger Dog.

Dodger Stadium remains one of the most beautiful parks in all of baseball.

Los Angeles Dodgers

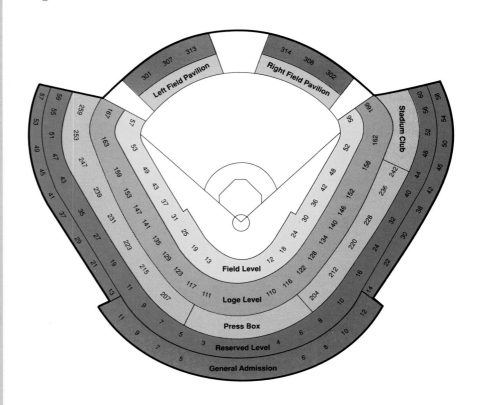

Dodger Stadium.

☐ Field Level
☐ Loge Level
☐ Club Level
☐ Reserved Level
■ Top Deck General Admission
☐ Lower Pavilion
☐ Upper Pavilion

Purchasing Tickets

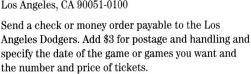

By mail:
Dodger Ticket Office
P.O. Box 51100
Los Angeles, CA 90051-0100

Send a check or money order payable to the Los Angeles Dodgers. Add $3 for postage and handling and specify the date of the game or games you want and the number and price of tickets.

In person:
Ticket Office
Dodger Stadium
1750 Stadium Way, adjacent to the Naval-Marine Center

The ticket office is open from March - October, Monday - Saturday, 8:30 a.m. - 5:30 p.m. For information, call 213/224-1400. Tickets are also available at Ticket-Master outlets in Music Plus stores, May Company stores, and Tower Records stores.

By phone:
213/224-1-HIT ($1 service charge per ticket)
Monday - Saturday, 8:30 a.m. - 5:30 p.m.

Directions to the Stadium

- From Freeway 101 South: Exit at Alvarado; turn left, then right on Sunset; go approximately two miles and turn left on Elysian Park Avenue. Go one mile more to stadium.

- From Freeway 101 North: Exit at Alvarado; turn right, then right on Sunset; go approximately two miles and turn left on Elysian Park Avenue. Go one mile more to stadium.

- From Freeway 110 South: Take the Dodger Stadium exit; turn left at the stop sign onto Stadium Way. Go past two stop signs; turn right on Elysian Park Avenue to the stadium.

- From Freeway 110 North: Take the Dodger Stadium exit; turn left onto Stadium Way. Go past a stop sign, then turn right on Elysian Park Avenue to the stadium.

- From Freeway 5 South: Exit at Stadium Way; turn left and follow Stadium Way to Academy Road. Make a quick right on Academy, then a quick left back to Stadium Way. Follow Stadium Way to Elysian Park Avenue; turn left on Elysian Park to the stadium.

- From Freeway 5 North: Exit at Stadium Way; turn left (Riverside). Turn left onto Stadium Way and follow Stadium Way to Academy Road. Make a quick right on Academy, then a quick left back to Stadium Way. Follow Stadium Way to Elysian Park Avenue, then turn left on Elysian Park to the stadium.

Public Transportation

Take RTD's bus line 635 to all Dodger games. Buses stop between parking lots 8 and 10 on the inner roads of the stadium.

Team Address
Los Angeles Dodgers
Dodger Stadium
1000 Elysian Park Ave.
Los Angeles, CA
90012-1199
213/224-1500

Franchise History
Brooklyn Dodgers 1890-1957
Los Angeles Dodgers 1958-

World Series Titles
1955 vs. New York Yankees
1959 vs. Chicago White Sox
1963 vs. New York Yankees
1965 vs. Minnesota Twins
1981 vs. New York Yankees
1988 vs. Oakland Athletics

National League Pennants
1890, 1899, 1900, 1916, 1920, 1941,
1947, 1949, 1952, 1953, 1955, 1956,
1959, 1963, 1965, 1966, 1974, 1977,
1978, 1981, 1988

West Division Titles
1974, 1977, 1978, 1981, 1983, 1985
1988

Hall of Fame Inductees
Willie Keeler, 1939]
Dan Brouthers, 1945
Hugh Jennings, 1945
Wilbert Robinson, 1945
Thomas McCarthy, 1946

Joe McGinnity, 1946
Paul Waner, 1952
Rabbit Maranville, 1954
Arthur "Dazzy" Vance, 1955
Zack Wheat, 1959
Max Carey, 1961
Jackie Robinson, 1962
Burleigh Grimes, 1964
Heinie Manush, 1964
Monte Ward, 1964
Casey Stengel, 1966
Branch Rickey, 1967
Lloyd Waner, 1967
Kiki Cuyler, 1968
Joe "Ducky" Medwick, 1968
Roy Campanella, 1969
Waite Hoyt, 1969
Dave Bancroft, 1971
Joe Kelley, 1971
Rube Marquard, 1971
Sandy Koufax, 1972
George Kelly, 1973
Billy Herman, 1975
Fred Lindstrom, 1976
Al Lopez, 1977
Larry MacPhail, 1978
Hack Wilson, 1979
Duke Snider, 1980
Frank Robinson, 1982
Walter Alston, 1983
Juan Marichal, 1983
Don Drysdale, 1984
Pee Wee Reese, 1984
Arky Vaughan, 1985
Hoyt Wilhelm, 1985
Ernie Lombardi, 1986
Tony Lazzeri, 1991

Award Winners
Cy Young Award
Don Newcombe, 1956
Don Drysdale, 1962
Sandy Koufax, 1963, 1965, 1966
Mike Marshall, 1974
Fernando Valenzuela, 1981
Orel Hershiser, 1988

Most Valuable Player
Dolph Camilli, 1941
Jackie Robinson, 1949
Roy Campanella, 1951, 1953, 1955
Don Newcombe, 1956
Maury Wills, 1962
Sandy Koufax, 1963
Steve Garvey, 1974}
Kirk Gibson, 1988

Rookie of the Year
Jackie Robinson, 1947
Don Newcombe, 1949
Joe Black, 1952
Jim Gilliam, 1953
Frank Howard, 1960
Jim Lefebvre, 1965
Ted Sizemore, 1969
Rick Sutcliffe, 1979
Steve Howe, 1980
Fernando Valenzuela, 1981
Steve Sax, 1982

Retired Uniform Numbers
1 Pee Wee Reese
4 Duke Snider
19 Jim Gilliam
24 Walter Alston
32 Sandy Koufax
39 Roy Campanella
42 Jackie Robinson
53 Don Drysdale

Parking

Extensive parking is available at Dodger Stadium. You can park in color-coded unreserved lots. The color on the baseball light stand should match the color of the level on which you'll be sitting; for example, if you have a yellow ticket, park in the yellow-coded lot.

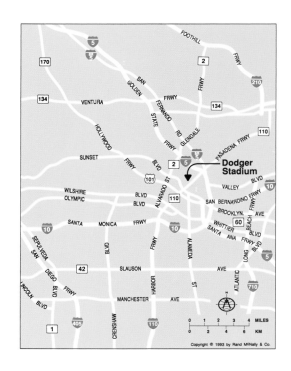

Los Angeles

Los Angeles means movie stars, beaches, palm trees, mountains, and a mild climate. The hotels and restaurants listed are all in the downtown area, convenient to the stadium.

Sports Spots

Active West Bowling Centers
21 centers throughout Southern California
310/447-2695
Bowling lanes, restaurants, cocktail lounges, supervised children's playrooms, game rooms.

Champions Sports Bar
Los Angeles Marriott Hotel
5855 W. Century Blvd.
310/641-5700
Sports bar/restaurant ($)

Griffith Park
Visitor Center
4730 Crystal Springs Drive
213/665-5188
Huge 4,105-acre park with 28 tennis courts, golf courses, horseback and hiking trails.

Little Joe's Restaurant
900 N. Broadway
213/489-4900
Sports bar/Northern Italian and American cuisine ($-$$)

Moody's
Sheraton Grande Hotel
333 S. Figueroa St.
213/617-6023
Sports bar/restaurant($$)

Restaurants

Bernard's
The Biltmore Hotel
506 S. Grand Ave.
213/612-1580
American and European cuisine, wild game ($$$)

El Cholo Restaurant
1122 S. Western Ave.
213/734-2773
Traditional Mexican cuisine ($$)

Seafood Bay Restaurant
1240 S. Soto St.
213/269-6874
Seafood, steak, chicken ($)

A friendly encounter on the tour at Universal Studios.

Stepps on the Court
Wells Fargo Center
330 S. Hope St.
213/626-0900
American cuisine ($$)

Tam O'Shanter Inn
2980 Los Feliz Blvd.
213/664-0228
Continental cuisine ($$)

Taylor's Steak House
3361 W. Eighth St.
213/382-8449
Steak, prime beef, seafood, clam chowder ($$)

Sports Spots & Restaurants (Dinner for two without beverage or tip):
$ Under $20
$$ $20-$40
$$$ More than $40

Accommodations

Best Western Executive Motor Inn Mid-Wilshire
603 S. New Hampshire Ave.
213/385-4444, 800/528-1234 ($)

The Biltmore Hotel
506 S. Grand Ave.
213/624-1011, 800/421-8000, 800/245-8673 (CA) ($$$)

Holiday Inn Downtown
750 Garland Ave.
213/628-5242, 800/465-4329 ($$)

Hyatt Regency Los Angeles
711 S. Hope St.
213/683-1234, 800/233-1234 ($$$)

Los Angeles Hilton & Towers
930 Wilshire Blvd.
213/629-4321, 800/445-8667 ($$$)

Westin Bonaventure, Los Angeles
404 S. Figueroa St.
213/624-1000, 800/228-3000 ($$$)

Wilshire Comfort Inn
3400 W. 3rd St.
213/385-0061, 800/228-5150 ($)

Price ranges: Double room during the week (lower rates are often available on weekends)
$ Under $75
$$ $75-$125
$$$ More than $125

Attractions

Disneyland
1313 S. Harbor Blvd., Anaheim
714/999-4000
Probably the most famous theme park in the world.

Hollywood Walk of Fame
Hollywood Boulevard from Gower to Sycamore and both sides of Vine Street from Yucca to Sunset Boulevard
Stars made of terrazzo and brass dedicated to motion picture luminaries line the streets. Stop at Mann's Chinese Theatre at 6925 Hollywood Blvd. to see footprints of the stars in cement.

La Brea Tar Pits
5801 Wilshire Blvd.
213/936-2230
Site of the richest discovery of fossils from the Ice Age. On-site George C. Page Museum houses fossils recovered from the pits.

Los Angeles County Museum of Art
5905 Wilshire Blvd.
213/857-6000
Contains paintings, sculpture, decorative arts, textiles.

Los Angeles Zoo
5333 Zoo Drive
213/666-4650
Animals from various continents. Animal and bird shows.

The January Rose Parade in Pasadena.

Universal Studios Hollywood
100 Universal City Plaza, Universal City
818/508-9600
Narrated tour by tram of the back lot of this busy motion picture and television studio.

For More Information

Los Angeles Convention & Visitors Bureau
515 S. Figueroa
Los Angeles, CA 90071
213/624-7300
[At presstime, the bureau was scheduled to move; please call for current information.]

Milwaukee County Stadium is synonymous with having a good time.

Start in the parking lot. There are plenty of places to park and plenty of activities. Tailgating is a year-round sport in the Badger State, no matter what game is being played. Pack a small grill, a frisbee, a cooler, and you're set for baseball, Wisconsin-style.

Inside, fans enjoy a comfortable ballpark with good sightlines, great food, and a friendly atmosphere. Fan areas at the stadium are impeccably clean, and the ushers are cheerfully helpful.

County Stadium was one of the first ballparks built with public monies and its first tenants were the National League Milwaukee Braves, which played here from 1953 to 1965. The present-day Milwaukee Brewers started life in 1969 as the Seattle Pilots. Within a year, the Pilots relocated to Milwaukee, were renamed the Brewers, and took up residence at County Stadium.

The stadium's original seating capacity of 36,000 was expanded in 1954, 1974, and 1975 to the present capacity of 53,192. Other improvements included a new outfield wall and permanent bleachers built in 1984. Milwaukee County Stadium was also the first stadium built with lights for night games.

Food fact: Milwaukee County Stadium has the best bratwurst in baseball. Don't forget to slather on the famous "Secret Sauce."

It's no secret that inside and out, Milwaukee County Stadium provides a great baseball experience for fans.

Milwaukee Brewers

Milwaukee County Stadium.

- Lower Deck Boxes
- Lower Deck Grandstand
- Loge and Mezzanine
- Upper Deck Boxes
- Upper Deck Grandstand
- Bleachers

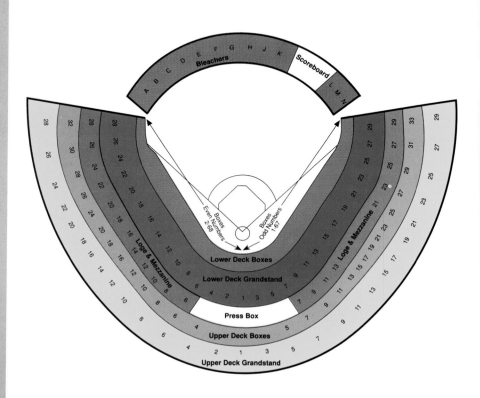

Purchasing Tickets

By mail:
Milwaukee Brewers Ticket Office
Milwaukee County Stadium
Milwaukee, WI 53214

In person:
Brewers Ticket Office is located on the northwest side of Milwaukee County Stadium and is open Monday - Friday, 9 a.m. - 7 p.m.; Saturday, 9 a.m. - 5 p.m.; Sunday, 11 a.m. - 3 p.m.; and until after the game is over for home night games. For information, call 414/933-1818.

By phone:
414/933-9000
800/933-7890
To fax a credit card order, dial 414/933-3547. Include the name, number, and expiration date of your credit card and your signature. Also, indicate date of game, type of seat requested, and your mailing address.

Directions to Stadium

- From the east: Take I-94 to highway U.S. 41 south and enter at Gate 6.

- From the west: Take I-94 to the VA/County Stadium exit and enter at Gate 1, or go east on Bluemound Road and enter at Gates 1 or 2.

- From the north: Take U.S. 41 to County Stadium exit and enter at Gate 6, or take Bluemound Road and enter at Gates 1 or 2.

- From the south: Take U.S. 41 (South 43rd Street) to the stadium and enter at Gate 6.

Public Transportation

The Milwaukee County Transit System operates bus Route 90 along Wisconsin Avenue directly to County Stadium. Most major bus routes connect with Route 90. For information, call 414/344-6711.

Parking

County Stadium parking lots can accommodate 13,000 vehicles. General parking costs $4, limited preferred parking at Gates 1, 2, and 5 costs $6. On-street parking in neighboring residential areas is prohibited. Handicapped parking is available at all gates for $4.

Emergency road service is available in the stadium parking lots beginning in the seventh inning to aid motorists who are locked out of their cars or have dead batteries and to provide free local towing. For assistance, go to Gate X at Section 6 of the main concourse.

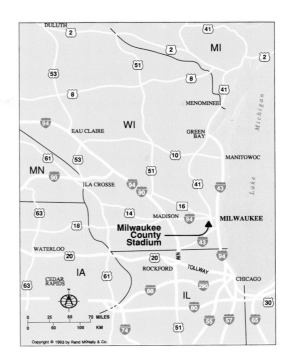

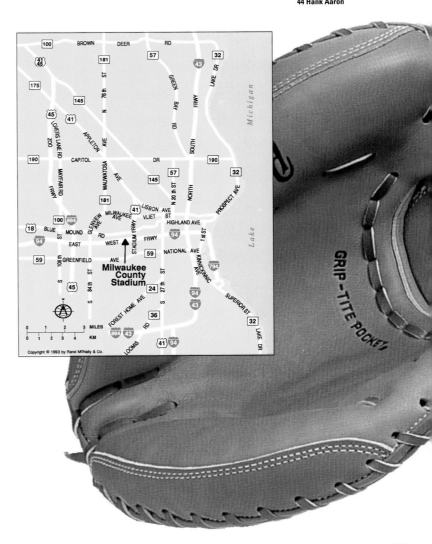

Profile

Team Address
Milwaukee Brewers
Milwaukee County Stadium
201 S. 46th St.
Milwaukee, WI 53214
414/933-4114

Franchise History
Seattle Pilots 1969
Milwaukee Brewers 1970-

American League Pennants
1982 vs. California Angels

East Division Titles
1982

Hall of Fame Inductees
Hank Aaron, 1982
Rollie Fingers, 1992

Award Winners
Cy Young Award
Rollie Fingers, 1981
Pete Vuckovich, 1982

Most Valuable Player
Rollie Fingers, 1981
Robin Yount, 1982, 1989

Retired Uniform Numbers
34 Rollie Fingers
44 Hank Aaron

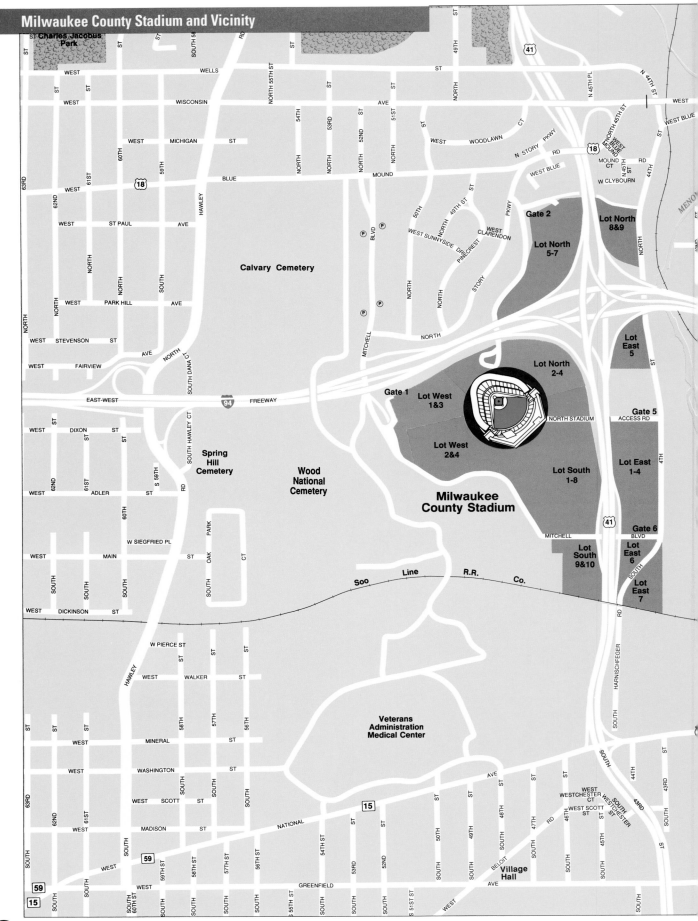

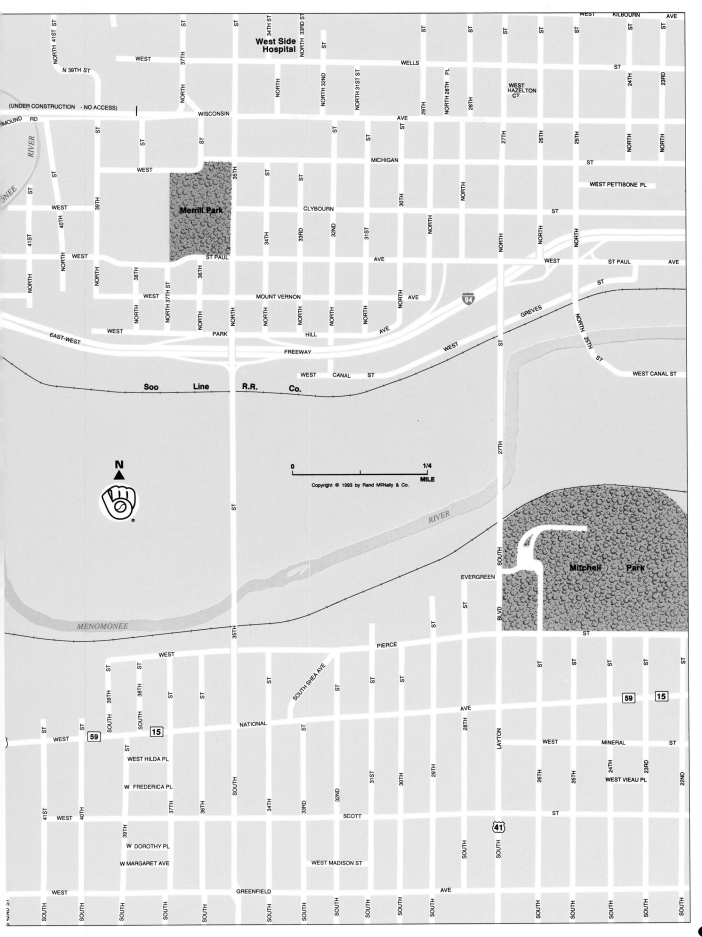

Milwaukee

County Stadium is located on the west end of town, close to the suburb of Wauwatosa. The hotels and restaurants listed are downtown (near the lakefront) or near the stadium.

Sports Spots

Dairyland Greyhound Park
5522 104th Ave., Kenosha
414/657-8200, 800/233-3357
Greyhound racing. Sports
lounge/restaurant ($$)

Geneva Lakes Kennel Club
Highway 50 East, Delavan
414/728-8000
Greyhound racing. Sports
bar/restaurant, food court, picnic
areas ($-$$)

Luke's Sports Spectacular
1225 N. Water St.
414/223-3210
Sports bar/restaurant ($)

**Milwaukee Brewers
Clubhouse Shop**
95 N. Moorland Road, Brookfield
414/789-1148
Official licensed memorabilia.

**Milwaukee County Golf
Courses**
Located throughout the county
414/257-6100
Regulation 9- and 18-hole
courses.

Pettit National Ice Center
Wisconsin State Fair Park
I-94 at 84th St., West Allis
414/271-6066
Enclosed training and competi-
tion center. Public skating
offered.

Saz's
5539 W. State St.
414/453-2410
Sports bar/restaurant; convenient to the stadium ($-$$)

Seagull Charters
McKinley Marina
1750 N. Lincoln Memorial Drive
414/442-4855, 414/224-7707
Steel clipper offers sportfishing
for chinook, coho, and steelhead.
Boat rentals, tackle store.

The Domes at Mitchell Park.

Restaurants

Alioto's
3041 N. Mayfair Road,
Wauwatosa
414/476-6900
Seafood, ribs, steak ($$-$$$)

Ciatti's Italian Restaurant
1118 N. 4th St.
414/223-4400
Northern, southern Italian cui-
sine ($$)

Jake's
6030 W. North Ave., Wauwatosa
414/771-0550
21445 W. Capitol Dr., Brookfield
414/781-7995
Prime rib, duckling, seafood ($$)

**Karl Ratzsch's Old World
Restaurant**
320 E. Mason St.
414/276-2720
German and Continental cuisine
($$$)

Mader's German Restaurant
1037-41 N. Old World Third St.
414/271-3377, 800/558-7171
Classic German and Continental
specialties ($$)

Major Goolsby's
340 W. Kilbourn Ave.
414/271-3414
Sandwiches/appetizers in casual
atmosphere ($)

Mandarin Restaurant
11120 W. Bluemound Road,
Wauwatosa
414/453-5340
Cantonese, Szechuan, and American cuisine ($-$$)

Nantucket Shores
924 E. Juneau
414/278-8660
Seafood, prime rib ($$)

*Sports Spots & Restaurants
(Dinner for two without
beverage or tip):*
$ *Under $20*
$$ *$20-$40*
$$$ *More than $40*

Accommodations

**Best Western Midway Motor
Lodge—Highway 100**
251 N. Mayfair Road, Wauwatosa
414/774-3600 ($$)

Camelot Inn
10900 W. Bluemound Road,
Wauwatosa
414/258-2910 ($)

**Excel Inn of Milwaukee—
West**
115 N. Mayfair Road, Wauwatosa
414/257-0140 ($)

Holiday Inn—West
201 N. Mayfair Road, Wauwatosa
414/771-4400 ($$)

**Howard Johnson Lodge
West—Wauwatosa**
2275 N. Mayfair Road,
Wauwatosa
414/771-4800 ($)

Hyatt Regency Milwaukee
333 W. Kilbourn Ave.
414/276-1234 ($$$)

Pfister Hotel
424 E. Wisconsin Ave.
414/273-8222 ($$$)

Sheraton Mayfair
2303 N. Mayfair Road,
Wauwatosa
414/257-3400 ($$)

*Price ranges: Double room
during the week (lower rates
are often available on
weekends)*
$ *Under $75*
$$ *$75-$125*
$$$ *More than $125*

Attractions

The Grand Avenue
275 W. Wisconsin Ave.
414/224-9720
Downtown retail center with
turn-of-the-century architecture.

Miller Brewing Company
4251 W. State St.
414/931-BEER
Free guided tours of Wisconsin's
largest brewery.

Milwaukee County Zoo
10001 W. Bluemound Road
414/771-3040
Natural environment for animals.

Milwaukee Public Museum
800 W. Wells St.
414/278-2702
Exhibits ranging in time from the
dinosaur age to the information
age.

Several breweries offer free guided tours.

**Mitchell Park Horticultural
Conservatory (The Domes)**
524 S. Layton Blvd.
414/649-9800
Tropical, arid, and seasonal plant
displays in three huge glass
domes.

For More Information

*Greater Milwaukee Convention &
Visitors Bureau*
510 W. Kilbourn Ave.
Milwaukee, WI 53202
414/273-3950

The Metrodome lives up to its multipurpose billing.

It has hosted NFL football and the Super Bowl, the NCAA basketball Final Four, tractor pulls, and two World Series, among other events. It is also, since 1982, the home-dome of the Minnesota Twins.

Construction of the Hubert H. Humphrey Metrodome started in 1979 after the Minnesota legislature approved a $55 million grant. The domed structure sits on a 20-acre site in the Industrial Square district just east of downtown Minneapolis. The dome itself is constructed of 1/32-inch thick Teflon-coated fiberglass.

The 13-foot wall in leftfield, which includes a 6-foot Plexiglas extension, and 23-foot wall in rightfield, including a 16-foot canvas cover, thwart cheap home runs and create some interesting bounces. And you can literally lose balls in the roof. Dave Kingman's pop up in 1984 has yet to come down.

In 1990, the 55,883-seat stadium got a $6-million addition that included new parking facilities and food and beverage areas.

The indoor acoustics assure that fan fervor is translated into home-field advantage. Minnesotans like to root for the Twins and, as their enthusiasm rises, so does the decibel level. Minnesota's fans like the noise because it means their Twins are winning.

The stadium is less than a two-mile walk from downtown.

Minnesota Twins

Hubert H. Humphrey Metrodome.

☐ Club Level
■ Lower Deck Reserved
☐ Upper Deck Reserved
☐ Lower Left Field
■ Upper Deck Outfield

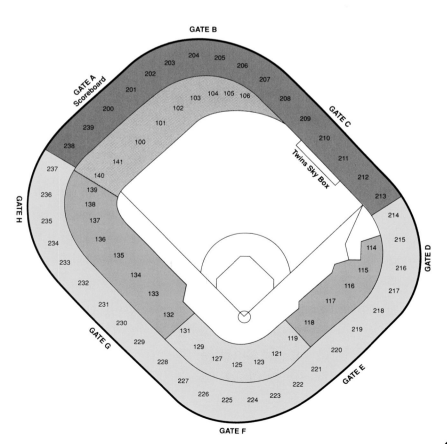

Purchasing Tickets

By mail:
Minnesota Twins, NW 8187
P.O. Box 66117
St. Paul, MN 55166-8187
Send check or money order payable to the Minnesota
Twins.

In person:
Metrodome Ticket Office
501 Chicago Ave. S.
Minneapolis
Ticket office hours: Monday - Friday, 9 a.m. - 5 p.m.;
Saturday, 9 a.m. - 4 p.m.; 9 a.m. - 9 p.m. on days when
night games are scheduled. For ticket information,
call 612/375-1116 or 800/28-TWINS.

Tickets are also sold at Twins Pro Shops in two locations: 2401 Fairview Ave. N., Roseville, and the "Hub"
Shopping Center at 66th and Nicollet in Richfield.

By phone:
Twins Ticket Office—612/375-1116 or 800/28-TWINS.

Directions to the Stadium

- From the north: Take I-35W south to the Washington
  Avenue exit. Turn right on Washington.

- From the south: Take I-35W north to the
  3rd Street exit.

- From the northwest: Take I-94 East to I-35W North to
  the 3rd Street exit.

- From the west: Take Highway 394 (Highway 12) to I-94
  East to the 3rd Street exit.

- From the east: Take I-94 West to the 5th Street exit.
  Or, take I-94 West to the 11th Street exit for parking in
  the downtown area.

Public Transportation

A shuttle bus service operates three routes covering
the downtown area for one hour preceding Twins
games with more than 30,000 anticipated attendance.
Bus stops are marked with special shuttle bus signs.
The buses also operate for one hour after the games.
For information, call 612/827-7733.

Parking

About 15,000 parking spaces are available in lots, on
ramps, and at meters within six blocks north and west
of the Metrodome. All areas marked "No Stadium
Parking Area" are subject to tagging and towing. Handicapped parking is available between 3rd and 5th
streets on both sides of Chicago Avenue (on the west
side of the Metrodome) and at any hooded meters at
no charge. Many downtown ramps and lots also provide parking spaces for handicapped individuals.

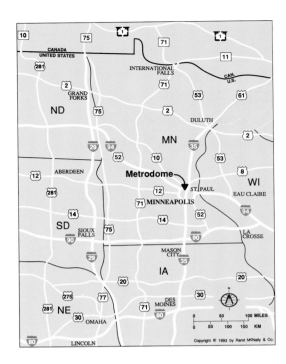

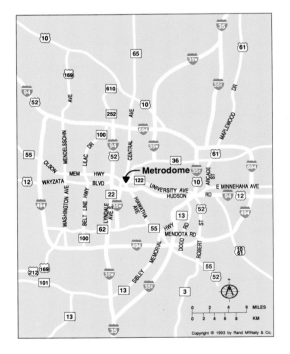

A drop-off zone for handicapped individuals is located
on Chicago Avenue and is accessible to those
displaying proper licenses. A parking lot exclusively
for handicapped individuals is located at 4th Street
and Chicago Avenue.

Minneapolis

The Twin Cities are blessed with natural beauty. The Metrodome is near downtown Minneapolis, so most hotels and restaurants are in the downtown area as well.

Sports Spots

Bunker Hills Regional Park
Foley Boulevard and Highway 242, Coon Rapids
612/757-3920
Wave pool, horseback riding, golf, biking.

Hennepin Parks
Located throughout the Twin Cities area
612/559-9000
Outdoor recreation centers, golf courses, beaches, boat launches, biking trails, and hiking trails.

Hoops on Hennepin
1110 Hennepin Ave.
612/375-1900
Sports bar/restaurant with game room ($-$$)

Hubert's
601 Chicago Ave. S.
612/332-6062
Sports bar/restaurant near the Metrodome ($)

Mac's Sports Grill and Bar
301 Central Ave. S.E.
612/379-0272
Sports bar/restaurant ($)

National Sports Center
1700 105th Ave. N.E., Blaine
612/785-5600
Olympic training center for cycling, track and field, soccer, and weight lifting.

Skyways make it easy to stroll in downtown Minneapolis.

Restaurants

Ciatti's Italian Restaurant
1346 LaSalle Ave.
612/339-7747
Northern, Southern Italian cuisine ($$)

Grandma's Saloon and Deli
1810 Washington Ave. S.
612/340-0516
Seafood, sandwiches, soups ($-$$)

Ichiban Japanese Steak House
1333 Nicollet Mall
612/339-0540
Japanese cuisine ($$-$$$)

J.D. Hoyt's
301 Washington Ave. N.
612/338-1560
Beef, ribs, chops ($$$)

Jax Cafe
1928 University Ave. N.E.
612/789-7297
Steak, seafood, pasta ($$-$$$)

Leeann Chin Chinese Cuisine
International Centre, 9th Street and 2nd Avenue S.
612/338-8488
Cantonese, Szechuan cuisine ($$)

Nankin
2 S. 7th St.
612/333-3303
Chinese, Cantonese, Szechuan cuisine ($$)

Pronto Ristorante
1300 Nicollet Mall
612/333-4414
Northern Italian cuisine ($$-$$$)

Rudolph's
1933 Lyndale Ave. S.
612/871-8969
Barbecued ribs, chops ($-$$)

Accommodations

Best Western Normandy Inn
405 8th St. S.
612/370-1400 ($$)

Days Inn—University
2407 University Ave. S.E.
612/623-3999 ($)

Holiday Inn Metrodome
1500 Washington Ave. S.
612/333-4646 ($$)

Hotel Luxeford Suites
1101 LaSalle Ave.
612/332-6800 ($$)

Hyatt Regency Minneapolis
1300 Nicollet Mall
612/370-1234 ($$$)

The Marquette Hotel
7th and Marquette streets
612/332-2351, 800/328-4782 ($$$)

Minneapolis Metrodome Hilton
1330 Industrial Blvd.
612/331-1900, 800/HILTONS ($$)

Radisson Metrodome Hotel
615 Washington Ave. S.E.
612/379-8888 ($$)

Attractions

The Guthrie Theater
725 Vineland Place
612/377-2224
Renowned regional theater.

Sculpture Garden near downtown.

Mall of America
60 E. Broadway, Bloomington
612/851-3500
The nation's largest indoor shopping mall.

Minneapolis Institute of Arts
2400 3rd Ave. S.
612/870-3000
Comprehensive fine arts museum.

The Guthrie, the city's prominent regional theater.

Ordway Music Theatre
345 Washington St., St. Paul
612/224-4222
Performing arts center features Broadway musicals, operas.

Riverplace
43 Main St. S.E.
612/378-1969
Historic district with shops, restaurants, entertainment.

The Science Museum of Minnesota
30 E. 10th St., St. Paul
612/221-9488
Exhibits of natural history and science; Omnitheater.

Valleyfair Family Amusement Park
One Valleyfair Drive, Shakopee
612/445-7600
Rides, entertainment, and attractions; IMAX theater.

Walker Art Center
Vineland Place
612/375-7600
Modern art and special exhibitions as well as music, film, dance.

For More Information

Minneapolis Convention & Visitors Association
1219 Marquette Ave.
Minneapolis, MN 55403
612/348-4313

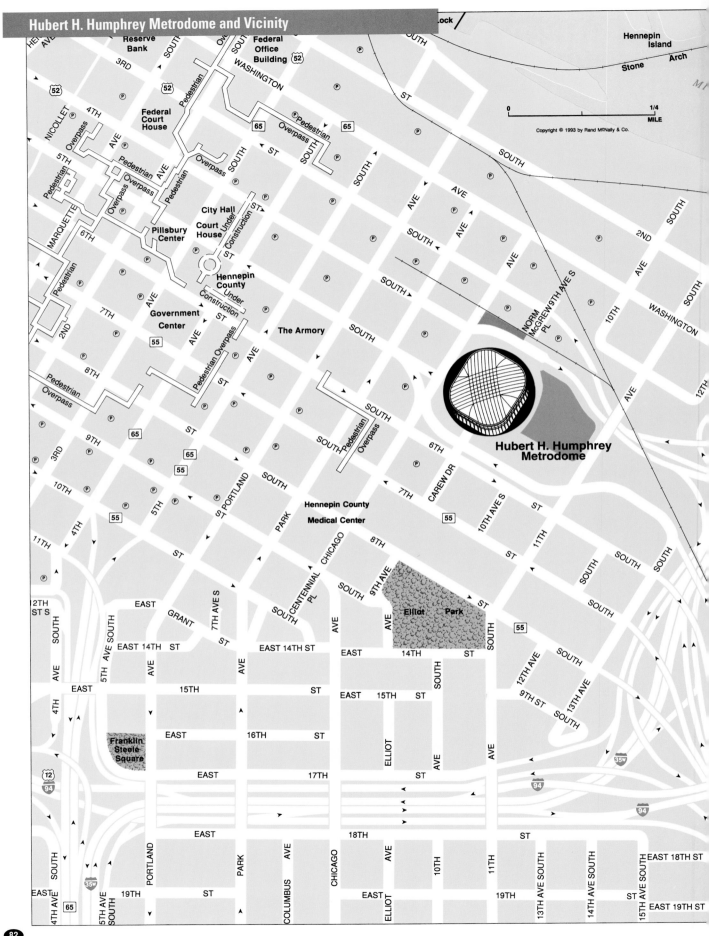

Hubert H. Humphrey
Metrodome

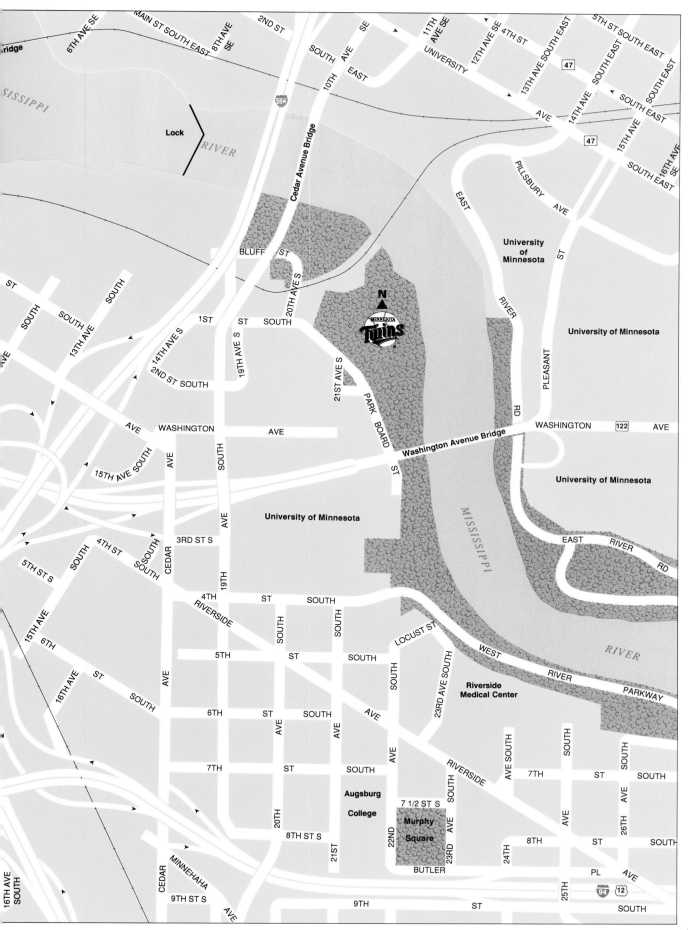

MISSISSIPPI

6TH AVE SE

MAIN ST SOUTH EAST

8TH AVE SE

2ND ST

SOUTH

AVE

EAST

SE

11TH AVE SE

UNIVERSITY

12TH AVE SE

4TH ST

5TH ST SOUTH EAST

13TH AVE SOUTH EAST

14TH AVE SOUTH EAST

47

SOUTH EAST

15TH AVE SOUTH EAST

16TH AVE SOUTH EAST

10TH

35W

Lock

RIVER

47

AVE

Cedar Avenue Bridge

EAST

PILLSBURY

AVE

University of Minnesota

BLUFF ST

20TH AVE S

N

MINNESOTA Twins

University of Minnesota

RIVER

ST

ST

SOUTH

SOUTH

1ST

ST SOUTH

19TH AVE S

21ST AVE S

PLEASANT

SOUTH

13TH AVE

14TH AVE S

2ND ST SOUTH

PARK

WASHINGTON

122

AVE

AVE

WASHINGTON

AVE

BOARD

Washington Avenue Bridge

15TH AVE SOUTH

AVE

ST

University of Minnesota

MISSISSIPPI

5TH ST S

4TH ST

3RD ST S

19TH

EAST RIVER RD

SOUTH

SOUTH

CEDAR

4TH

ST

SOUTH

RIVER

15TH AVE

6TH

SOUTH

5TH

ST

SOUTH

LOCUST ST

WEST

RIVER

16TH AVE

ST

SOUTH

23RD AVE SOUTH

RIVER

PARKWAY

16TH AVE SOUTH

AVE

6TH

ST

SOUTH

AVE

Riverside Medical Center

SOUTH

7TH

ST

SOUTH

26TH

AVE

7TH

ST

SOUTH

RIVERSIDE

AVE SOUTH

7TH

ST

SOUTH

Augsburg College

7 1/2 ST S

AVE

8TH

ST

SOUTH

20TH

22ND

Murphy Square

23RD

24TH

8TH ST S

21ST

BUTLER

PL

AVE

CEDAR

MINNEHAHA

25TH

94

12

9TH ST S

9TH

ST

SOUTH

AVE

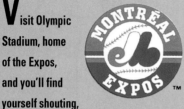

Visit Olympic Stadium, home of the Expos, and you'll find yourself shouting, "Vive baseball!"

Montréal, a city that combines French and English traditions, gave a Gallic welcome to the Expos from the team's inception in 1969. Part of that welcome included the promise of a new stadium to be built for the 1976 Olympics and then to become the Expos' home.

Olympic Stadium, or *Stade Olympique*, is uniquely designed with a retractable roof. Twenty-six cables connect to a 60,696-square-foot round section of the roof, which can be lifted by a 552-foot high tower. The dome itself is made up of more than 200,000 square feet of fabric (Kevlar) that weighs 65 tons.

In 1991, the stadium underwent renovations to increase fan comfort. The seating capacity was reduced from 60,011 to 43,739, and two stands for bleachers were erected behind the outfield fences. The entire playing field was then moved 40 feet towards the stands, bringing fans closer to the game.

Olympic Stadium is also one of the easiest ballparks to reach in the Major Leagues. Just take the Metro, Montréal's efficient subway system (Pie IX Metro station). Once at the stadium, you'll know you're not in Kansas by the bilingual announcements and signage.

The Expos prove that baseball is fun no matter what language you speak.

Montréal Expos

Olympic Stadium.

☐ VIP Box Seat
☐ Box Seat
☐ Terrace
☐ Promenade
☐ General Admission Reserved
☐ Bleachers

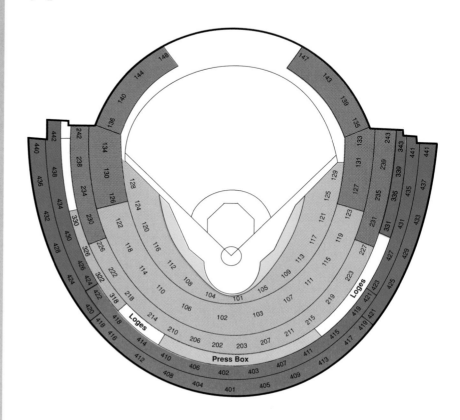

Purchasing Tickets

By mail:

P.O. Box 500
Station M
Montreal, Quebec H1V 3P2
Canada

Send a check or money order payable to Montreal Baseball Club Inc. There is a $4 (Canadian) service charge for mail orders. You may also pay by credit card. For information, call 514/253-3434.

In person:

Olympic Stadium
4549 Pierre de Coubertin Ave.
Ticket office hours: Monday - Saturday, 9 a.m. - 5 p.m., and home game days an hour before game time.

By phone:

Admission Network
514/790-1245 (in Montreal)
800/361-4595 (elsewhere in Canada)
800/678-5440 in the United States

Directions to the Stadium

- From New England: Take I-87 north from Vermont to Quebec Highway 15 to the Jacques Cartier Bridge. Stay left on the bridge as you exit; go to the first stoplight; turn right onto Sherbrooke Street, which goes directly to the stadium.

- From upstate New York: Take I-81 north to Canada's Highway 401; then east to Quebec Highway 20; north to Highway 40 to the Boulevard Pie IX exit south to the stadium.

- From Ontario: Take Highway 417 east to Quebec Highway 40 (Autoroute Metropolitaine) north to the Boulevard Pie IX exit south to the stadium. Or, take Highway 401 east to Quebec Highway 20; take 20 north to Highway 40 (Autoroute Metropolitaine) to the Boulevard Pie IX exit south to the stadium.

Public Transportation

Metro trains run directly from downtown Montreal to the Olympic Stadium, which is designated the Pie IX Metro station.

Parking

Olympic Stadium operates a six-level underground garage with 3,711 parking spaces. Each level has six to 12 spaces reserved for handicapped. Parking on the street around the stadium is not advised, since it is reserved for residents.

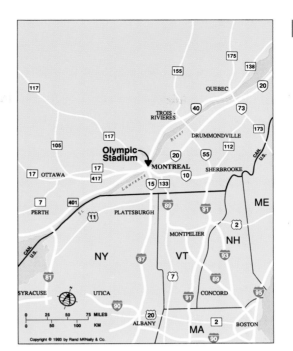

Profile

Team Address
Montreal Expos
Olympic Stadium
4549 Avenue Pierrre de Coubertin
Montreal, Quebec H1V 3N7
Canada
514/253-3434

Franchise History
Montreal Expos 1969 -

East Division Titles
1981

Award Winners
Rookie of the Year
Carl Morton, 1970
Andre Dawson, 1977

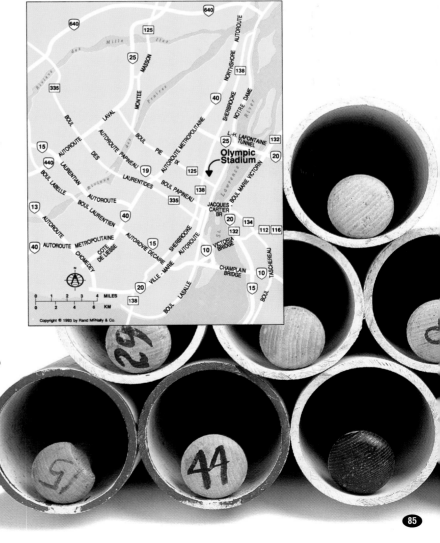

L'Assomption-
Métro

Oliver
Guimond

Thibodeau

ONNEAU

Underground

AVE
Underground

DE MARSE

RUE

BOUL

RUE

PIERRE-DE-COUBERTIN

L'ASSOMPTION

HOCHELAGA

RUE

VIMONT

RUE DE VILLE-MARIE

ST-CLEMENT

ROUEN

BÉNARD

ONTARIO

RUE

RUE

RUE

RUE

LA
FONTAINE

ST-CLEMENT

THEODORE

LECLAIRE

SICARD

ADAM

RUE
BECHARD

VIAU

VILLE-MARIE

RUE DE

VIMONT

CATHERINE

ST-

NOTRE-DAME

RUE

Parc
St-Clement

RUE MONSABRE

CORDAIRE

RUE
BOILEAU

RUE

DICKSON

RUE

RUE

DESAULNIERS

RUE

RUE

LOUIS-VEUILLOT

RUE LANDRY

RUE

LACORDAIRE

MONSABRE
AVE

DE

BOSSUET

TOULOUSE

RUE DE MEAUX

SOULIGNY

DE

CADILLAC

DUQUESNE

AVE

DUBUISSON

RUE

RUE

RUE

RUE

ONTARIO

DE

DUQUESNE

LAFONTAINE

CADIL

BOSSUET

DICKSON

ROUSEMONT

NOTRE-DAME

RUE

RIVER

LAWRENCE

SAINT

MONTREAL
EXPOS

0   1/4
MILE

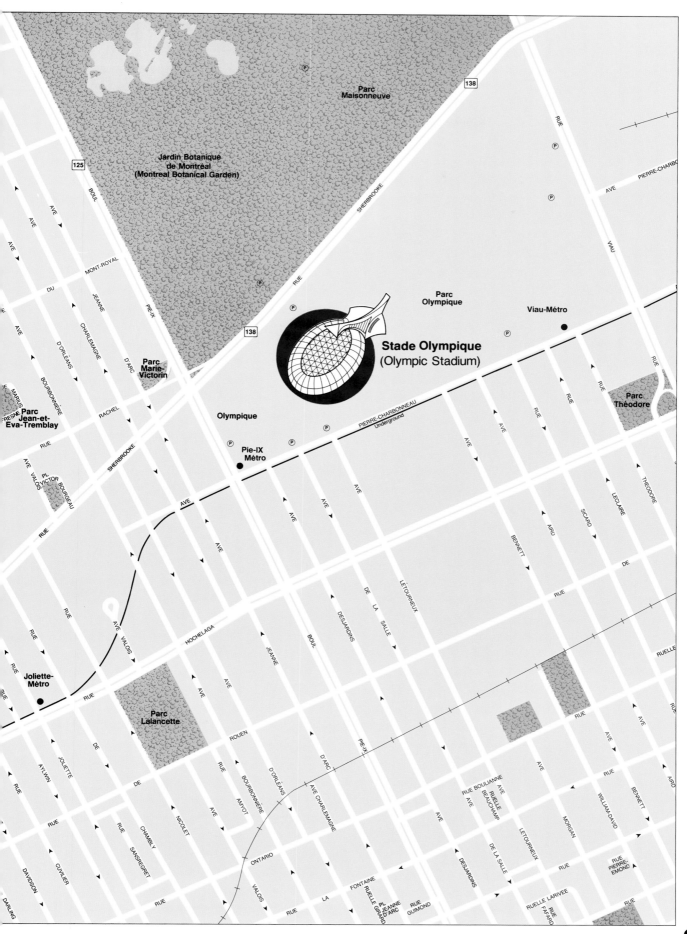

Parc
Maisonneuve

138

125

Jardin Botanique
de Montréal
(Montreal Botanical Garden)

MONT-ROYAL

SHERBROOKE

RUE

Parc
Olympique

Viau-Métro

138

Stade Olympique
(Olympic Stadium)

Parc
Marie-
Victorin

Parc
Théodore

Parc
Jean-et-
Eva-Tremblay

Olympique

PIERRE-CHARBONNEAU
Underground

Pie-IX
Métro

SHERBROOKE

AVE

HOCHELAGA

Joliette-
Métro

Parc
Lalancette

ROUEN

AVE CHARLEMAGNE

RUE BOULIANNE

ONTARIO

PL
JEANNE
D'ARC

87

Montréal

Montréal is a city where English and French cultures meet. Most of the hotels and restaurants listed are located downtown or near the stadium.

Sports Spots

Cycling Paths of Montréal
A network of cycling paths covers 240 kilometers throughout the city. Bicycles can be rented by calling 514/525-8888 (Acces Cible) or 514/393-1528 (Cyclo-Touriste).

Ecole de Voile de Lachine
2105 Saint Joseph Blvd., Lachine
514/634-4326
Light sailboats and windsurfers for rent.

La Cage aux Sports
2250 Guy St.
514/931-8588
Sports bar/restaurant with 10 locations in the city ($)

Lachine Rapids Tours
Foot of Berri at Victoria Pier
514/284-9607
Jet boats shoot the Lachine rapids.

Maisonneuve Park
4601 Sherbrooke St. E.
514/872-5558
Covers 525 acres; includes a municipal golf course (514/872-1143) and a cycling track.

Olympic Basin and Beach
Ile Notre Dame
Sailboats, sailboards, canoes, kayaks, hiking trails.

Olympic Park
4141 Pierre de Coubertin Ave.
514/252-8687
Park surrounding Olympic Stadium has six public swimming pools.

Montréal–a sophisticated world city.

Restaurants

Cafe Les Pres
6060 Sherbrooke St. E.
514/252-1828
Chicken, burgers, lasagna. Convenient to stadium ($$)

Chez La Mere Michel
1209 Guy St.
514/934-0473
French cuisine ($$$)

Le St. Amable
188 St. Amable St.
514/866-3471
French cuisine ($$$)

Le Vieux Munich
1170 St. Denis St.
514/288-8011
German cuisine ($-$$)

Les Chenets
2075 Bishop St.
514/844-1842
French cuisine ($$)

Les Halles
1450 Crescent St.
514/844-2328
French cuisine ($$$)

Restaurant Lotte
215 Blvd. Rene Levesque E.
514/393-3838
Szechuan and Cantonese cuisine, entertainment ($$)

Stadium Club
Auberge Universel Hotel
5000 Sherbrooke St. E.
514/253-3365
Seafood, veal, beef ($$)

William Tell
2055 Stanley St.
514/288-0139
Swiss cuisine ($$$)

Sports Spots & Restaurants (Dinner for two without beverage or tip - in $Canadian):
$ Under $20
$$ $20-$40
$$$ More than $40

Accommodations

Auberge des Glycines
819 Blvd. de Maisonneuve E.
514/526-5511, 800/361-6896 ($)

Auberge Ramada Centre-Ville
1005 Guy St.
514/938-4611, 800/272-6232 ($$)

Auberge Universel Hotel
5000 Sherbrooke St. E.
514/253-3365 ($$)

Bonaventure Hilton International
1 Place Bonaventure
514/878-2332 ($$$)

Hotel le Sherbrooke
12555 Sherbrooke St. E.
514/640-5500 ($)

Hotel Saint-Denis
1254 St. Denis St.
514/849-4526 ($)

La Tour Centre-Ville
400 Blvd. Rene Levesque W.
514/866-8861, 800/361-2790 ($)

Lord Berri Hotel
1199 Berri St.
514/845-9236 ($$)

Price ranges: Double room during the week (lower rates are often available on weekends - in $Canadian);
$ Under $75
$$ $75-$125
$$$ More than $125

Attractions

Biodôme
4777 Pierre de Coubertin Ave.
514/872-3034
A "living" museum of nature and environmental science. Four simulated ecosystems.

Botanical Garden
4101 Sherbrooke St. E.
514/872-1400
More than 30 gardens.

La Ronde
Ile Sainte-Helene
514/872-6222
Rides, water slides, a circus, entertainment.

Museum of Fine Arts
1379 Sherbrooke St. W.
514/285-1600
The oldest art museum in Canada. Features Canadian and Quebecois art.

Dining alfresco along the Rue Prince Arthur.

Notre-Dame Basilica
116 Notre Dame St. W.
514/849-1070
Neo-Gothic architecture; museum with priceless art.

Old Montreal
Extends from St. Lawrence River to St. Antoine and McGill to Berri Street
Renovated 17th- to 19th-century buildings. Shops, restaurants, museums, historic sites.

Old Port
Between McGill & Berri
514/496-7678
Lively historical district with tours, cruises, cafes, theaters.

A street in Montréal's colorful Chinatown.

Olympic Stadium Tower
4141 Pierre de Coubertin Ave., in Olympic Park
514/252-8687
Sightseeing tower. Cable car rides to the top.

For More Information

Greater Montréal Convention & Visitors Bureau
1555 Peel St., Suite 600
Montreal, Quebec H3A 1X6
Canada
514/844-5400

Shea Stadium, home of the New York Mets, has the largest scoreboard in the majors—86-feet high by 175-feet long. All the better to announce every Mets run, and there are a lot of them. Of course, it wasn't always that way.

The Mets were formed in 1962, a NL expansion team located in the very long shadows of the New York Yankees, Brooklyn Dodgers, and New York Giants. The Dodgers and Giants had moved to warmer quarters, and the Mets were the great NewYork-National League hope.

For the first two seasons, the team played at the venerable Polo Grounds. The Mets moved into Shea Stadium near Flushing Meadow Park in Queens in 1964. (The stadium is also near busy LaGuardia Airport, so expect to hear jets coming and going throughout most games.) Built near the site of the 1939-1940 and 1964-1965 World's Fair, the five-tier stadium has hosted three World Series since it opened.

Remember the 1969 Miracle Mets and Cy Young winner Tom Seaver? Shea has hosted two more championship teams: The 1973 "Ya Gotta Believe" club, which rallied from last place and 11-1/2 games out in early August to win the National League East. And the 1986 team that ran away with the East but had to rally in the series against Boston.

When Shea is filled to its 55,777-seat capacity, which it often is, fans expect success, and they frequently get it.

New York Mets

Shea Stadium.

- ■ Field Level
- ■ Loge
- ■ Mezzanine
- ■ Upper Level
- □ Picnic Bleachers
- ■ Picnic Area

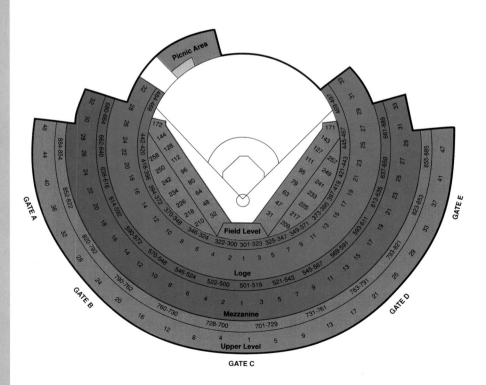

Purchasing Tickets

By mail:

Mets Ticket Department
Shea Stadium
Flushing, NY 11368.

Specify game date(s) and number and price of tickets. Enclose check or money order payable to New York Mets, or include credit card number (MasterCard, Visa, American Express), expiration date, and signature.

In person:

Advance Ticket Window at Shea Stadium
126th Street and Roosevelt Avenue, near Gate D

Ticket office hours: Monday - Friday, 9 a.m. - 6 p.m.; Saturdays, Sundays, and holidays, 9 a.m. - 5 p.m., and until one hour past the scheduled game time for night games. Cash, MasterCard, Visa, and American Express accepted.

You may also purchase tickets and officially licensed Mets merchandise in person at any of the following Mets Clubhouse Shop locations: 575 Fifth Ave. at 47th Street; Menlo Park Mall, Edison, NJ; 30-93 Steinway St., Long Island City, NY.

By phone:

Call the Mets Ticket Office at 718/507-TIXX to purchase Mets tickets by phone (MasterCard, Visa, or American Express) or for information on the Mets home schedule and additional information regarding the purchase of tickets in person or by mail.

Directions to the Stadium

- From Northern Queens: Cross Island North to Whitestone Expressway then exit Northern Boulevard/Shea Stadium.

- From Southern Queens: Take Northern Boulevard east to Shea Stadium.

- From the Bronx and Westchester: Take the Cross Bronx Expressway to the Bronx-Whitestone Bridge, then take the bridge to the Whitestone Expressway to the Northern Boulevard/Shea Stadium exit. Or, take the Triborough Bridge to Grand Central Parkway to the Northern Boulevard/Shea Stadium exit.

- From Brooklyn: Take the Brooklyn-Queens Expressway eastbound to the Grand Central Parkway eastbound and exit at Northern Boulevard/Shea Stadium. Or, take the Belt Parkway eastbound to the Van Wyck Expressway northbound to the Northern Boulevard West exit to Shea Stadium.

- From Manhattan: Take the Triborough Bridge to the Grand Central Parkway to the Northern Boulevard/Shea Stadium exit.

Public Transportation

For bus and subway information, call:
718/830-1234

Parking

Parking is available at five lots surrounding Shea Stadium, with parking for handicapped individuals at Gates B, C, and D. Alternate Shea Stadium parking is located in Flushing Meadow–Corona Park.

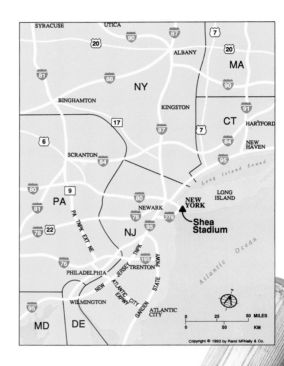

New York

Take a bite of the Big Apple and its stellar theater, art, shopping, and entertainment offerings. Hotels and restaurants listed are in Manhattan or near Shea Stadium.

Sports Spots

The Boathouse
In Central Park near 72nd Street park entrance
212/517-3623
Boat rentals on Central Park Lake; bicycle rentals also available; outdoor cafe ($$)

Flushing Meadow—Corona Park
Jewel and Roosevelt, Queens
718/760-6600
Marina, ice skating, pool, tennis courts, two zoos.

Legends
17 Murray St. (between Broadway and Church)
212/608-3900
Sports bar/restaurant ($-$$)

Mickey Mantle's
42 Central Park South
212/688-7777
Sports bar/restaurant ($$)

New York Mets Clubhouse Shops
575 Fifth Ave.
212/986-4887
414 Menlo Park, Edison, NJ
908/548-1955
30-93 Steinway St., Astoria
718/204-0927
Official licensed memorabilia shops.

New York Road Runners Club
9 E. 89th St.
212/860-4455
Sponsors New York City Marathon, other races, running classes, seminars.

The famous Manhattan skyline.

Runyon's
305 E. 50th St. (between First and Second)
212/223-9592
932 Second Ave. (between 49th and 50th)
212/759-7800
Sports bars/restaurants ($$)

Sporting Club
99 Hudson St. (between Franklin and Leonard)
212/219-0900
Sports bar/restaurant ($$-$$$)

Sports
2182 Broadway (between 77th and 78th)
212/874-7208
Sports bar/restaurant ($-$$)

Restaurants

Christo's
143 E. 49th St.
212/355-2695
Steak, Italian specialties ($$-$$$)

Foro Italico
455 W. 34th St.
212/564-6619
Italian cuisine ($$)

Gallagher's Steak House
228 W. 52nd St.
212/245-5336
Steak, chops, fish ($$$)

Il Vagabondo
351 E. 62nd St.
212/832-9221
Northern Italian cuisine ($$)

P.J. Clarke's
Third Avenue at 55th Street
212/759-1650
Burgers, steak, chili ($-$$)

Sam's Cafe
1406 Third Ave. at 80th Street
212/988-5300
Burgers, steak, seafood ($$)

Sports Spots & Restaurants (Dinner for two without beverage or tip):
$ Under $20
$$ $20-$40
$$$ More than $40

Accommodations

Days Inn–New York
440 W. 57th St.
212/581-8100, 800/325-2525 ($$$)

Grand Hyatt New York Hotel
Park Avenue at Grand Central
212/883-1234, 800/233-1234 ($$$)

Holiday Inn Crown Plaza
104-04 Ditmars Blvd.
East Elmhurst
718/457-6300 ($$$)

LaGuardia Marriott
102-05 Ditmars Blvd.
East Elmhurst
718/565-8900 ($$$)

Ramada Hotel
90-10 Grand Central Pkwy.
East Elmhurst
718/446-4800 ($$-$$$)

Price ranges: Double room during the week (lower rates often available on weekends)
$ Under $75
$$ $75-$125
$$$ More than $125

Wall Street, the financial center of America.

Attractions

American Museum of Natural History
Central Park West at 79th Street
212/769-5100
Exhibits, interactive displays, planetarium.

Empire State Building
34th Street and Fifth Avenue
212/736-3100
Panoramic view of New York from outdoor observatories. King Kong display.

Metropolitan Museum of Art
82nd Street and Fifth Avenue
212/535-7710
Vast collection of world art.

Museum of Modern Art
11 W. 53rd St.
212/708-9480
Excellent collection of 20th-century art, architecture, design, photography, film.

Rockefeller Center
48th Street to 51st Street, west of Fifth Avenue
212/698-8500
Shopping and restaurants.

Rockefeller Center offers several dining areas.

South Street Seaport
Fulton and South streets
212/SEA-PORT
Restored piers and landmark buildings filled with shops, restaurants, pubs.

Statue of Liberty National Monument/Ellis Island
Liberty Island
212/363-3200
Ferry boats depart from Battery Park (212/269-5755).

Wall Street
Lower Manhattan
America's financial center lined with brokerages and financial institutions; nearby, the twin towers of the World Trade Center.

For More Information

New York City Convention & Visitors Bureau
2 Columbus Circle
New York, NY 10019
212/397-8200

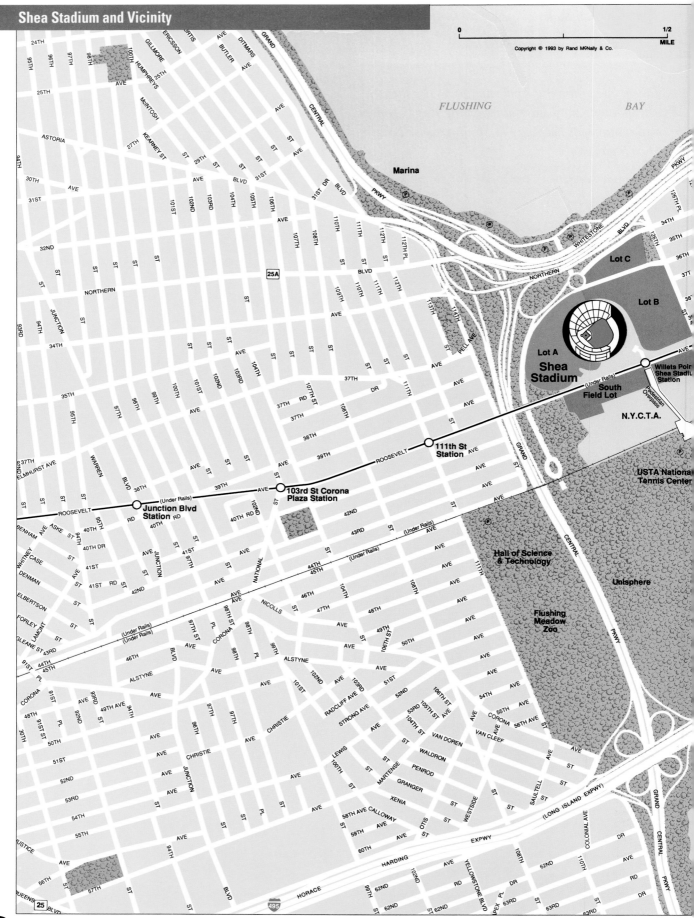

FLUSHING   BAY

Marina

Lot C

Lot B

Lot A

Shea Stadium

Willets Poin
Shea Stadium
Station

South
Field Lot

N.Y.C.T.A.

**111th St
Station**

**103rd St Corona
Plaza Station**

**Junction Blvd
Station**

USTA National
Tennis Center

Hall of Science
& Technology

Unisphere

Flushing
Meadow
Zoo

Copyright © 1993 by Rand McNally & Co.

0   1/2
MILE

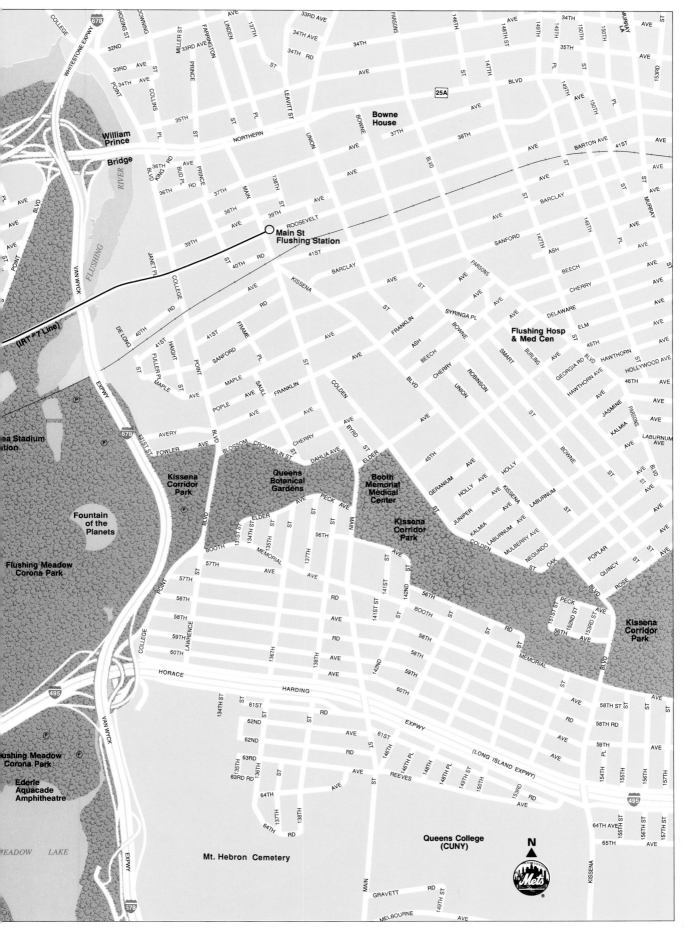

Yankee Stadium reflects baseball's greatest traditions and its legendary past.

The stadium, which hosted its first game on April 18, 1923, ranks high on the "don't miss" list of any baseball fan.

Fans can recapture baseball history at Yankee Stadium by visiting Monument Park adjacent to centerfield. It is here that Babe Ruth, Lou Gehrig, and Miller Huggins, manager of three World Championship and six American League Championship teams, are honored with statues.

Originally, the memorials were located in fair territory. Casey Stengel once saw a long drive to center get by his outfielder and bounce behind the statues. When the fielder had trouble retrieving the ball, legend says that Stengel yelled, "Ruth, Gehrig, Huggins—someone throw the ball." To clear the playing field, the statues were moved to the area between the bullpens when the stadium was remodeled in the mid-1970s.

Eighteen plaques also line the stadium walls, celebrating Yankee notables, and a special walk honors players whose uniform numbers have been retired.

Heroes are the tradition at Yankee Stadium: Joe DiMaggio started his 56-game hitting streak at Yankee Stadium on May 15, 1941, a mark that may never be broken. Roger Maris hit his record-breaking 61st home run on October 1, 1961, here. Don Larsen pitched the World Series' only perfect game on this site in 1956.

New York Yankees

Field Level Boxes
Main Level Boxes
Club Level Boxes
Loge Level Boxes
Tier Level Boxes
Main Level Reserved
Tier Level Reserved
Bleachers

Yankee Stadium.

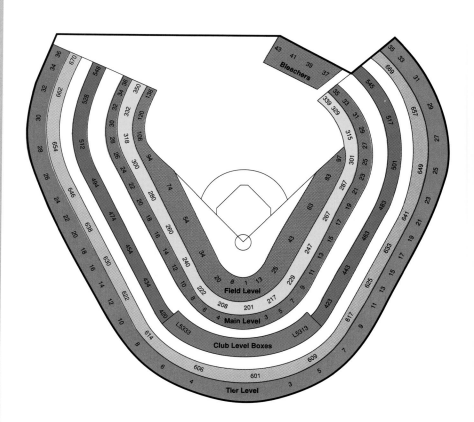

Purchasing Tickets

By mail:
Mail Order Department
Yankee Stadium
Bronx, NY 10451

Send a check or money order payable to the New York Yankees (add $2 for the cost of postage and handling). Specify the number of tickets, the date, and the price of the tickets you want.

In person:
Advance Ticket Windows
161st Street and River Avenue

Ticket office hours: Daily, 9 a.m. - 5 p.m. and through the conclusion of all home night games. For ticket information, call 718/293-6000.

Tickets are also available at New York Yankees clubhouse stores at 393 Fifth Ave., 212/685-4693, and 110 E. 59th St., 212/758-7844.

By phone:
212/307-1212	215/336-2000	609/520-8383
516/888-9000	914/454-3388	617/931-2000
203/624-0033	201/507-8900	518/476-1000

Directions to the Stadium

- From Brooklyn and Staten Island: Take F.D.R. Drive north to Harlem River Drive northbound to either West 155th Street or Frederick Douglas Boulevard to West 154th Street east (via Macombs Dam Bridge) to Jerome Avenue. Or take Brooklyn-Queens Expressway north to Grand Central Parkway eastbound to Triborough Bridge to the Bruckner Expressway eastbound to East 149th Street to River Avenue.

- From Manhattan: Take West Side Highway north to Henry Hudson Parkway to George Washington Bridge Highway (I-95) eastbound to Edward L. Grant Highway south to Jerome Avenue. Or take F.D.R. Drive north to Harlem River Drive northbound to West 155th Street east (via Macombs Dam Bridge) to Jerome Avenue. Or take F.D.R. Drive north to Harlem River Drive northbound to West 155th Street east (via Macombs Dam Bridge) to East 157th Street to East 153rd Street.

- From Queens and Long Island: Take Throgs Neck Bridge or Bronx Whitestone Bridge to Cross Bronx Expressway westbound to Jerome Avenue south. Or take the Triborough Bridge to Harlem River Drive northbound to Frederick Douglas Boulevard to West 154th Street east (via Macombs Dam Bridge) to Jerome Avenue. Or take Throgs Neck Bridge or Bronx Whitestone Bridge to Cross Bronx Expressway westbound to Jerome Avenue south to River Avenue. Or take Grand Central Parkway westbound to Triborough Bridge to Bruckner Expressway eastbound to East 149th Street to River Avenue. Or take Grand Central Parkway westbound to Triborough Bridge to Bruckner Expressway eastbound to East 163rd Street west to Washington Avenue south to East 161st Street west to stadium.

Team Address
New York Yankees
Yankee Stadium
Bronx, NY 10451
718/293-4300

Franchise History
Baltimore Orioles 1901-02
New York Yankees 1903-

World Series Titles
1923 vs. New York Giants
1927 vs. Pittsburgh Pirates
1928 vs. St. Louis Cardinals
1932 vs. Chicago Cubs
1936 vs. New York Giants
1937 vs. New York Giants
1938 vs. Chicago Cubs
1939 vs. Cincinnati Reds
1941 vs. Brooklyn Dodgers
1943 vs. St. Louis Cardinals
1947 vs. Brooklyn Dodgers
1949 vs. Brooklyn Dodgers
1950 vs. Philadelphia Phillies
1951 vs. New York Giants
1952 vs. Brooklyn Dodgers
1953 vs. Brooklyn Dodgers
1956 vs. Brooklyn Dodgers
1958 vs. Milwaukee Braves
1961 vs. Cincinnati Reds
1962 vs. San Francisco Giants

1977 vs. Los Angeles Dodgers
1978 vs. Los Angeles Dodgers

American League Pennants
1921, 1922, 1923, 1926, 1927, 1928, 1932, 1936, 1937, 1938, 1939, 1941, 1942, 1943, 1947, 1949, 1950, 1951, 1952, 1953, 1955, 1956, 1957, 1958, 1960, 1961, 1962, 1963, 1964, 1976, 1977, 1978, 1981

East Division Titles
1976, 1977, 1978, 1980, 1981

Hall of Fame Inductees
Babe Ruth, 1936
John McGraw, 1937
Lou Gehrig, 1939
Willie Keeler, 1939
Clark C. Griffith, 1945
Wilbert Robinson, 1945
Frank Chance, 1946
Jack Chesbro, 1946
Joe McGinnity, 1946
Herb Pennock, 1948
Paul Waner, 1952
Edward G. Barrow, 1953
Bill Dickey, 1954
Frank "Home Run" Baker, 1955

Joe DiMaggio, 1955
Dazzy Vance, 1955
Joe McCarthy, 1957
Burleigh Grimes, 1964
Miller Huggins, 1964
Casey Stengel, 1966
Branch Rickey, 1967
Red Ruffing, 1967
Stan Coveleski, 1969
Waite Hoyt, 1969
Earle Combs, 1970
George M. Weiss, 1970
Joe Kelley, 1971
Yogi Berra, 1971
Lefty Gomez, 1972
Whitey Ford, 1974
Mickey Mantle, 1974
Bucky Harris, 1975
Joe Sewell, 1977
Larry MacPhail, 1978
Johnny Mize, 1981
Enos Slaughter, 1985
Catfish Hunter, 1987
Tony Lazzeri, 1991
Gaylord Perry, 1991

Award Winners
Cy Young Award
Bob Turley, 1958
Whitey Ford, 1961
Sparky Lyle, 1977
Ron Guidry, 1978

Most Valuable Player
Lou Gehrig, 1936
Joe DiMaggio, 1939, 1941, 1947
Joe Gordon, 1942
Spud Chandler, 1943
Phil Rizzuto, 1950
Yogi Berra, 1951, 1954, 1955
Mickey Mantle, 1956, 1957, 1962
Roger Maris, 1960, 1961
Elston Howard, 1963
Thurman Munson, 1976
Don Mattingly, 1985

Rookie of the Year
Gil McDougald, 1951
Bob Grim, 1954
Tony Kubek, 1957
Tom Tresh, 1962
Stan Bahnsen, 1968
Thurman Munson, 1970
Dave Righetti, 1981

Retired Uniform Numbers
1 Billy Martin
3 Babe Ruth
4 Lou Gehrig
5 Joe DiMaggio
7 Mickey Mantle
8 Bill Dickey and Yogi Berra
9 Roger Maris
10 Phil Rizzuto
15 Thurman Munson
16 Whitey Ford
32 Elston Howard
37 Casey Stengel

Public Transportation

For subway and bus information, call:
718/830-1234

Parking

Fourteen parking lots surround Yankee Stadium.

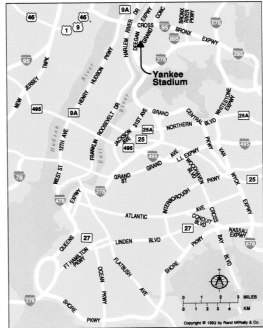

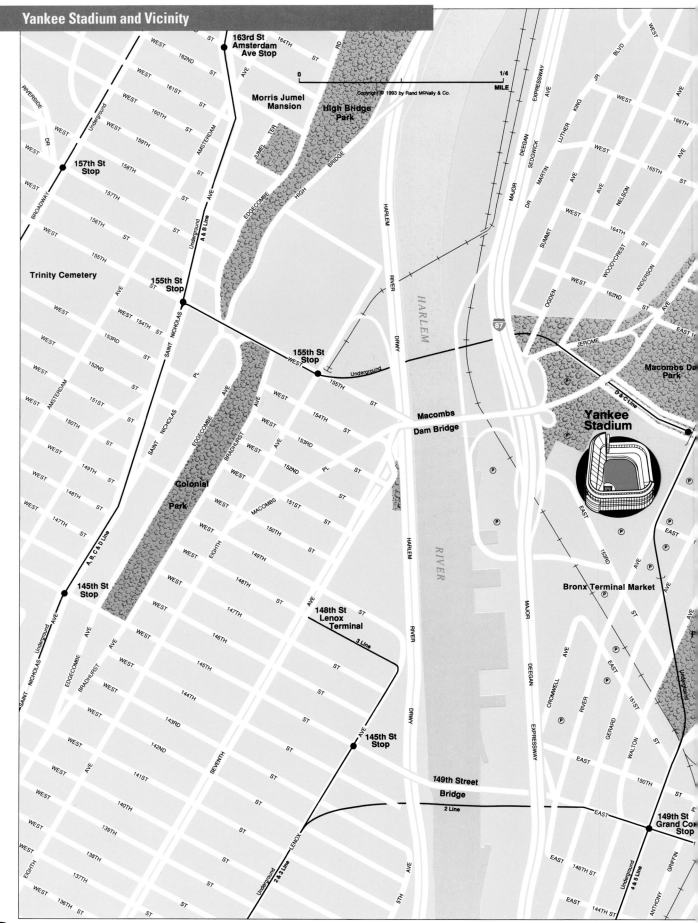

163rd St
Amsterdam
Ave Stop

Morris Jumel
Mansion

High Bridge
Park

0   1/4
         MILE

Copyright© 1993 by Rand McNally & Co.

157th St
Stop

WEST

RIVERSIDE DR

BROADWAY

UNDERGROUND

AMSTERDAM AVE

A & B Line

Trinity Cemetery

155th St
Stop

SAINT NICHOLAS

EDGECOMBE

155th St
Stop

Underground

HARLEM RIVER DRWY

HARLEM

RIVER

I-87

Macombs
Dam Bridge

Yankee
Stadium

Macombs Dam
Park

D & C Line

JEROME

OGDEN AVE

SUMMIT AVE

WOODYCREST AVE

ANDERSON AVE

NELSON AVE

MAJOR DEEGAN

MARTIN LUTHER KING JR

SEDGWICK AVE

Colonial

Park

BRADHURST

EDGECOMBE

A, B, C & D Line

EIGHTH

SEVENTH

LENOX

145th St
Stop

148th St
Lenox
Terminal

3 Line

145th St
Stop

SAINT NICHOLAS AVE

Underground

AMSTERDAM AVE

BRADHURST AVE

EDGECOMBE AVE

Underground 2 & 3 Line

5TH AVE

Bronx Terminal Market

CROMWELL AVE

RIVER AVE

GERARD AVE

WALTON AVE

MAJOR DEEGAN EXPRESSWAY

149th Street
Bridge

2 Line

149th St
Grand Con
Stop

Underground 4 & 5 Line

ANTHONY

GRIFFIN

New York

Restaurants listed are either in Manhattan or near the stadium in the Bronx. The hotels are in Manhattan or in New Jersey convenient to the George Washington Bridge.

Sports Spots

The Boathouse
In Central Park near 72nd Street park entrance
212/517-3623
Boat rentals on Central Park Lake; bicycle rentals also available. Outdoor cafe ($$)

Legends
17 Murray St. (between Broadway and Church)
212/608-3900
Sports bar/restaurant ($-$$)

Mickey Mantle's
42 Central Park South
212/688-7777
Sports bar/restaurant ($$)

New York Yankees Clubhouse Stores
393 Fifth Ave.
212/685-4693
110 E. 59th St.
212/758-7844
Licensed merchandise and ticket sales.

Runyon's
305 E. 50th St. (between First and Second)
212/223-9592
932 Second Ave. (between 49th and 50th)
212/759-7800
Sports bars/restaurants ($$)

Sporting Club
99 Hudson St. (between Franklin and Leonard)
212/219-0900
Sports bar/restaurant ($$-$$$)

Sports
2182 Broadway (between 77th and 78th)
212/874-7208
Sports bar/restaurant ($-$$)

Restaurants

Alex and Henry's
862 Cortlandt Ave., Bronx
718/585-3290
Italian cuisine ($$-$$$)

Elaine's
1703 Second Ave. at 88th Street
212/534-8103
American, Italian cuisine ($$-$$$)

Gallagher's Steak House
228 W. 52nd St.
212/245-5336
Steak, chops, fish ($$$)

Il Vagabondo
351 E. 62nd St.
212/832-9221
Northern Italian cuisine ($$)

Mamma Leone's
261 W. 44th St.
212/586-5151
A New York landmark ($$$)

P.J. Clarke's
Third Avenue at 55th Street
212/759-1650
Burgers, steak, chili ($-$$)

Sam's Cafe
1406 Third Ave. at 80th Street
212/988-5300
Burgers, steak, seafood ($$)

Yolanda's Restaurant
292 E. 149th St., Bronx
718/993-2709
Southern Italian cuisine ($$)

Sports Spots & Restaurants (Dinner for two without beverage or tip):
$ Under $20
$$ $20-$40
$$$ More than $40

Accommodations

Days Inn–New York
440 W. 57th St.
212/581-8100, 800/325-2525 ($$$)

Doral Inn
541 Lexington Ave. at 49th Street
212/755-1200, 800/22-DORAL ($$$)

Grand Hyatt New York Hotel
Park Avenue at Grand Central
212/883-1234, 800/233-1234 ($$$)

Loews New York Hotel
569 Lexington Ave. at 51st Street
212/752-7000, 800/223-0888 ($$$)

Ramada Hotel
375 W. Passaic St., Rochelle Park, New Jersey
201/845-3400 ($$)

Sheraton–Hasbrouck Heights
650 Terrace Ave., Hasbrouck Heights, New Jersey
201/288-6100 ($$)

Price ranges: Double room during the week (lower rates often available on weekends)
$ Under $75
$$ $75-$125
$$$ More than $125

Attractions

Broadway Theater District
Midtown Manhattan, along Broadway and adjoining streets
The latest plays and some of the best talent in the world.

Bronx Zoo
185th Street and Seventh Boulevard, Bronx
212/367-1010
Exhibits include Jungleworld, Great Ape House, Mouse House, and rides.

Towers surround Central Park.

Central Park
From 59th to 110th streets between Fifth Avenue and Central Park West
Zoo, tennis courts, theater, Tavern on the Green restaurant, and two rowing lakes.

Empire State Building
34th Street and Fifth Avenue
212/736-3100
Panoramic views of New York and suburbs from outdoor promenade and observatories. King Kong display.

Metropolitan Museum of Art
82nd Street and Fifth Avenue
212/535-7710
Vast collection representative of the history of world art.

Rockefeller Center attracts visitors year-round.

Museum of Modern Art
11 W. 53rd St.
212/708-9480
Excellent collection of 20th-century fine art.

The New York Stock Exchange, located on Wall Street.

Statue of Liberty National Monument / Ellis Island
Liberty Island
212/363-3200
Ferryboats depart from Battery Park (212/269-5755).

For More Information

New York City Convention & Visitors Bureau
2 Columbus Circle
New York, NY 10019
212/397-8200

Oakland-Alameda County Coliseum is a great place to see baseball...and tennis, track, and roller derby.

Home to the Oakland A's, the 47,313-seat stadium boasts a concert-quality sound system, easy parking, nearly perfect weather conditions, and great food.

The Athletics resided in Philadelphia from 1901 through 1954 when the team was moved to Kansas City. In 1960, the A's were sold to Charles O. Finley, who moved the team to Oakland in 1968.

It was magic from year one. The A's finished the first season in sixth place. But on May 8, 1968, an amazed crowd watched Jim "Catfish" Hunter retire 27 consecutive Twins batters in a 4-0 game, thus becoming at age 22, the century's youngest "perfect game" pitcher. Clearly the A's were on to something.

In 1972, they showed the world exactly what that something was. They won the American League Championship Series three games to two over the Detroit Tigers and went on to beat the Cincinnati Reds in the World Series. The amazing A's followed that feat with a World Series win over the New York Mets in 1973 and over the Los Angeles Dodgers in 1974. Three consecutive World Series titles is indeed an amazing story.

In 1988, the team reintroduced the Athletics' original mascot, the Elephant. This lovable pachyderm turned out to be quite a good luck charm. The A's won three straight American League crowns between 1988 and 1991, and they won the World Series in 1989, sweeping the Giants in four games. When you set foot in the Oakland Coliseum, you're visiting a field of champions.

Oakland Athletics

Oakland-Alameda County Coliseum.

- ☐ MVP
- ■ Field Level Infield
- ☐ Field Level
- ■ Plaza Level Infield
- ■ Plaza Level
- ▨ Upper Reserved
- ☐ Bleachers
- ■ Sky Boxes

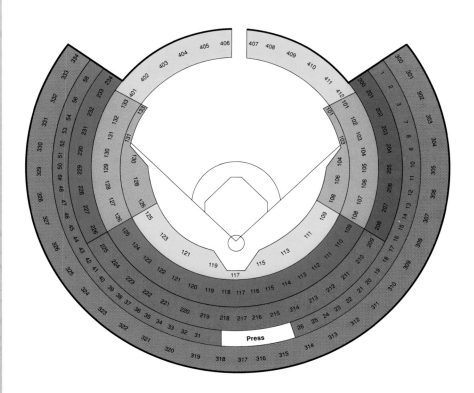

Press

Purchasing Tickets

By mail:
Oakland A's Tickets
P.O. Box 2220
Oakland, CA 94621
510/638-0500

Send a check or money order payable to the Oakland Athletics Baseball Company or a Visa or MasterCard number and expiration date. Specify the date of game, price, location of tickets. Include $4 handling fee.

In person:
Coliseum Box Office
Hegenberger Road off I-880

Box office hours: Monday - Friday, 9 a.m. - 6 p.m.; Saturday, 10 a.m. - 4 p.m.; Sunday, noon - 4 p.m. On game days, the office is open until one half-hour after the game. Tickets are also available at all BASS Ticket Centers and at the A's Clubhouse Stores in Southland Mall in Hayward and Hilltop Mall in Richmond.

NOTE: Half-price tickets are available to all fans every Tuesday night except opening night for all upper reserved (third deck) seats and for all games for seats in the mezzanine, plaza level, and upper reserved section for children 14 and under, senior citizens 65 and older, members of active military, and persons using wheelchairs. Field-level seats are also available at half price for people using wheelchairs.

By phone:
510/762-BASS   707/546-BASS
408/998-BASS   916/923-BASS

Directions to the Stadium

- From San Jose: Go north on I-880 (the Nimitz Freeway) to Oakland and exit at 66th Avenue, then follow signs to the Coliseum.

- From San Mateo (via the San Mateo Bridge): Go east on the San Mateo Bridge to I-880 to Oakland and exit at 66th Avenue, then follow the signs to the Coliseum.

- From Marin County: Go over the San Rafael Bridge (I-580) to I-80 westbound until you reach I-580 headed to Hayward. Take I-580 to I-980 toward Oakland, then get on I-880 south. Exit at 66th Avenue and follow signs to the Coliseum.

- From San Francisco: Go east on the Bay Bridge to I-580 toward Hayward, then take I-980 to downtown Oakland and I-880 south. Exit at 66th Avenue and follow the signs to the Coliseum.

- From Sacramento: Take I-80 west toward Oakland, then take I-580 toward Hayward and take I-980 to downtown Oakland, then I-880 south. Exit at 66th Avenue and follow the signs to the Coliseum.

- From Contra Costa County: Take Highway 24 through the Caldecott Tunnel and continue toward downtown Oakland, then get on I-980 to I-880 south. Exit at 66th Avenue and follow the signs to the Coliseum.

Team Address
Oakland Athletics
Oakland-Alameda County
Coliseum
Oakland, CA 94621
510/638-4900

Franchise History
Philadelphia Athletics 1901-54
Kansas City Athletics 1955-67
Oakland Athletics 1968-

World Series Titles
1910 vs. Chicago Cubs
1911 vs. New York Giants
1913 vs. New York Giants
1929 vs. Chicago Cubs
1930 vs. St. Louis Cardinals
1972 vs. Cincinnati Reds
1973 vs. New York Mets
1974 vs. Los Angeles Dodgers
1989 vs. San Francisco Giants

American League Pennants
1902, 1905, 1910, 1911, 1913, 1914,
1929, 1930, 1931, 1972, 1973, 1974,
1988, 1989, 1990

West Division Titles
1971, 1972, 1973, 1974, 1975, 1981,
1988, 1989, 1990, 1992

Hall of Fame Inductees
Ty Cobb, 1936
Nap Lajoie, 1937
Connie Mack, 1937
Tris Speaker, 1937
Eddie Collins, 1939
Jimmy Collins, 1945
Eddie Plank, 1946
Rube Waddell, 1946
Mickey Cochrane, 1947
Lefty Grove, 1947
Herb Pennock, 1948
Jimmie Foxx, 1951
Chief Bender, 1953
Al Simmons, 1953
Frank "Home Run" Baker, 1955
Zack Wheat, 1959
Elmer Flick, 1963
Stan Coveleski, 1969
Waite Hoyt, 1969
Luke Appling, 1964
Lou Boudreau, 1970
Satchel Paige, 1971
George Kell, 1983
Enos Slaughter, 1985
Willie McCovey, 1986
Jim "Catfish" Hunter, 1987
Billy Williams, 1987
Joe Morgan, 1990
Rollie Fingers, 1992

Award Winners
Cy Young Award
Vida Blue, 1971
Jim Hunter, 1974
Bob Welch, 1990
Dennis Eckersley, 1992

Most Valuable Player
Lefty Grove, 1931
Jimmie Foxx, 1932, 1933
Bobby Shantz, 1952
Vida Blue, 1971
Reggie Jackson, 1973
Jose Canseco, 1988
Rickey Henderson, 1990
Dennis Eckersley, 1992

Rookie of the Year
Harry Byrd, 1952
Jose Canseco, 1986
Mark McGwire, 1987
Walt Weiss, 1988

Retired Uniform Numbers
27 Jim "Catfish" Hunter

Public Transportation

Bay Area Rapid Transit (BART) trains run from San Francisco and other nearby communities directly to the Coliseum BART Station, which connects by bridge to the stadium. For information, call 510/465-2278 or 415/788-2278.

Parking

Extensive parking is available in lots surrounding the Coliseum. Parking for handicapped individuals is available in lots A, B, C, and D close to the stadium.

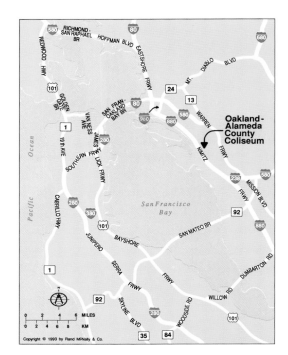

Oakland

The Coliseum is located near the Oakland Airport, so most of the hotels listed are near the airport or downtown; the restaurants are primarily downtown.

Sports Spots

Chabot Equestrian Center
14600 Skyline Blvd.
510/569-4428
Horses for hire; pack rides twice daily.

Golf Courses
Oakland has three public golf courses: Galbraith, 18 holes, 510/569-9411; Lake Chabot, 18 holes, 510/351-5812; and Montclair, 9 holes, 510/482-0422. Reservations are taken one week in advance.

Joaquin Miller Park
3450 Joaquin Miller Road
510/273-3091, 510/531-2205
Ten hiking trails with spectacular views.

Lake Merritt and Lakeside Park
Bordered by Lakeside Drive, Lake Shore Avenue, and Grand Avenue
155-acre saltwater lake in the heart of downtown with adjacent 122-acre park, jogging paths, boat rentals, putting greens, gardens.

Mac's Sports Bar and Grill
495 Embarcadero
510/451-MACS
Sports bar/restaurant ($)

Oakland A's Clubhouse Shops
390 Southland Mall, Hayward
510/732-5995
2248 Hilltop Mall Road
Richmond
510/758-1229
Official licensed shops.

Oakland offers great dining, entertainment and night life.

Ricky's Sports Lounge and Restaurant
15028 Hesperian Blvd.
San Leandro
510/352-0200
Sports bar/restaurant ($-$$)

Sports Edition Bar
Oakland Airport Hilton, One Hegenberger Road
510/635-5000
Sports bar/restaurant ($-$$)

Tennis Courts
510/238-3494
Oakland parks offer more than 50 tennis courts. Reservations: 510/238-3187.

Restaurants

Crogan's Seafood House
500 12th St.
510/464-3698
Seafood, pasta, steaks ($-$$)

Dai Ten Japanese Restaurant
1830 Webster St.
510/836-3021
Japanese cuisine ($$)

Francesco's Restaurant
8520 Pardee Drive at Hegenberger Road, near the Coliseum
510/569-0653
Italian cuisine ($$)

Lantern Restaurant
814 Webster St.
510/451-0627
Chinese cuisine ($-$$)

New Gulf Coast Grill
736 Washington St. at 8th Street
510/836-3663
Louisiana cuisine ($-$$)

The Old Spaghetti Factory
62 Jack London Square
510/893-0222
Italian cuisine ($)

Pacific Coast Brewing Co.
906 Washington St.
510/836-2739
Beer brewed on premises; chicken, sandwiches ($)

Sangthong Thai Restaurant
850 Broadway
510/839-4017
Thai cuisine ($$)

Scott's Seafood Grill and Bar
2 Broadway at Jack London's Waterfront
510/444-3456
Seafood, chops ($$-$$$)

Sports Spots & Restaurants (Dinner for two without beverage or tip):
$ Under $20
$$ $20-$40
$$$ More than $40

Accommodations

Claremont Resort Spa & Tennis Club
Ashby and Domingo
510/843-3000 ($$$)

Clarion at Oakland International
455 Hegenberger Road
510/562-6100 ($$)

Days Inn–Oakland Airport/Coliseum
8350 Edes Ave.
510/568-1880 ($)

Hampton Inn/Oakland Airport
8465 Enterprise Way
510/632-8900, 800/HAMPTON ($)

Paramount Theatre, a renovated Art Deco movie palace.

Oakland Airport Hilton
One Hegenberger Road
510/635-5000, 800/445-8667 ($$$)

Waterfront Plaza Hotel
10 Washington St.
510/836-3800 ($$$)

Price ranges: Double room during the week (lower rates are often available on weekends)
$ Under $75
$$ $75-$125
$$$ More than $125

Attractions

Children's Fairyland
540 Grand Ave.
510/452-2259
More than 60 three-dimensional sets depicting fairy tales, nursery rhymes.

Jack London's Waterfront and Village
Alice and Embarcadero
510/893-7956
Complex of shops, restaurants, and marina.

Oakland Museum
1000 Oak St.
510/834-2413
California art, history, and natural science exhibits.

The display on film at the Oakland Museum.

Oakland Zoo in Knowland Park
Golf Links Road off I-580
510/632-9523
More than 300 animals, reptiles, and birds.

Port of Oakland Tour
510/272-1100
Free 75-minute tour of outer harbor, estuary, and Jack London's Waterfront.

Western Aerospace Museum
8260 Boeing St.
International Airport, North Field
510/638-7100
Aircraft exhibits, artifacts, library.

For More Information

Oakland Convention & Visitors Bureau
1000 Broadway, Suite 200
Oakland, CA 94607
510/839-9000

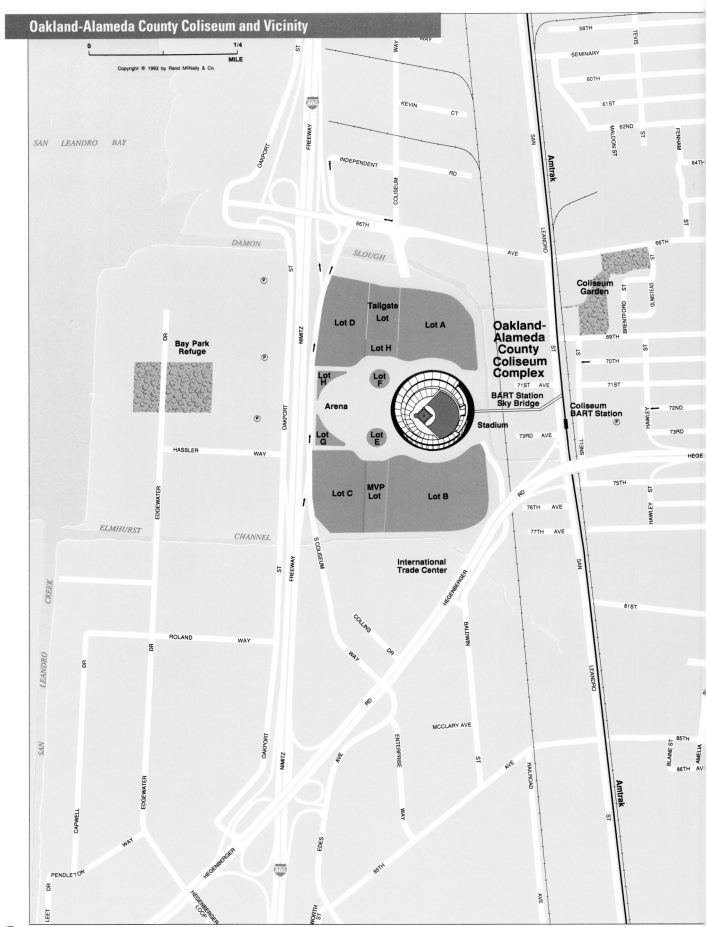

0   1/4
MILE

Copyright © 1993 by Rand McNally & Co.

SAN LEANDRO BAY

DAMON SLOUGH

Bay Park Refuge

Tailgate Lot

Lot D

Lot A

Lot H

Lot H

Lot F

Arena

Lot G

Stadium

Lot E

Lot C

MVP Lot

Lot B

International Trade Center

Oakland-Alameda County Coliseum Complex

BART Station Sky Bridge

Coliseum BART Station

Coliseum Garden

ELMHURST CHANNEL

SAN LEANDRO CREEK

It was an almost 90-year odyssey for the Phillies to get to "The Vet," Veterans Stadium. Opened in April 1971, this largest of all National League parks (capacity: 62,586) delivers fan comfort in a thoroughly modern facility.

Back in 1883, the Phillies played their first season in a small wooden stadium called Recreation Park at 23rd Street and Ridge Pike. From there, they moved to the Philadelphia Baseball Grounds in 1887, which later became known as Baker Bowl.

More than 50 years later, in 1938, the Phillies moved to Shibe Park (later called Connie Mack Stadium), a classic concrete and steel ballpark built in 1909. They shared field time with their AL rivals the Philadelphia Athletics until 1955 when the A's moved to Kansas City. Shibe Park was distinguished by a French Renaissance dome on the roof behind home plate.

The Phillies remained at Shibe Park until 1971 when Veterans Stadium opened at Broad Street and Pattison Avenue in South Philadelphia. With the team came the home plate from the old park. On opening day, April 10, 1971, the first ball was dramatically dropped from a helicopter.

The Vet is very visitor friendly. You'll find two miles of ramps, eight sets of escalators, and four elevators to help you get to your seat. The stadium is a multipurpose facility, also hosting the NFL Philadelphia Eagles.

Philadelphia Phillies

Rosemary Rahn/Philadelphia Phillies

- ☐ Deluxe Boxes
- ■ Field Boxes
- ☐ Terrace Boxes
- ■ Loge Boxes
- ☐ Reserved - 600 Level
- ☐ Reserved - 700 Level

Veterans Stadium.

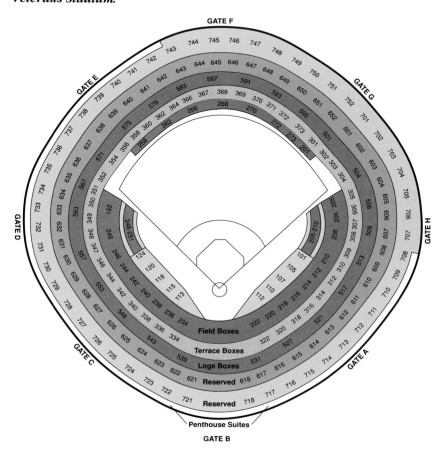

Purchasing Tickets

By mail:

Philadelphia Phillies
P.O. Box 7575
Philadelphia, PA 19101
215/463-1000 (information)
Send a check or money order payable to the Philadelphia Phillies. Include the date you want, number of tickets, and the price. Add a $4 service charge.

In person:

Veterans Stadium Ticket Office
Under Gate B on the Pattison Avenue side
Ticket office hours: Monday - Friday 9 a.m. - 8 p.m.; Saturday and Sunday 10 a.m. - 4 p.m. The office accepts cash, checks, money orders, and credit cards.

By phone:

Call 215/463-1000 and use your Visa, MasterCard, or American Express card.
Phone hours: weekdays 9 a.m. - 8 p.m.;
weekends 10 a.m. - 4 p.m.;
or fax your order to 215/463-9878.

Directions to the Stadium

- From I-76 West: Take exit 45, Sports Complex, Broad Street, and proceed south on Broad. Or, take exit 46, Packer Avenue, and proceed either west on Packer or south on Darien Street, then head west on Pattison Avenue. Or, take exit 43A, follow 26th Street to Penrose Avenue, then head east on Pattison.

- From Walt Whitman Bridge East: Take exit 46B, 7th Street South, then head west on either Packer Avenue or Pattison Avenue. Or, take exit 45, Sports Complex, Broad Street, to Broad Street South.

- From I-95 South: Take the Sports Complex, Broad Street exit and proceed north on Broad. Or, take the I-76 East, South Jersey exit and proceed west on Packer Avenue. Or, take the I-76 West, PA 291 Central Philadelphia exit. Proceed over George Platt Bridge, then bear right onto Pattison Avenue. Proceed east on Pattison to Broad.

- From I-95 North: Take the I-76, South Jersey exit to Front Street, then head south on Front and west on Packer Avenue or Pattison Avenue. Take the Broad Street PA 291 exit, then proceed north on Broad Street.

Public Transportation

The Broad Street subway line connects downtown Philadelphia (center city) with Veterans Stadium. The trip time is 10 minutes from City Hall Station to Pattison Avenue Station. Philadelphia also has an extensive bus and street car system that links to the subway system. For travel information, call 215/580-7800.

Parking

Philadelphia's sports complex contains both Veterans Stadium and the Spectrum, a stadium for basketball, hockey, and lacrosse. Parking lots surround the stadiums and provide extensive parking spaces.

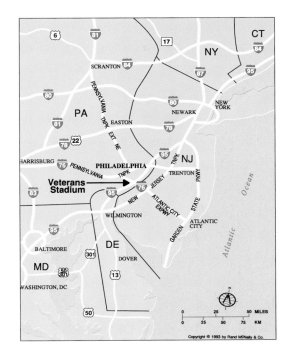

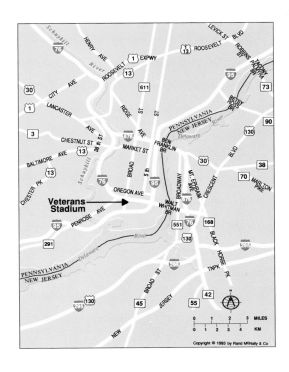

Profile

Team Address
Philadelphia Phillies
Veterans Stadium
P.O. Box 7575
Philadelphia, PA 19101
215/463-6000

Franchise History
Worcester Brown Stockings
1880-82
Philadelphia Phillies 1883-

World Series Titles
1980 vs. Kansas City Royals

National League Pennants
1915, 1950, 1980, 1983

East Division Titles
1976, 1977, 1978, 1980, 1983

Hall of Fame Inductees
Nap Lajoie, 1937
Grover Cleveland Alexander, 1938
Dan Brouthers, 1945
Ed Delahanty, 1945
Hugh Duffy, 1945
Hughie Jennings, 1945
Johnny Evers, 1946
Tommy McCarthy, 1946
Kid Nichols, 1949
Jimmie Foxx, 1951
Chief Bender, 1953
Harry Wright, 1953
Billy Hamilton, 1961
John Clarkson, 1963
Elmer Flick, 1963
Eppa Rixey, 1963
Tim Keefe, 1964
Casey Stengel, 1966
Lloyd Waner, 1967
Dave Bancroft, 1971
Sam Thompson, 1974
Bucky Harris, 1975
Roger Connor, 1976
Robin Roberts, 1976
Hack Wilson, 1979
Chuck Klein, 1980
Joe Morgan, 1990
Ferguson Jenkins, 1991

Award Winners
Cy Young Award
Steve Carlton, 1972, 1977,
1980, 1982
John Denny, 1983
Steve Bedrosian, 1987

Most Valuable Player
Chuck Klein, 1932
Jim Konstanty, 1950
Mike Schmidt, 1980, 1981, 1986

Rookie of the Year
Jack Sanford, 1957
Richie Allen, 1964

Retired Uniform Numbers
1 Richie Ashburn
20 Mike Schmidt
32 Steve Carlton
36 Robin Roberts

Smith Plgd

Wilson Park

Lutheran Cem

Girard Park

Playground

U S Defense Personnel Support Ctr

Naval Regional Medical Center

American Swedish Historical Museum

Swedish Manor House

F D Roosevelt   Golf Course

MEADOW

LAKE

F D Ro

To 95

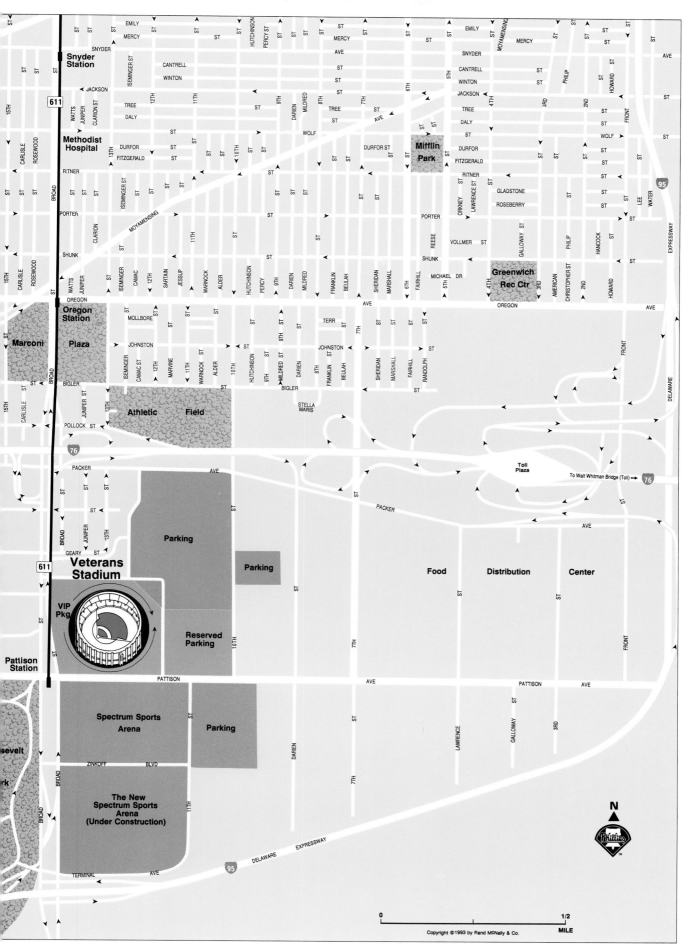

Snyder Station

611

Methodist Hospital

Mifflin Park

95

Greenwich Rec Ctr

Oregon Station

Marconi Plaza

Athletic Field

76

Veterans Stadium

VIP Pkg

Toll Plaza

To Walt Whitman Bridge (Toll) → 76

Parking

Parking

Reserved Parking

Food Distribution Center

Pattison Station

Spectrum Sports Arena

Parking

ZINKOFF BLVD

The New Spectrum Sports Arena (Under Construction)

TERMINAL AVE

DELAWARE EXPRESSWAY

95

N

Phillies

0   1/2
MILE

Philadelphia

Veterans Stadium is located in a sports complex in South Philadelphia, a short subway ride or drive from the downtown center city. The restaurants listed are either in the downtown area or around South Street, Philadelphia's restaurant row. The hotels listed are located in center city, near the University of Pennsylvania, or close to the airport.

An historic preserve: Philadelphia's Independence Hall.

Sports Spots

Dickens Inn
421 S. 2nd St.
215/928-9307
Sports bar/English cuisine ($$)

Fairmont Park
Begins at Benjamin Franklin Parkway
215/685-0000
More than 8,900 acres of park with baseball and softball diamonds, 115 tennis courts, 14 soccer fields, 13 football fields, a bowling green, an archery range, three bocce courts, six 18-hole golf courses, six swimming pools, hiking trails, bike paths, fishing stream, and boat and bike rentals.

Golf Corp Sports Center
7900 City Line Ave.
215/879-3536
Miniature golf, batting cages, golf driving range.

Sportz
21st and South
Sports bar/restaurant ($)

The famous Liberty Bell.

Restaurants

Alouette
334 Bainbridge St.
215/629-1126
French-Asian cuisine ($$$)

Bookbinders Seafood House
125 Walnut St.
215/925-7027
Seafood, lobster, crab ($$$)

Cafe Nola
328 South St.
215/627-2590
Cajun-Creole cuisine ($$-$$$)

DiLullo Centro
1407 Locust St.
215/546-2000
Northern Italian cuisine ($$-$$$)

Dock Street Brewing Company
18th and Cherry
215/496-0413
Brewery and pub ($$)

Downey's Pub
Front and South
215/625-9500
American cuisine, outdoor cafe, raw bar ($$)

Jim's Steaks
400 South St.
215/928-1911
Hoagies and Philadelphia cheesesteaks ($)

Magnolia Cafe
1602 Locust St.
215/546-4180
Cajun-Creole cuisine ($-$$)

Meiji-En
Pier 19, North Delaware Avenue at Callowhill Street
215/592-7100
Japanese cuisine ($$-$$$)

RIB-IT
52 S. 2nd St.
215/923-5511
Ribs, shrimp, sandwiches, chicken ($-$$)

Sports Spots & Restaurants (Dinner for two without beverage or tip):
$ Under $20
$$ $20-$40
$$$ More than $40

Accommodations

The Barclay
237 S. 18th St.
215/545-0300 ($$)

Comfort Inn at Penn's Landing
100 N. Columbus Blvd.
215/627-7900 ($$)

Days Inn Hotel
4101 Island Ave., adjacent to Philadelphia International Airport
215/492-0400 ($$)

Penn Tower Hotel
Civic Center Boulevard and 34th Street
215/387-8333 ($$-$$$)

The Philadelphia Museum of Art.

Philadelphia Hilton & Towers
Broad and Locust
215/893-1600 ($$$)

Ramada Inn Center City
501 N. 22nd St.
215/568-8300 ($)

Sheraton Society Hill
One Dock St.
215/238-6000 ($$$)

Sheraton University City
36th and Chestnut
215/387-8000 ($$$)

Price ranges: Double room during the week (lower rates are often available on weekends)
$ Under $75
$$ $75-$125
$$$ More than $125

Attractions

Academy of Natural Sciences Museum
19th Street and Benjamin Franklin Parkway
215/299-1020
Features dinosaurs, gems, and minerals.

Afro-American Historical and Cultural Museum
701 Arch St.
215/574-0380
Art and artifacts reflecting African-American culture.

Betsy Ross House
239 Arch St.
215/627-5343
Restored Colonial house.

Franklin Institute Science Museum
20th Street and Benjamin Franklin Parkway
215/448-1200
Hands-on exhibits cover four floors.

Independence National Historical Park
Visitor Center, 3rd and Chestnut
215/597-8974
Historic square mile that includes the Liberty Bell Pavilion, Independence Hall, Congress Hall.

Philadelphia Museum of Art
26th Street and Benjamin Franklin Parkway
215/763-8100
More than 500,000 paintings, drawings, prints, sculptures.

Philadelphia Zoo
34th Street and Girard Avenue
215/243-1100
More than 1,700 species, many in natural habitats.

United States Mint
5th and Arch
215/597-7350
Self-guided tours.

For More Information

Philadelphia Convention & Visitors Bureau

1555 Market St., Suite 2020
Philadelphia, PA 19102
215/636-3300

T hree Rivers Stadium, built in 1970, signifies the point at which the past and the present meet.

Its name comes from the nearby junction of the Allegheny, Monongahela, and Ohio Rivers (pirates once lived along the Ohio River, so it is appropriate that the Pittsburgh Pirates landed nearby). The club got its nickname in 1891 when they allegedly "pirated" a player from the Philadelphia club. The team played its first games at Union Park. From 1891 through 1908, they called Exposition Park home (on the same site as today's Three Rivers Stadium); from 1908 through 1970, they played at Forbes Field.

From the moment the Pirates stepped onto the field at Three Rivers, they seemed intent on making history. During the '70s, they amassed a 916-695 won-lost record for a .569 winning percentage. They won six division championships, two National League pennants, and two World Series (1971 and 1979).

At Three Rivers, Pirate history is all around you. A section of outfield wall from Forbes Field is enshrined in the Allegheny Club. Other displays in the Allegheny Club include a plaque showing where Babe Ruth hit his 714th home run at Forbes Field.

The 58,729-seat Three Rivers Stadium has been called "The House That Clemente Built," in recognition of the success and influence of the first Hispanic elected to the Hall of Fame, Roberto Clemente, who played his entire career in Pittsburgh.

Pittsburgh Pirates

Andrew A. Wagner/ Greater Pittsburgh C&VB

- ■ Club Boxes
- □ Terrace Boxes
- ■ Terrace Reserved & Outfield Reserved
- ■ Family Section
- ■ General Admission

Three Rivers Stadium.

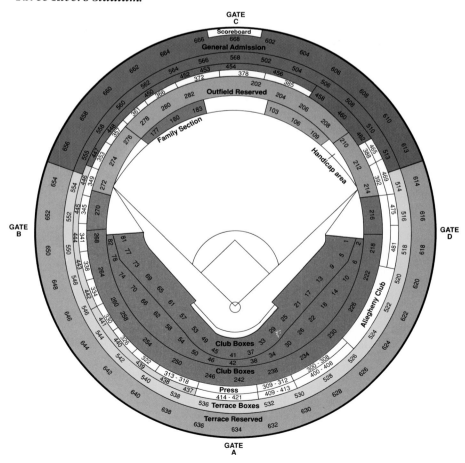

Purchasing Tickets

By mail:

Pittsburgh Pirates
Three Rivers Stadium
P.O. Box 7000
Pittsburgh, PA 15212

Send a check or money order payable to the Pittsburgh Pirates; add $2.50 for processing charges. Specify the date you want, the number of tickets, and the price.

In person:

Three Rivers Stadium Advance Ticket Office
under Gate A
600 Stadium Circle
Ticket office hours: Monday - Saturday 9 a.m. - 6 p.m. For information, call 412/323-5000. You may use MasterCard, Visa, American Express, or Discover card to purchase tickets in advance at the stadium.

Tickets are also available in person at all Pittsburgh-area Kaufmann's Department Stores, National Record Marts, Oasis Stores, and at special Pirate Clubhouse Stores located at the Westin William Penn Hotel downtown, the Allegheny Center Mall in Pittsburgh, and the Logan Valley Mall in Altoona.

By phone:

Pirates TicketMaster
412/323-1919 or 800/366-1212
(outside Allegheny County)

Directions to the Stadium

- From the south and I-279: Take exit 7B to U.S. 19 North across the West End Bridge. Turn right onto Western Avenue to Allegheny Center.

- From the south and Routes 51, 19, and 88: Travel north to the West End Bridge. Cross the bridge and turn right onto Western Avenue to Allegheny Center.

- From the east and I-376: Take exit 5 to Route 885; turn right to Crosstown Boulevard (I-579); exit left to 7th Avenue; go left onto Liberty Avenue and immediately right to the 9th Street Bridge. Cross the Bridge and go left onto Isabella Street and left again into parking.

- From the north and I-279: Take exit 15 to East Street; go right on North Avenue or East Ohio Street to Allegheny Center.

- From the north and Route 28: Exit to East Ohio Street and the Allegheny Center.

Public Transportation

Provided by Port Authority Transit. For information, call 412/231-5707.

Parking

There are approximately 7,500 parking spaces within a 10-minute walk of the stadium.

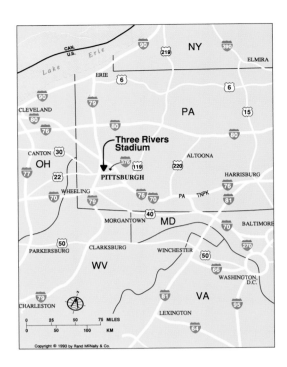

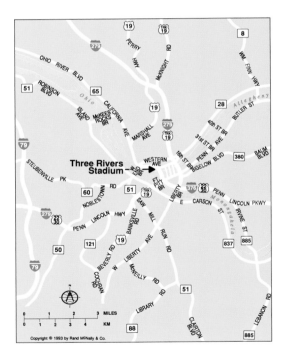

Pittsburgh

Three Rivers Stadium stands where three rivers meet. Hotels and restaurants listed are in the downtown area or a convenient drive from the stadium.

Sports Spots

Allegheny County Parks
Headquartered at 1520 Penn Ave.
412/392-8480
Nine parks featuring golf courses, tennis courts, wave pools, fishing lakes, and free concerts in the summer.

Chauncy's
Commerce Court
The Shops at Station Square
412/232-0601
Sports bar/restaurant ($$)

Pittsburgh's PA Motor Speedway
Route 22 West, Noblestown Exit
412/279-RACE
Stock car racing on clay track.

Pittsburgh Pirates Clubhouse Shop
300 Monroeville Mall Blvd., Monroeville
412/856-7610
Official licensed shop.

Pittsburgh Sports Garden
1 Station Square Drive East
(corner of Smithfield and East Carson streets)
412/281-1511
Sports bar/restaurant ($)

The Pub Sports Bar
Pittsburgh Hilton and Towers,
600 Commonwealth Place
412/391-4600, ext. 5305
Sports bar/restaurant ($)

Seven Springs Mountain Resort
RD 1, Champion
814/352-7777
Golf, water sports in summer, skiing in winter.

Pittsburgh's impressive skyline.

Restaurants

Blarney Stone Restaurant
30 Grant Ave.
412/781-1666
Irish and American cuisine ($$)

Brandy's Meeting, Eating, and Drinking Place
2323 Penn Ave.
412/566-1000
Sandwiches, seafood, salads ($$)

Froggy's Inc.
100 Market St.
412/471-3764
Sandwiches, seafood, chops, chicken ($$)

Grand Concourse
One Station Square
412/261-1717
Seafood, pasta, steak ($$)

Kiku Japanese Restaurant
Station Square
412/765-3200
Japanese cuisine ($$)

Spaghetti Warehouse
2601 Smallman St.
412/261-6511
Pasta, lasagna, veal ($)

F. Tambellini Restaurant
139 7th St.
412/391-1091
Northern Italian cuisine ($$)

Top of the Triangle
600 Grant St.
USX Tower, 62nd Floor
412/471-3807
Seafood, beef, pasta ($$-$$$)

Sports Spots & Restaurants
(Dinner for two without beverage or tip):
$ Under $20
$$ $20-$40
$$$ More than $40

Accommodations

NOTE: The Pittsburgh Convention and Visitors Bureau has a toll-free information number to call for special Pirates games hotel packages, 800/927-8376.

Best Western Parkway Center Inn
875 Greentree Road
412/922-7070 ($$)

ClubHouse Inn Pittsburgh
5311 Campbells Run Road
412/788-8400 ($$)

Holiday Inn at University Center
100 Lytton Ave.
412/682-6200 ($$)

Pittsburgh Hilton and Towers
600 Commonwealth Place
412/391-4600, 800/HILTONS
($$$)

Pittsburgh Vista Hotel
1000 Penn Ave.
412/281-3700 ($$$)

Station Square is home to popular restaurants and shops.

Sheraton Hotel at Station Square
7 Station Square Drive
412/261-2000 ($$$)

Price ranges: Double room during the week (lower rates are often available on weekends)
$ Under $75
$$ $75-$125
$$$ More than $125

Attractions

The Carnegie
4400 Forbes Ave.
412/622-3131
Cultural center includes Library of Pittsburgh, Museum of Art, Museum of Natural History, and Music Hall.

The Carnegie Science Center
Next to Three Rivers Stadium
412/237-3300
Omnimax Theater, hands-on exhibits, planetarium.

Duquesne and Monongahela Inclines
1220 Grandview Ave.
412/381-1665
2235 Beaver Ave.
412/237-7000
Spectacular views from cable cars traveling down city slopes.

Gateway Clipper Fleet
9 Station Square Dock
412/355-7980
Sightseeing riverboats.

Heinz Hall for the Performing Arts
600 Penn Ave.
412/392-4843
Concert hall; touring Broadway shows.

The sun sets on Kennywood Park.

Kennywood Park
4800 Kennywood Blvd., West Mifflin
412/461-0500
Rides, arcades, and games.

Pittsburgh Zoo
Highland Park
412/665-3639
Natural habitats, children's zoo, aqua zoo, tropical forest.

The Shops at Station Square
Station Square
412/471-5808
65 retail shops, restaurants, nightclubs.

For More Information

Pittsburgh Convention & Visitors Bureau
4 Gateway Center, Suite 514
Pittsburgh, PA 15222
412/281-7711

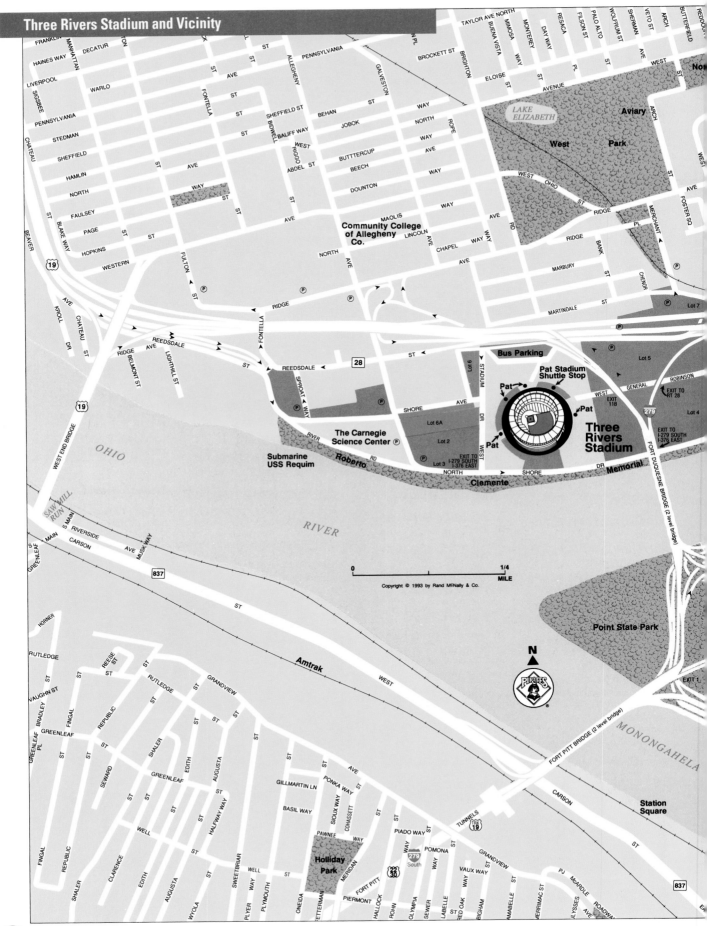

Copyright © 1993 by Rand McNally & Co.

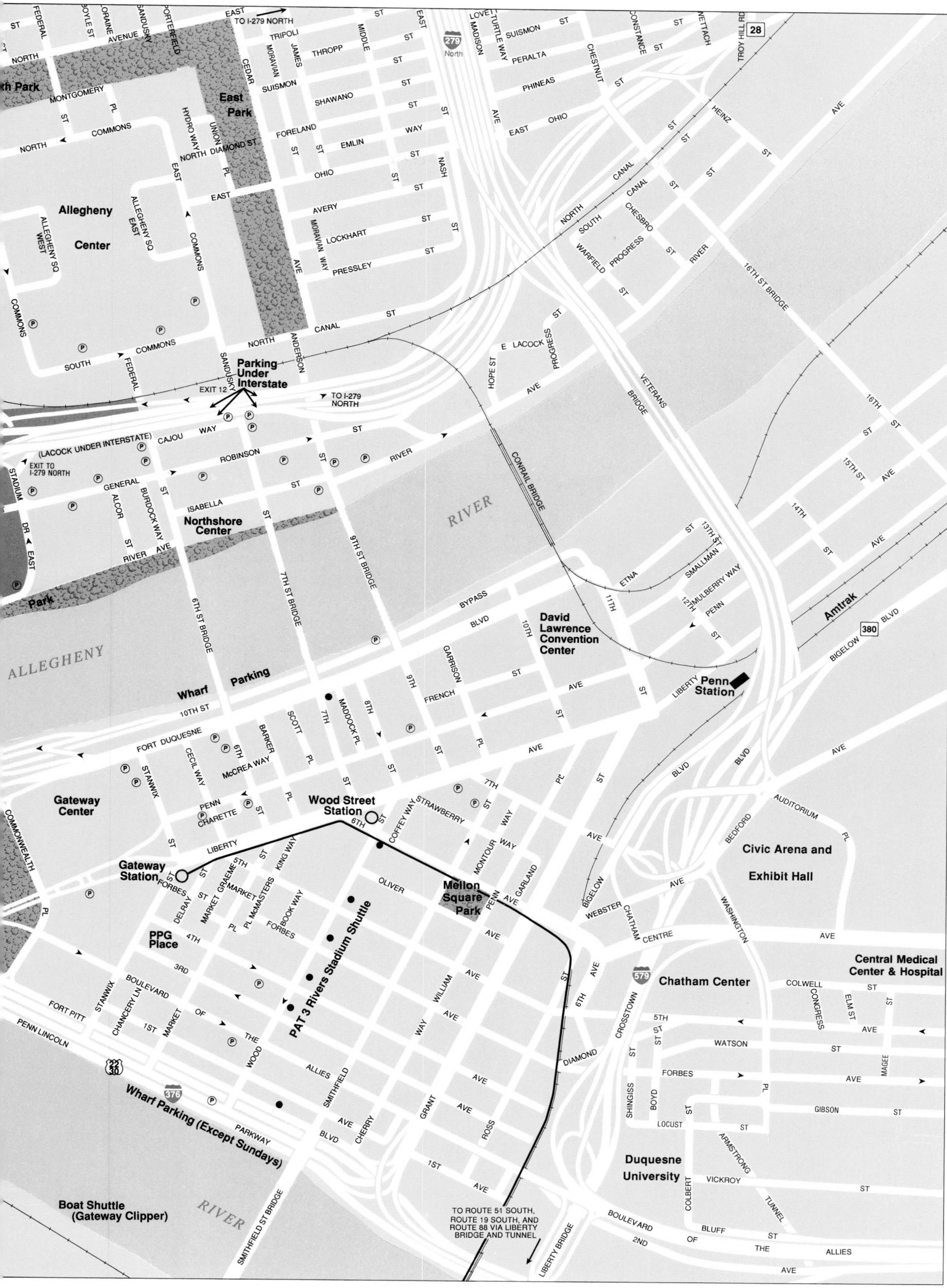

East Park

Allegheny Center

Allegheny Square West

Allegheny Square East

North Park

EAST TO I-279 NORTH

TO I-279 NORTH

28

279 North

FEDERAL ST
BOYLE ST
LORAINE ST
SANDUSKY
PORTERFIELD
CEDAR ST
MORAVIAN
JAMES ST
THROPP
TRIPOLI ST
MADISON AVE
LOVET
TURTLE WAY
SUISMON WAY
PERALTA ST
PHINEAS ST
CONSTANCE
CHESTNUT ST
NETTACH
TROY HILL RD

AVENUE
MONTGOMERY
PL
COMMONS
SHAWANO ST
MIDDLE ST
EAST ST
ST
WAY
ST
EAST OHIO ST
HEINZ ST

NORTH
HYDRO WAY
UNION PL
DIAMOND ST
FORELAND ST
EMLIN ST
NASH ST
AVE
CANAL ST
CHESBRO ST
RIVER ST
16TH ST BRIDGE

Allegheny
Center

EAST
ALLEGHENY AVE
OHIO ST
AVERY ST
MORAVIAN WAY
LOCKHART ST
PROGRESS ST
WARFIELD ST

COMMONS
EAST COMMONS
PRESSLEY ST
NORTH CANAL ST
ANDERSON ST
NORTH
SOUTH
CANAL ST

SOUTH
FEDERAL
COMMONS
Parking Under Interstate
EXIT 12
E LACOCK ST
HOPE ST
PROGRESS ST
VETERANS BRIDGE
16TH ST
14TH

Park
STADIUM DR
EXIT TO I-279 NORTH
(LACOCK UNDER INTERSTATE)
CAJOU WAY
ROBINSON ST
RIVER AVE
TO I-279 NORTH
ST
15TH ST

ALLEGHENY
ALCOR
GENERAL
BURDOCK WAY
ISABELLA ST
9TH ST BRIDGE
RIVER
13TH ST
SMALLMAN ST
PENN
MULBERRY WAY
14TH
Amtrak
380 BLVD

Northshore
Center
7TH ST BRIDGE
6TH ST BRIDGE
BYPASS
BLVD
ETNA ST
11TH
12TH ST
BIGELOW BLVD

RIVER

ALLEGHENY

Wharf   Parking
10TH ST
SCOTT ST
MADDOCK PL
8TH
7TH
9TH ST
GARRISON PL
FRENCH ST
David Lawrence Convention Center
AVE
LIBERTY AVE
Penn Station

Gateway Center
FORT DUQUESNE
CECIL WAY
BARKER PL
McCREA WAY
6TH
PENN
CHARETTE
STANWIX
Wood Street Station
COFFEY WAY
STRAWBERRY
7TH
PL
ST
AVE
BLVD
AUDITORIUM PL

COMMONWEALTH
Gateway Station
FORBES
DELRAY ST
MARKET
GRAEME ST
5TH
KING WAY
Mellon Square Park
OLIVER
MONTOUR WAY
GARLAND
BEDFORD AVE
Civic Arena and Exhibit Hall
WASHINGTON

PPG Place
LIBERTY
4TH
PL
PL
McMASTERS
BOOK WAY
FORBES
PENN
WEBSTER AVE
CHATHAM
CENTRE AVE

3RD
CHANCERY LN
1ST
MARKET
THE
WOOD
PAT 3 Rivers Stadium Shuttle
WAY
WILLIAM AVE
6TH
579
Chatham Center
BIGELOW
Central Medical Center & Hospital
COLWELL
CONGRESS ST
ELM ST
MAGEE ST

FORT PITT
STANWIX
BOULEVARD OF
ALLIES
SMITHFIELD ST
WAY
GRANT AVE
DIAMOND ST
CROSSTOWN
5TH
WATSON ST
FORBES AVE
ST
GIBSON ST

PENN LINCOLN
22 30
376
Wharf Parking (Except Sundays)
PARKWAY
BLVD
CHERRY WAY
ROSS ST
SHINGISS ST
BOYD ST
LOCUST ST
ARMSTRONG TUNNEL
VICKROY ST

Boat Shuttle (Gateway Clipper)

RIVER

SMITHFIELD ST BRIDGE
1ST AVE
TO ROUTE 51 SOUTH, ROUTE 19 SOUTH, AND ROUTE 88 VIA LIBERTY BRIDGE AND TUNNEL
LIBERTY BRIDGE
BOULEVARD OF THE ALLIES
Duquesne University
COLBERT ST
BLUFF ST
2ND AVE

Busch Stadium, baseball, beer, and the city of St. Louis.

Professional baseball has been part of St. Louis since the National League formed in 1876, although the team has sported several names. The Browns were first; they became the Perfectos. Throughout this long history, the teams played in many stadiums, each located on almost the same spot.

Until Gussie Busch came along. He wanted something new.

Beer baron August Busch, Jr., persuaded his board of directors to purchase the Cards in 1953. He remodeled Sportsman's Park and renamed it Busch Stadium. That was the old Busch Stadium, where a signature Busch eagle atop the leftcenter scoreboard flapped its wings after every Cardinal homer.

Busch wasn't satisfied. He resolved to build a bigger, better park for his team. The "new" Busch Stadium opened in 1966 when a helicopter carried home plate from the old to the new.

Busch Stadium pays attention to baseball fans and traditions. The concrete superstadium is circular and constructed with two decks, which means no posts or columns obstruct the view. When a Card hits a homer, watch as a cardinal takes flight—on the scoreboard.

A statue of Stan "The Man" Musial is outside the main entrance, and the park itself houses a St. Louis Hall of Fame. But the name on the front says it all: This is the house that Busch built.

St. Louis Cardinals

Busch Stadium.

- ■ Field Boxes
- ■ Loge Boxes
- □ Loge Reserved
- ■ Terrace Boxes
- ■ Terrace Reserved
- ■ General Admission
- □ Bleachers

St.Louis C&VC

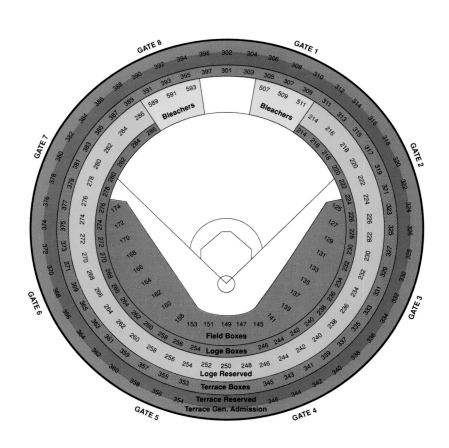

Purchasing Tickets

By mail:

St. Louis Cardinals
P.O. Box 8787
St. Louis, MO 63102
Send a check or money order payable to the St. Louis Cardinals. Specify date of game or games, number and price of tickets you want. Add $4 for postage and handling.

In person:

Busch Stadium
250 Stadium Plaza
Ticket office hours: Monday - Saturday 9 a.m. - 5:30 p.m., and 9 a.m. until game time on game days.

By phone:

314/421-2400

Directions to the Stadium

- From Illinois: Take I-55 South, I-64 West, I-70 West, or US 40 West across the Mississippi River (Poplar Street Bridge) to Busch Stadium exit.

- In Missouri: Take I-55 North, I-64 East, I-70 East, I-44 East, or US 40 East to downtown St. Louis and Busch Stadium exit.

Public Transportation

Bi-State Development buses stop at the stadium. For information, call 314/231-2345.

Parking

Stadium parking lots (with spaces for handicapped) are located east and west of the stadium; private lots also surround the stadium.

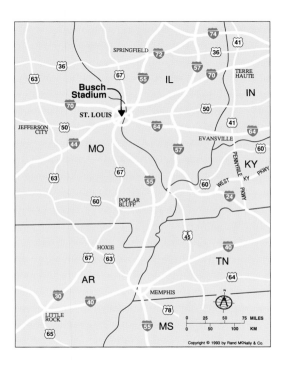

Team Address
St. Louis Cardinals
Busch Stadium
250 Stadium Plaza
St. Louis, MO 63102
314/421-3060

Franchise History
St. Louis Cardinals 1892 -

World Series Titles
1926 vs. New York Yankees
1931 vs. Philadelphia Athletics
1934 vs. Detroit Tigers
1942 vs. New York Yankees
1944 vs. St. Louis Browns
1946 vs. Boston Red Sox
1964 vs. New York Yankees
1967 vs. Boston Red Sox
1982 vs. Milwaukee Brewers

National League Pennants
1926, 1928, 1930, 1931, 1934, 1942, 1943, 1944, 1946, 1964, 1967, 1968, 1982, 1985,1987

East Division Titles
1982, 1985, 1987

Hall of Fame Inductees
John McGraw, 1937
Cy Young, 1937
Grover Cleveland Alexander, 1938
Rogers Hornsby, 1942
Roger Bresnahan, 1945
Wilbert Robinson, 1945
Frank Frisch, 1947
Jesse Burkett, 1948
Mordecai Brown, 1949
Kid Nichols, 1949
Dizzy Dean, 1953
Bobby Wallace, 1953
Rabbitt Maranville, 1954
Arthur (Dazzy) Vance, 1955
Bill McKechnie, 1962
Burleigh Grimes, 1964
Miller Huggins, 1964
James (Pud) Galvin, 1965
Branch Rickey, 1967
Joe (Ducky) Medwick, 1968

Stan Musial, 1969
Jesse Haines, 1970
Jake Beckley, 1971
Chick Hafey, 1971
Jim Bottomley, 1974
Roger Connor, 1976
Bob Gibson, 1981
John Mize, 1981
Walter Alston, 1983
Lou Brock, 1985
Enos Slaughter, 1985
Hoyt Wilhelm, 1985
Albert (Red) Schoendienst, 1989

Award Winners
Cy Young Award
Bob Gibson, 1968, 1970

Most Valuable Player
Frank Frisch, 1931
Dizzy Dean, 1934
Joe Medwick, 1937
Mort Cooper, 1942
Stan Musial, 1943, 1946, 1948
Marty Marion, 1944
Ken Boyer, 1964
Orlando Cepeda, 1967
Bob Gibson, 1968
Joe Torre, 1971
Keith Hernandez, 1979 (tie)
Willie McGee, 1985

Rookie of the Year
Wally Moon, 1954
Bill Virdon, 1955
Bake McBride, 1974
Vince Coleman, 1985
Todd Worrell, 1986

Retired Uniform Numbers
6 Stan Musial
14 Ken Boyer
17 Dizzy Dean
20 Lou Brock
45 Bob Gibson
85 August A. Busch, Jr.

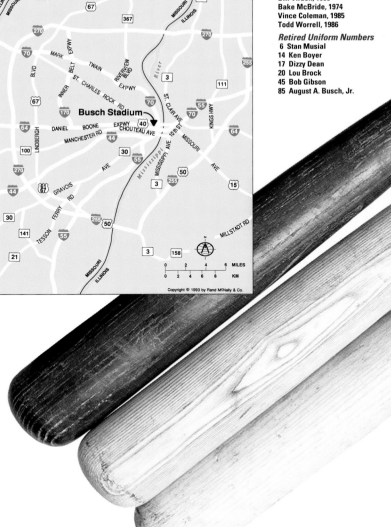

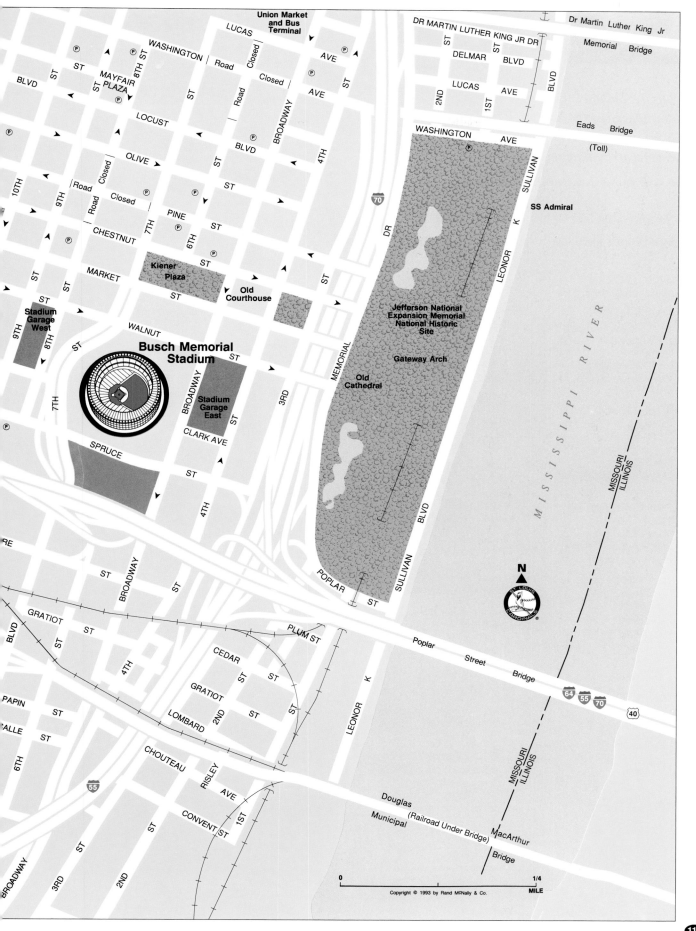

St. Louis

Busch Stadium is part of the renovated downtown/riverfront area. Hotels and restaurants listed are downtown, within an easy walk or bus ride from the stadium.

Sports Spots

Lynn Dickey's Sports Cafe
1820 Market St. (at Union Station)
314/436-1314
Sports bar/restaurant ($-$$)

Mike Shannon's
100 N. 7th St., near the stadium
314/421-1540
Sports bar/restaurant named for the Cardinals radio announcer who once played for the Red-birds ($$-$$$)

National Bowling Hall of Fame
111 Stadium Plaza (across from Busch Stadium)
314/231-6340
Photographs, paintings, and bowling memorabilia.

Quail Creek Golf Club
6022 Wells Road
314/487-1988
18-hole public golf course; reservations required.

Ozzie's Restaurant /Sports Bar
645 West Port Plaza
314/434-1000
Sports bar/restaurant named for Cardinals shortstop Ozzie Smith ($-$$)

St. Louis Sports Hall of Fame, Gift Shop & Museum
100 Stadium Plaza (in Busch Stadium)
314/421-FAME
St. Louis sports history. Stadium and Hall of Fame tours.

A riverboat travels past the Gateway Arch.

Restaurants

Amighetti's Bakery and Cafe
101 N. Broadway
314/241-3700
Bakery, deli, pasta, pizza, ice cream ($)

Boston's
1820 Market St. (at Union Station)
314/241-9030
Seafood, prime rib, oyster bar ($$-$$$)

Caleco's Bar and Grill
420 Olive St.
314/421-0708
Italian, American specialties ($-$$)

Dierdorf and Hart's
1820 Market St. (at Union Station)
314/421-1772
Steak, chops, chicken ($$$)

Hannegan's
719 N. Second St. (at Laclede's Landing)
314/241-8877
Steak, seafood, chicken ($$)

Hunan Manor Restaurant
606 Pine St.
314/231-2867
Hunan, Mandarin, Szechuan cuisine ($)

La Sala
513 Olive St.
314/231-5620
Mexican cuisine ($)

Lt. Robert E. Lee
100 S. L.K. Sullivan Blvd., aboard a reproduction of a Mark Twain-era sternwheeler
314/241-1282
Seafood, steak, pasta ($$-$$$)

Tony's
410 Market
314/231-7007
Italian pasta, veal, chicken ($$$)

Sports Spots & Restaurants (Dinner for two without beverage or tip):
$ Under $20
$$ $20-$40
$$$ More than $40

Accommodations

Courtyard by Marriott
2340 Market St.
314/241-9111, 800/321-2211 ($$)

Days Inn at the Arch
333 Washington Ave.
314/621-7900, 800/325-2525 ($)

Drury Inn Gateway Arch
711 N. Broadway
314/231-8100 ($$)

Embassy Suites Hotel
901 N. First St.
314/241-4200, 800/362-2779 ($$)

Holiday Inn Riverfront
200 N. Fourth St.
314/621-8200 ($$)

Hyatt Regency St. Louis at Union Station
One Union Station
314/231-1234, 800/233-1234 ($$$)

Price ranges: Double room during the week (lower rates are often available on weekends)
$ Under $75
$$ $75-$125
$$$ More than $125

At historic Union Station, visitors enjoy paddle boats.

Attractions

Anheuser-Busch Brewery
12th and Lynch
314/577-2626
Tours of the bottling plant, Budweiser Clydesdale stables.

The Forum (Arts Center)
3540 Washington Ave.
314/535-4660
Exhibitions of art, architecture, design, video.

Gateway Arch
11 N. Fourth St.
314/425-4465
Passenger tram carries visitors to an observation room at the top; Museum of Westward Expansion.

Gateway Riverboat Cruises
St. Louis Levee, below Gateway Arch
314/621-4040
Day trips, dinner cruises, sightseeing cruises aboard replicas of 19th-century riverboats.

The Missouri Botanical Garden.

Missouri Botanical Garden
4344 Shaw
314/577-5100
Founded in 1859 by Henry Shaw, this National Historic Landmark offers gardens, a geodesic-domed greenhouse, a tropical rain forest.

St. Louis Zoo
Forest Park
314/781-0900
More than 3,400 animals in natural habitats.

Six Flags Over Mid-America—St. Louis
About 30 miles southwest of St. Louis on I-44
314/938-5300
More than 100 rides, shows, entertainment.

Union Station
18th and Market
314/421-6655
Historic train station renovated as a shopping center with restaurants, hotels, entertainment.

For More Information

St. Louis Convention & Visitors Bureau
#10 South Broadway, Suite 1000
St. Louis, MO 63102
314/421-1023

San Diego Jack Murphy Stadium, home to the San Diego Padres, was formally dedicated in August 1967—with a football game. The first baseball game played here occurred in April 1968, but it was the Pacific Coast League Padres then.

The next year, the city was awarded a National League franchise, and the San Diego Padres were formed. Their 59,700-seat stadium is a terrific spot to go to after a day at the beach.

Start with the setting: Mountains provide a great backdrop to the ballpark. This is also an engineering marvel. The San Diego River flowed just under the stands. It had to be diverted to accommodate the structure.

The stadium consists of 1,715 giant pieces of pre-cast concrete in 234 different shapes. The structure is circular, but the stadium is open in rightfield. It is the only park in the Majors in which the bullpen dirt area touches the foul line. A foul ball can be caught in the bullpens, out of the sight of the umpires.

The stadium honors Jack Murphy, sports editor at the *San Diego Union*, who tirelessly lobbied for a modern stadium and Major League sports for the city of San Diego. He succeeded. The stadium is Major League in every way: there's plenty of parking, and the Southern California weather provides lots of pleasant afternoons and evenings at the ballpark.

San Diego Padres

San Diego Jack Murphy Stadium.

- Field, Press, Plaza, View Boxes
- Loge, View Reserved
- Grandstand Reserved
- General Admission

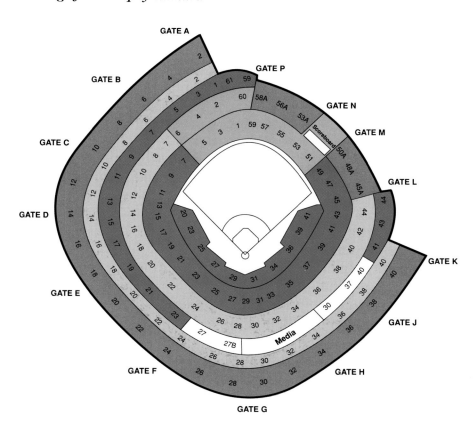

Purchasing Tickets

By mail:
San Diego Padres
Ticket Department
P.O. Box 2000
San Diego, CA 92112-2000
Send a check or money order payable to the San Diego
Padres. Please specify the date of the game or games
and the number and location of the seats you want.
Call 619/283-4494 for information.

In person:
Ticket Office
near Gate C
San Diego Jack Murphy Stadium
9449 Friars Road
Ticket office hours: Daily during the season
9 a.m. - 5 p.m. For information, call 619/283-4494.

By phone:
619/452-SEAT or 800/876-SEAT

Directions to the Stadium

• From the North: Take I-805 east to I-8 east to I-15
  north to Friars Road west to the stadium. Or take
  Highway 163 (Cabrillo Freeway) south to Friars Road
  east to the stadium.

• From the West (or I-5): Take I-8 east and turn off at
  Stadium Way, which leads onto Friars Road and the
  stadium.

• From the East: Take I-8 west and turn off at I-15 north
  to Friars Road west to the stadium.

Public Transportation

San Diego Transit, in conjunction with the Padres,
provides a shuttle bus to and from Padres home games
from these locations: downtown/Hillcrest, Market
Place at the Grove, Grossmont Trolley Station, and El
Cajon Transit Center. Buses depart from parking area
P-2 20 minutes after the conclusion of each game.
For information, call 619/233-3004.

North County Transit also provides a shuttle bus to
home games, available Thursday - Sunday. For information, call 619/722-NCTD (from coastal cities) or
619/743-NCTD (from inland cities).

Parking

There are approximately 18,700 parking spaces.
Special areas are provided for each seating section.
About 135 spaces are reserved for handicapped individuals and are located in the first row of parking
nearest the stadium gates and along the concrete
fingerwalks. Access ramps to the sidewalks are
located in front of every entrance gate except Gates
C and E. Unloading zones for handicapped individuals
are located on the fingerwalks near Gates F and N.

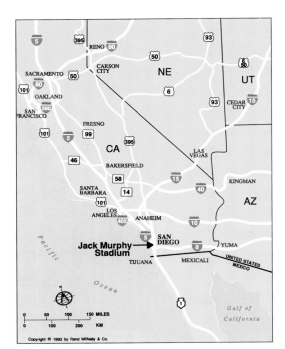

San Diego

San Diego Jack Murphy Stadium is in the Mission Valley section, with a good selection of restaurants and hotels. Another good restaurant spot is the Harbor Island area.

Trolley cars pass through downtown.

Sports Spots

Bike Coronado
1201 First St., Coronado
619/437-4888
Bike rentals.

Buhrow Into Surf and Dive
1536 Sweetwater Road, National City
619/477-5946
Surf and dive lessons and trips.

Hamel's Action Sports Center
704 Ventura Place, Mission Beach
619/488-5050
Rental of bikes, skates, and boogie boards.

Lake Cuyamaca Recreation and Park District
15027 Highway 79, Julian
619/447-8123
Trout and bass fishing in the San Diego mountains, hiking trail around lake.

Padres Pub
Mission Valley Hilton
901 Camino del Rio South
619/543-9000
Sports bar/restaurant ($)

San Diego Padres Clubhouse Shop
272 E. Via Rancho Pkwy., Escondido
619/745-9656
Official licensed memorabilia shop.

San Diego Parasail Adventures, Inc.
1641 Quivira Road
619/223-4386
Parasailing.

Seaforth Boat Rental
1641 Quivira Road
619/223-1681
Rentals of jet skis, ski boats, sail boats, speed boats, fishing boats, bikes. Parasailing.

Telly's Sports Bar
Sheraton Harbor Island Hotel
1380 Harbor Island Drive
619/291-2900
Sports bar/restaurant ($)

Trophy's Sports Grill
7510 Hazard Center Drive
619/296-9600
Sports bar/restaurant ($)

Restaurants

The Boathouse—Harbor Island
2040 Harbor Island Drive
619/291-8011
Seafood. Bay view ($$)

Butcher Shop Restaurant
5255 Kearny Villa Road
619/565-2272
American cuisine ($$)

Mister A's Restaurant
2550 Fifth Ave.
619/239-1377
Continental cuisine. Panoramic ocean and bay views ($$$)

Smugglers Inn
402 Fashion Valley
619/291-7170
Seafood, steaks, prime rib ($$-$$$)

Sports Spots & Restaurants (Dinner for two without beverage or tip):
$ **Under $20**
$$ **$20-$40**
$$$ **More than $40**

Flamingos and other exotic animals make their home at the San Diego Zoo.

Accommodations

Budget Motels of America
641 Camino del Rio South
619/295-6886, 800/624-1257 ($)

Comfort Suites—Mission Valley
631 Camino del Rio South
619/294-3444, 800/228-5150 ($$)

Handlery Hotel & Country Club
950 Hotel Circle North
619/298-0511, 800/223-0888 ($$)

Holiday Inn—Mission Valley
595 Hotel Circle South
619/291-5720, 800-HOLIDAY ($-$$)

Mission Valley Hilton
901 Camino del Rio South
619/543-9000, 800/445-8667 ($$)

Radisson Hotel
1433 Camino del Rio South
619/260-0111, 800/333-3333 ($$)

San Diego Marriott Mission Valley
8757 Rio San Diego Drive
619/692-3800, 800/842-5329 ($$)

Vagabond Inn
625 Hotel Circle South
619/297-1691, 800/522-1555 ($)

Price ranges: Double room during the week (lower rates are often available on weekends)
$ **Under $75**
$$ **$75-$125**
$$$ **More than $125**

A seal's antics are among the fun at Sea World.

Attractions

Balboa Park
1,074 acres, just north of downtown
619/239-0512
Gardens, museums, theaters, sports facilities, zoo, and lots of open space.

Old Town
North of San Diego Bay, near Hotel Circle
The first European settlement in California, this renovated historic district has interesting buildings, gardens, shops, restaurants.

San Diego Bay
Home port for Navy ships, a sport-fishing fleet, pleasure craft, and cruise ships. Maritime Museum is next to the Broadway pier; harbor cruises and ferry to Coronado.

San Diego Museum of Art
1450 El Prado, Balboa Park
619/232-7931
Dutch, Flemish, Baroque, and Italian and Spanish Renaissance art.

San Diego Zoo
2920 Zoo Drive
619/234-3153
Rare and exotic animals in a 100-acre tropical garden.

Sea World of California
1720 S. Shores Road, Mission Bay
619/226-3901, 619/222-6363
Aquatic animals, water shows.

Seaport Village
West Harbor Drive at Kettner Boulevard
619/235-4013
Shopping, entertainment, and dining complex.

For More Information

San Diego Convention & Visitors Bureau
1200 Third Ave., Suite 824
San Diego, CA 92101
619/232-3101

Jack Murphy Stadium

Mission Valley Shopping Center

0   1/2
MILE

Copyright © 1993 by Rand McNally & Co.

Mission Gorge
Navy Golf Course

RIVER

SAN DIEGO

SAN DIEGO

Kaiser Hospital

Mission San Diego De Alcala

Grantville Park

15

8

8

15

123

When Candlestick Park opened in 1960, 1.8 million fans headed to the 42,500-seat stadium in the first year. It's been the Giants' home field ever since.

The Giants headed west to San Francisco at the end of the 1957 season; they had spent more than 60 years in New York. For their first two seasons on the West Coast, the Giants played in Seals Stadium, a minor league park at 16th and Potrero Avenue. Then they moved into Candlestick Park.

The Giants' home is constantly being tested by the elements. The wind whips in so many different directions, it's sometimes almost impossible to track fly balls. In the 1961 All-Star Game, Stu Miller was blown off the pitcher's mound.

The temperature also can change direction quickly: During night games, temperatures have been known to dip into the 40s in July.

Candlestick was the site of the 1989 World Series between the Giants and their cross-Bay neighbors, the Oakland A's. Just a half-hour before Game 3 at Candlestick, an earthquake rumbled through the Bay Area and the park. The quake caused major damage to the city and put baseball on hold for 10 days. Remarkably, the park itself, the first Major League stadium constructed entirely of reinforced concrete, sustained only minor damage.

San Francisco Giants

Lower Boxes
Lower Reserved
Upper Boxes
Upper Reserved
Pavilion
General Admission

Dennis Despros/ San Fransisco Giants

Candlestick Park.

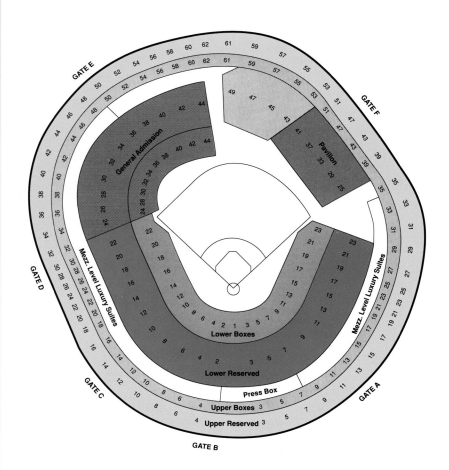

Purchasing Tickets

In person:
Candlestick Park
eight miles south of San Francisco
via the Bayshore Freeway (Route 101)
Ticket office hours: Monday - Friday 9 a.m. - 5 p.m.
For ticket information, call 415/467-8000.

Tickets are also available at the Giants Dugout Stores:
170 Grant Ave.
San Francisco

Serramonte Center
Daly City

Valley Fair Mall
near Stevens Creek and Winchester
Santa Clara

Stanford Shopping Mall
El Camino Real, north of University Avenue
Palo Alto

Coddington Center
Highway 101 at Steele Lane exit
Santa Rosa

By phone:
You can also purchase tickets at any of the 120 BASS/TM ticket outlets:

415/762-BASS in San Francisco; 707/762-BASS in North Bay; 209/266-BASS in Stockton; 408/998-BASS in San Jose; 916/923-BASS in Sacramento; 800/225-BASS outside California

Directions to the Stadium

• From San Francisco and the North: Take the Cow Palace-Brisbane exit from U.S. 101 (rather than the Candlestick Park exit). Proceed to Third Street and turn left over the freeway. Proceed on Third Street. Turn right on Jamestown Avenue; proceed to main lot.

• From the Peninsula and the South: Take the Third Street exit from U.S. 101 and continue on Third Street as instructed above.

Public Transportation

The Municipal Railway (MUNI) and the San Mateo County Transit District (SamTrans) offer regular bus service. For information, call 415/673-MUNI or Sam-Trans at one of the following numbers: in San Francisco 415/761-8000; in North County 415/871-2200; in Central County 415/348-8858; or in South County 415/367-1500.

Team Address
San Francisco Giants
Candlestick Park
San Francisco, CA 94124
415/468-3700

Franchise History
New York Gothams 1883-85
New York Giants 1886-1957
San Francisco Giants 1958-

World Series Titles
1905 vs. Philadelphia Athletics
1921 vs. New York Yankees
1922 vs. New York Yankees
1933 vs. Washington Senators
1954 vs. Cleveland Indians

National League Pennants
1888, 1889, 1904, 1905, 1911, 1912,
1913, 1917, 1921, 1922, 1923, 1924,
1933, 1936, 1937, 1951, 1954, 1962,
1989

West Division Titles
1971, 1987, 1989

Hall of Fame Inductees
Christy Mathewson, 1936
John McGraw, 1937
William (Buck) Ewing, 1939
Willie Keeler, 1939
Rogers Hornsby, 1942
Roger Bresnahan, 1945
Dan Brouthers, 1945
Mike (King) Kelly, 1945
James O'Rourke, 1945
Jesse Burkett, 1946
Joe McGinnity, 1946
Frankie Frisch, 1947
Carl Hubbell, 1947
Mel Ott, 1951
Bill Terry, 1954
Charles (Gabby) Hartnet, 1955
Ray Schalk, 1955
Bill McKechnie, 1962
Edd Roush, 1962
Burleigh Grimes, 1964
Tim Keefe, 1964
Monte Ward, 1964
Casey Stengel, 1966
Joe (Ducky) Medwick, 1968
Waite Hoyt, 1969
Dave Bancroft, 1971

Jake Beckley, 1971
Rube Marquard, 1971
Ross Youngs, 1972
Monte Irvin, 1973
George Kelly, 1973
Warren Spahn, 1973
Mickey Welch, 1973
Roger Conner, 1976
Fred Lindstrom, 1976
Amos Rusie, 1977
Willie Mays, 1979
Hack Wilson, 1979
Duke Snider, 1980
Johnny Mize, 1981
Travis Jackson, 1982
Juan Marichal, 1983
Hoyt Wilhelm, 1985
Ernie Lombardi, 1986
Willie McCovey, 1986
Joe Morgan, 1990
Gaylord Perry, 1991

Award Winners
Cy Young Award
Mike McCormick, 1967

Most Valuable Player
Carl Hubbell, 1933, 1936
Willie Mays, 1954, 1965
Willie McCovey, 1969
Kevin Mitchell, 1989

Rookie of the Year
Willie Mays, 1951
Orlando Cepeda, 1958
Willie McCovey, 1959
Gary Matthews, 1973
John Montefusco, 1975

Retired Uniform Numbers
Christy Mathewson
John McGraw
3 Bill Terry
4 Mel Ott
11 Carl Hubbell
24 Willie Mays
27 Juan Marichal
44 Willie McCovey

Parking

Extensive parking is available in lots to the north and east of Candlestick Park. Parking for handicapped individuals is located close to Gates A, E, and F. A shuttle service is available to transport handicapped, elderly, or other fans who require special assistance from the parking lot to the turnstiles. The eight-passenger trams stop at the handicapped parking areas and other specially marked locations.

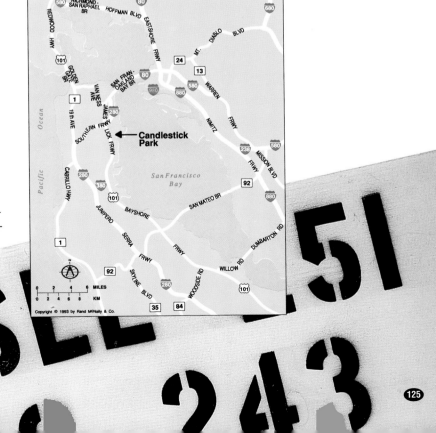

Bayview Playground

Visitacion Plg

Bayshore Station

Little Hollywood Plgd

Paul Avenue Station

Caltrain

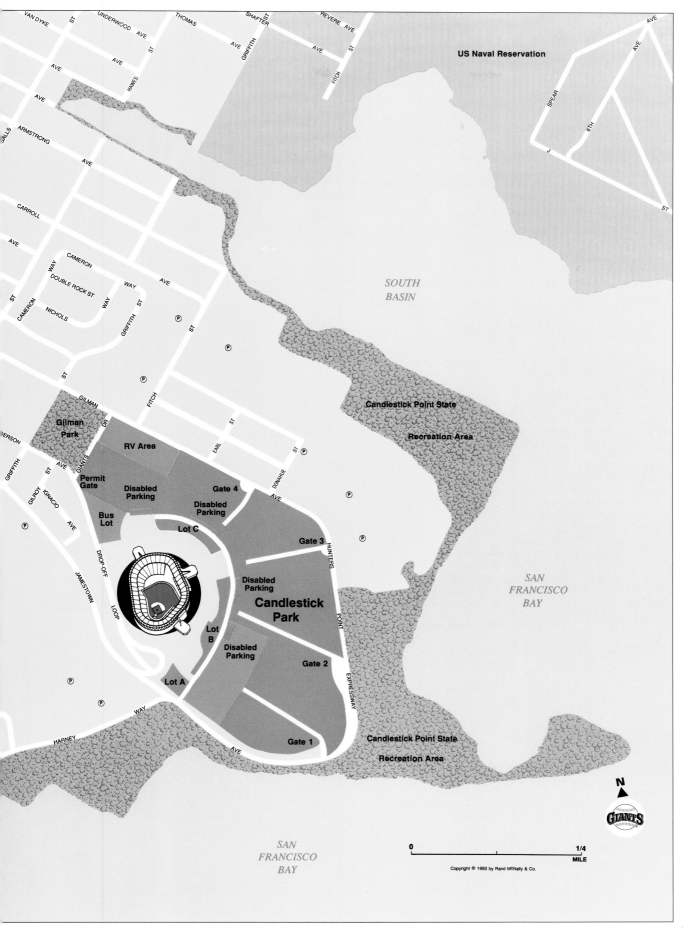

US Naval Reservation

SOUTH BASIN

Candlestick Point State

Recreation Area

SAN FRANCISCO BAY

Gilman Park

RV Area

Permit Gate

Disabled Parking

Bus Lot

Gate 4

Disabled Parking

Lot C

Gate 3

Disabled Parking

Candlestick Park

Lot B

Disabled Parking

Gate 2

Lot A

Gate 1

Candlestick Point State

Recreation Area

SAN FRANCISCO BAY

VAN DYKE ST
UNDERWOOD AVE
THOMAS
SHAFTER ST
ST
REVERE AVE
AVE
HAWES
AVE
GRIFFITH
AVE
ST
FITCH
SPEAR
6TH
ST
CARROLL
AVE
ARMSTRONG
AVE
ST
CAMERON WAY
DOUBLE ROCK ST
WAY
CAMERON AVE
NICHOLS
GRIFFITH ST
ST
FITCH
ST
GILMAN
GILMAN
ERSON
GRIFFITH ST
AVE
GIANTS DR
GILROY
IGNACIO AVE
JAMESTOWN
DROP-OFF
LOOP
HARNEY
WAY
EARL
ST
ST
DONAHUE AVE
HUNTERS
POINT
EXPRESSWAY
WAY
AVE

N

GIANTS

0   1/4
MILE

Copyright © 1993 by Rand McNally & Co.

127

San Francisco

Candlestick Park is about eight miles from the city center. Hotels listed are along the Van Ness corridor close to Highway 101; restaurants are scattered in the central city.

Sports Spots

Bicycling
There are two marked bike routes through San Francisco: one through Golden Gate Park to Lake Merced; the other from the south end of the city north across Golden Gate Bridge to Marin County. Bike rental shops line streets around Golden Gate Park, especially Stanyan Street and Geary Boulevard.

Big Nate's BBQ
1665 Folsom St.
415/861-4242
Sports bar/carry-out owned by Nate Thurmond ($$)

Golden Gate Park
Bounded by Stanyan and Fell, Lincoln Way, and Great Highway
A 1,017-acre park with museums, lakes, tennis courts, soccer fields, a golf course, riding stables, fly-casting pools, polo field, gardens, conservatory.

Lefty O'Doul's
333 Geary St.
415/982-8900
Sports bar/restaurant ($)

Pat O'Shea's Mad Hatter
3848 Geary Blvd.
415/752-3148
Sports bar/restaurant ($)

The San Francisco-Oakland Bay Bridge at dusk.

Restaurants

Basta Pasta
1268 Grant Ave.
415/434-2248
Italian pasta, pizza ($-$$)

Chevys Mexican Restaurant
150 Fourth St. at Howard Street
415/543-8060
Mexican cuisine ($-$$)

Ernie's Restaurant
847 Montgomery St.
415/397-5969
Contemporary French cuisine ($$$)

Fior d'Italia
601 Union St.
415/986-1886
Northern Italian cuisine ($$)

MacArthur Park
607 Front St.
415/398-5700
Ribs, seafood, steak ($$-$$$)

Max's Diner
311 Third St. at Folsom Street
415/546-6297
Deli sandwiches, meat loaf, chicken fried steak ($-$$)

North Beach Restaurant
1512 Stockton St.
415/392-1700
Northern Italian pasta ($$-$$$)

Scoma's
Pier 47, Fisherman's Wharf
415/771-4383
Seafood Italian style ($$-$$$)

Sports Spots & Restaurants (Dinner for two without beverage or tip):
$ Under $20
$$ $20-$40
$$$ More than $40

Accommodations

Cathedral Hill Hotel
1101 Van Ness Ave.
415/776-8200, 800/227-4730, 800/622-0855 (California) ($$$)

Holiday Inn—Golden Gateway
1500 Van Ness Ave.
415/441-4000, 800-HOLIDAY ($$)

Holiday Lodge
1901 Van Ness Ave.
415/776-4469, 800/367-8504 ($$)

Hotel Richelieu
1050 Van Ness Ave.
415/673-4711, 800/227-3608 ($$)

Quality Hotel
2775 Van Ness Ave.
415/928-5000, 800/221-2222 ($$)

Price ranges: Double room during the week (lower rates are often available on weekends)
$ Under $75
$$ $75-$125
$$$ More than $125

Attractions

Alcatraz Tours
Red and White Fleet
Pier 41, Fisherman's Wharf
415/546-BOAT, 800/BAY-CRUISE (California)
Self-guided tours of former federal penitentiary.

California Academy of Sciences
Golden Gate Park
415/221-5100, 415/750-7145 (tape)
Includes Steinhart Aquarium, Morrison Planetarium, and natural science exhibits.

Chinatown
Entrance at Grant Avenue and Bush Street
24-block area filled with restaurants, shops, food markets, museums.

Fisherman's Wharf
North end of Powell Street at the waterfront
Outdoor seafood stands, dozens of seafood restaurants, shopping, bay cruises.

A streetcar descends a San Francisco hill with Alcatraz in the distance.

Golden Gate Bridge
Highway 101 at the north end of the Presidio
Landmark suspension bridge that links San Francisco with Marin County to the north.

M.H. de Young Memorial Museum
Golden Gate Park
415/750-3600
Galleries of art from around the world.

North Beach
Between Telegraph Hill and Russian Hill
415/403-0666
Traditional Italian neighborhood featuring cabarets, jazz clubs, restaurants, gelato parlors.

Union Street
1500 to 2200 blocks, from Van Ness Avenue to the Presidio
415/441-7055
Boutiques, galleries, coffee houses, restaurants, and night spots.

For More Information

San Francisco Convention & Visitors Bureau
Powell & Market (Hallidie Plaza, Lower Level)
San Francisco, CA 94142
415/974-6900

The Kingdome not only defies Seattle's rainy weather, it also sometimes defies the law of gravity: What goes up does not necessarily come down in this domed stadium.

That's because the Kingdome, which was built for the AL expansion Mariners, is completely covered by a concrete dome that rises to a height of 250 feet.

At least twice since the ballpark opened, batted balls have been lost in the speakers hanging from the roof over the dugout at first base. On other occasions, fair balls have bounced off speakers and remained in play. Because of these unique possibilities, the Kingdome has some special rules: A batted ball that hits a suspended object in fair territory is fair or foul, depending on where it lands or is touched by a fielder. A batted ball that sticks to or in any suspended object in fair territory is a ground-rule double.

This 58,539-seat stadium even has a language of its own. You'll want to speak "dome" when you come to a game. The rightfield wall was nicknamed "Walla Walla" in 1982 when it was raised 23 feet. The carpet on the field is rolled out by a "rhinoceros" (machine) and smoothed by a "grasshopper" (another machine). But whatever langage you speak, you'll enjoy the Kingdome.

Seattle Mariners

The Kingdome.

Corky Trewin/ Seattle Mariners

- ☐ Box
- ☐ Field
- ☐ Club
- ☐ View
- ☐ Family
- ☐ General Admission

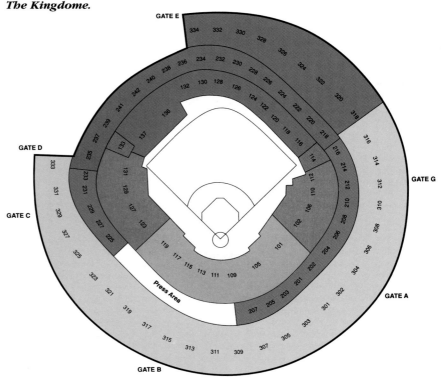

Purchasing Tickets

By mail:

Seattle Mariners Ticket Office
P.O. Box 4100
411 1st Ave. S.
Seattle, WA 98104
Send a check or money order payable to the Seattle Mariners. Please specify the date of the game or games, number of tickets, and price. For information, call 206/628-3555.

In person:

Advance ticket window
near Gate D
201 S. King St.
Ticket window hours: Monday - Saturday 8:30 a.m. - 5:30 p.m.; Sunday noon - 5:00 p.m. For information, call 206/628-3555.

Tickets are also available at various TicketMaster outlets (cash only) throughout Washington state, in Oregon, and in the greater Vancouver, B.C., area.

By phone:

TicketMaster 206/628-0888; in Vancouver 604/280-4444

Directions to the Stadium

- From the North (outside the city limits): Take the main line section of I-5, exit at Airport Way (Exit 164) off-ramp at Dearborn Street, turn right onto Dearborn, go to Fourth Avenue South; turn left onto Fourth Avenue South and go to South Royal Brougham Way. Turn right and proceed to Kingdome Lot B or C.

- From the North (inside the city limits): From west of I-5, go to Aurora Avenue southbound to First Avenue exit ramps (exits from left lane). Follow First Avenue southbound to South Royal Brougham Way; turn left, proceed to Kingdome Lot B or C. From east of I-5, follow the directions for traveling from the north from outside the city limits.

- From the South (outside the city limits): Exit I-5 North at the Spokane Street (Exit 163) off-ramp, follow Spokane (lower level) to Fourth Avenue South; turn right and go north to South Royal Brougham Way. Turn left and proceed to Kingdome Lot B or C.

- From the South (inside the city limits): Follow First Avenue or Fourth Avenue north to South Royal Brougham Way; turn left from Fourth (or right from First) onto South Royal Brougham, and proceed to Kingdome Lot B or C.

- From the East (via I-90): Exit I-90 at Dearborn Street (exit is from the left lane), on Dearborn. Go to Fourth Avenue South, turn left, go to South Royal Brougham Way. Turn right, and proceed to Kingdome Lot B or C.

- From the East (via S.R. 520): Exit 520 onto I-5 Southbound, follow the directions for traveling from the north from outside the city limits.

Public Transportation

From downtown, take any bus going south on 3rd Avenue (except bus Number 3 or 4, or an express bus). Get off at 3rd and Jackson. For more information, call Metro Transit, 206/553-3000.

Parking

Stadium parking lots are located to the north and south of the Kingdome. Additional off-street parking lots are scattered throughout the neighborhood surrounding the stadium.

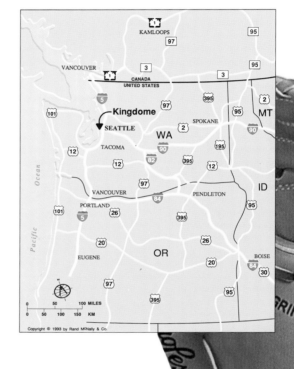

Profile

Team Address
Seattle Mariners
The Kingdome
P.O. Box 4100
411 1st Ave. S.
Seattle, WA 98104
206/628-3555

Franchise History
Seattle Mariners 1977-

Hall of Fame Inductee
Gaylord Perry, 1991

Award Winners
Rookie of the Year
Alvin Davis, 1984

Seattle

Seattle, on Puget Sound, is surrounded by scenic mountain ranges and three national parks. Hotels and restaurants listed are close to the downtown area.

The Seattle skyline as night falls.

Sports Spots

Charlie Mac's
15221 Pacific Highway S.
206/242-9999
Sports bar/restaurant ($)

Gasoline Alley Sports
6501 20th Ave. N.E.
206/524-1606
Antique shop with baseball collectibles.

Golden Age Collectables (sic)
Pike Place Public Market, in Public Market
206/622-9799
Large collectible shop.

Keystone Corner Baseball Cards
534 Queen Ave. N.
206/285-9277
Used-sports-equipment store with baseball cards and collectibles.

Sneakers Bar and Restaurant
567 Occidental Ave. S.
6/625-1340
Sports bar/restaurant ($)

Swannie's
222 S. Main St.
206/622-9353
Oldest sports bar/restaurant in Seattle ($)

Triple C Collectibles
15200 Aurora Ave. N.
206/368-0333
Large selection of baseball cards and collectibles.

Restaurants

Dante's Steak and Grog
5300 Roosevelt Way N.E.
206/525-1300
Steak, sandwiches ($)

F.X. McRory's Steak, Chop and Oyster House
419 Occidental Ave. S., near the Kingdome
206/623-4800
Recreates a classic New York City chop house ($$)

Il Terrazzo
411 First Ave. S.
206/467-7797
Northern Italian cuisine ($$-$$$)

Larry's Greenfront Restaurant and Lounge
209 First Ave. S., in Pioneer Square
206/624-7665
Pre-game brunch, meat loaf, burgers, blue-plate specials, fish and chips ($)

Metropolitan Grill
818 Second Ave.
206/624-3287
Steak, seafood ($$-$$$)

New Orleans Creole Restaurant
114 First Ave. S., in Pioneer Square
206/622-2563
Creole-Cajun cuisine ($-$$)

Vito's
927 Ninth Ave.
206/682-2695
Italian cuisine ($$)

Sports Spots & Restaurants (Dinner for two without beverage or tip):
$ Under $20
$$ $20-$40
$$$ More than $40

Seattle's waterfront bustles with activity.

Accommodations

Best Western Executive Inn
200 Taylor Ave. N.
206/448-9444 ($$)

Days Inn Town Center
2205 Seventh Ave.
206/448-3434 ($$)

Edgewater Inn
Pier 67, 2411 Alaskan Way
206/728-7000 ($$$)

Park Inn
225 Aurora Ave. N.
206/728-7666 ($-$$)

Quality Inn City Center
2224 Eighth Ave.
206/624-6820 ($$)

Sixth Avenue Inn
2000 Sixth Ave.
206/441-8300 ($$)

West Coast Camlin Hotel
1619 Ninth Ave.
206/682-0100 ($$)

West Coast Vance Hotel
620 Stewart St.
206/441-4200 ($$)

Price ranges: Double room during the week (lower rates are often available on weekends)
$ Under $75
$$ $75-$125
$$$ More than $125

A ferry travels Puget Sound with Mt. Rainier in the distance.

Wild Waves Water Park

36201 Enchanted Pkwy. S., Federal Way, in the same complex with Enchanted Village
206/838-7003, 206/927-4113
Features 24,000 square-foot wave pool, water slides.

Attractions

Enchanted Village
36201 Enchanted Pkwy. S., Federal Way
206/838-7003, 206/661-8000
Rides, petting zoo, bird aviary, 13-hole Krogolf, wax museum, water slides.

Museum of Flight
9404 E. Marginal Way S.
206/764-5720
Historic airplanes; exhibits and film on aviation history.

Museum of History and Industry
2700 24th Ave. E.
206/324-1125
History of Seattle, King County, and the Puget Sound region.

Pacific Science Center
200 2nd Ave. N.
206/443-2001
Hands-on science exhibits, IMAX theater, planetarium.

The Seattle Aquarium
Pier 59, Waterfront Park
206/386-4320
A variety of marine life in natural environments.

The Seattle Space Needle
203 Sixth Ave. N.
206/443-2100
Spectacular views of the Pacific Northwest. Two revolving restaurants at top.

Underground Seattle Tour
610 First Ave.
206/682-1511
Explore the city beneath the city in a guided tour of Pioneer Square.

Waterfront Area
Alaskan Way, Piers 52-70
Shops, restaurants; Pike Place Market.

For More Information

Seattle/King County Convention & Visitors Bureau
520 Pike St., Suite 1300
Seattle, WA 98101
206/461-5840

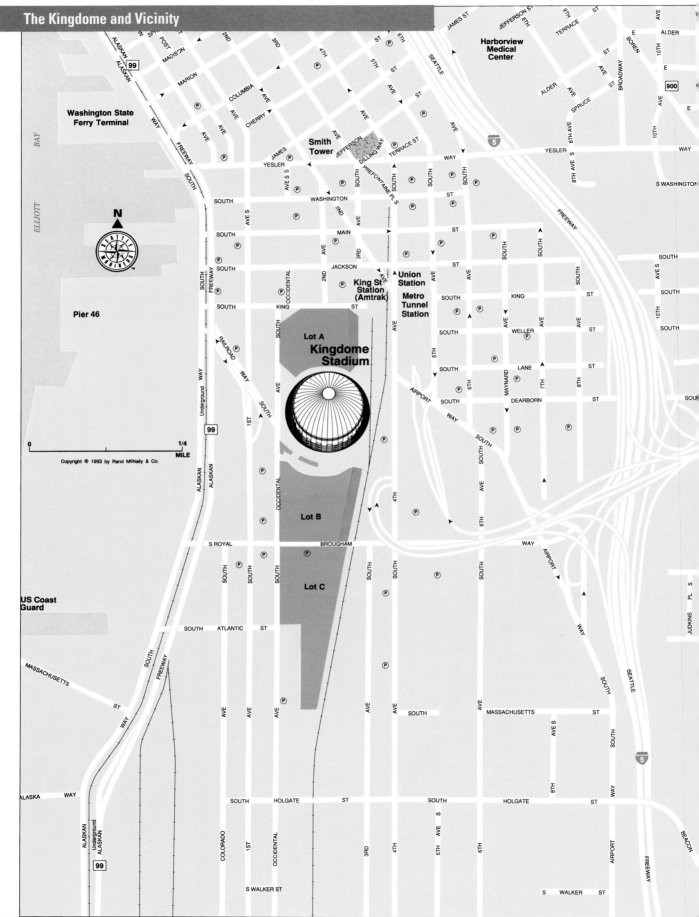

Harborview
Medical
Center

Washington State
Ferry Terminal

N

Pier 46

Smith
Tower

0   1/4
         MILE

Copyright © 1993 by Rand McNally & Co.

King St
Station
(Amtrak)

Union
Station

Metro
Tunnel
Station

Lot A

Kingdome
Stadium

Lot B

US Coast
Guard

Lot C

Arlington Stadium is a hot spot for baseball.

In fact, the Rangers play every Sunday game at night to take advantage of cooler evening temperatures. Even so, there are more home runs because warm, humid air does not cause as much resistance to the flight of the ball as dense, cooler air.

The Rangers came to Texas via Washington, DC. When the original Washington Senators moved to Minnesota to become the Twins in 1961, AL expansion created a new Senators team in Washington. After the 1971 season, they moved to Arlington, midway between Dallas and Fort Worth, and were renamed the Texas Rangers.

The Rangers play at a former minor league ballpark. In 1972, it was renamed Arlington Stadium and eventually expanded from 10,000 seats to 43,521.

Several interesting construction notes: Before the upper deck was added in 1978, fans actually entered at the top of the park because it was built below the parking lot level. The stadium also has the largest bleacher section in the majors (more than 16,000), which spans the outfield from foul pole to foul pole.

In 1994, the Rangers plan to move into a new stadium adjacent to their current home. Fans and players alike will enjoy the open-air, natural grass ballpark. The centerpiece of a 160-acre complex, it will include a sports hall of fame, amphitheater, little league park, jogging paths, bike trails, and other facilities.

Texas Rangers

Arlington C&VB

Arlington Stadium.

■ Infield Boxes
□ Reserved Boxes
□ Plaza
■ Grandstand Reserved
■ General Admission

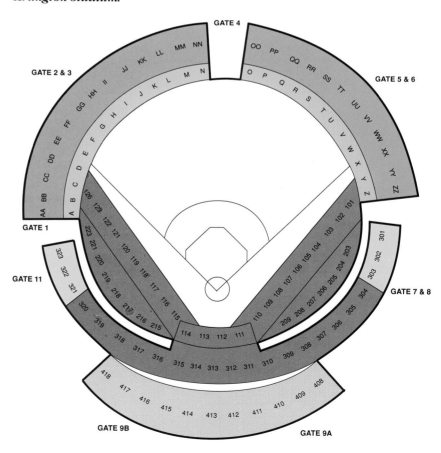

Purchasing Tickets

By mail:

Ticket Office
Texas Rangers Baseball Club
P.O. Box 90111
Arlington, TX 76004

Send a check or money order payable to the Texas Rangers; add a $3 postage and handling fee. Specify the date of the game or games you want to see as well as the number and price of tickets.

In person:

Arlington Stadium Ticket Office
1700 Copeland Road

Ticket office hours: Monday - Friday 9 a.m. - 6 p.m.; Saturday 10 a.m. - 4 p.m.; on days of home games 9 a.m. - 9 p.m.; Saturday and Sunday 9 a.m. - 3:30 p.m. for day games and noon - 9 p.m. for night games. For ticket information, call 817/273-5100.

Tickets are also available at Rainbow TicketMaster and TicketQuik outlets, including Sound Warehouse and all major Sears stores in the Dallas-Fort Worth metroplex and in Denton.

By phone:

817/273-5100

Directions to the Stadium

- From Dallas: Take I-30 to the Highway 360 exit and turn south on the service road. Turn west (right) on Six Flags Drive. Turn west (right) to Road to Six Flags. Follow road to Toll Plaza #4. Or, take Highway 183 west to Highway 360. Head south on 360 to Randol Mill Road. Head west on Randol Mill to Toll Plaza #3 (south of the stadium). Or, take I-30 to the F.M. 157 exit (Collins Street) and go south on 157 to Road to Six Flags, then turn east to Toll Plaza #2.

- From Fort Worth: Take I-30 east to Fielder Road, then go south on Fielder to Randol Mill Road to Toll Plaza #3 (south of the stadium). Or, take I-30 east to F.M. 157 (Collins Street). Go south on 157 to Road to Six Flags to Toll Plaza #2. Or, take I-30 east to Pennant Drive. Go straight down Pennant Drive to Toll Plaza #2.

Public Transportation

For local transport, call Yellow Cab 817/534-7777.

Parking

All toll plazas to the stadium open approximately two hours before game time and are located off Copeland Road, Road to Six Flags, Randol Mill Road, and Stadium Drive east. Extensive parking is available in lots surrounding the stadium.

Profile

Team Address
Texas Rangers
Arlington Stadium
1250 Copeland Road, Suite 1100
Arlington, TX 76011
817/273-5222 (office)
817/273-5000 (stadium)

Franchise History
Washington Senators 1961-71
Texas Rangers 1972-

Hall of Fame Inductees
Ted Williams, 1966
Ferguson Jenkins, 1991
Gaylord Perry, 1991

Award Winners
Most Valuable Player
Jeff Burroughs, 1974
Rookie of the Year
Mike Hargrove, 1974

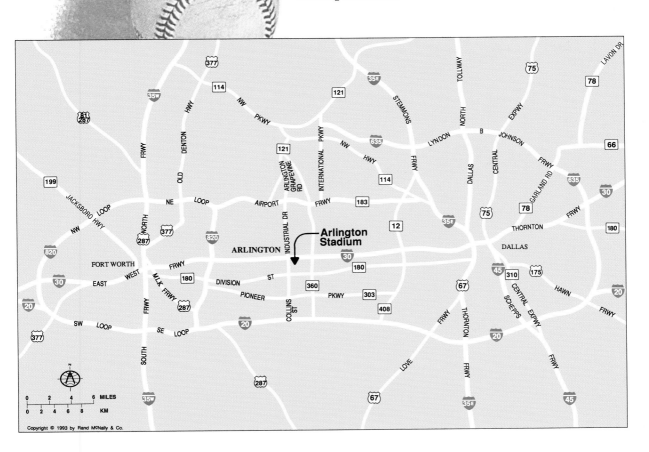

Copyright © 1993 by Rand McNally & Co.

135

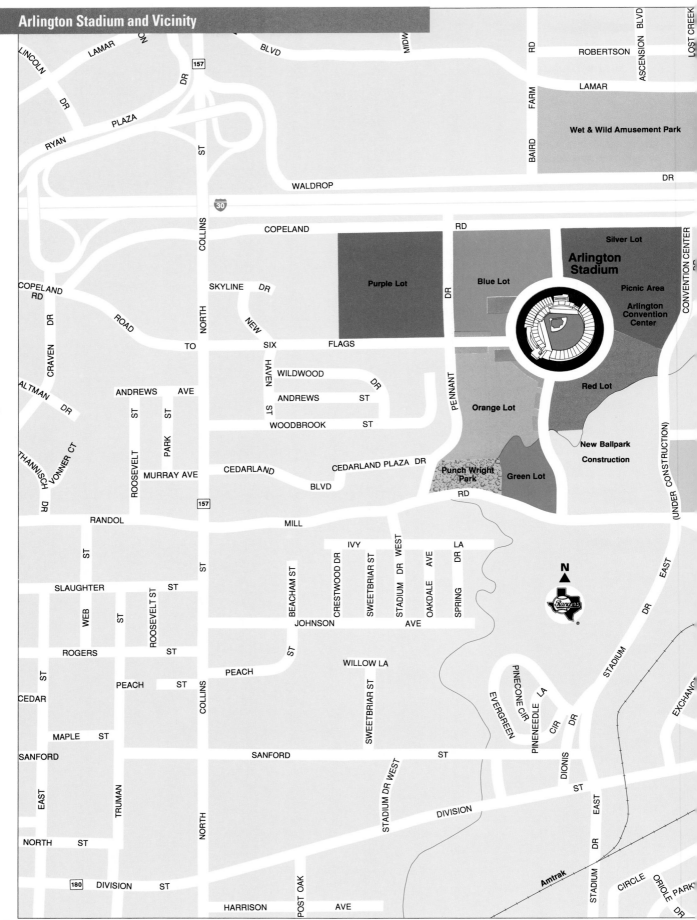

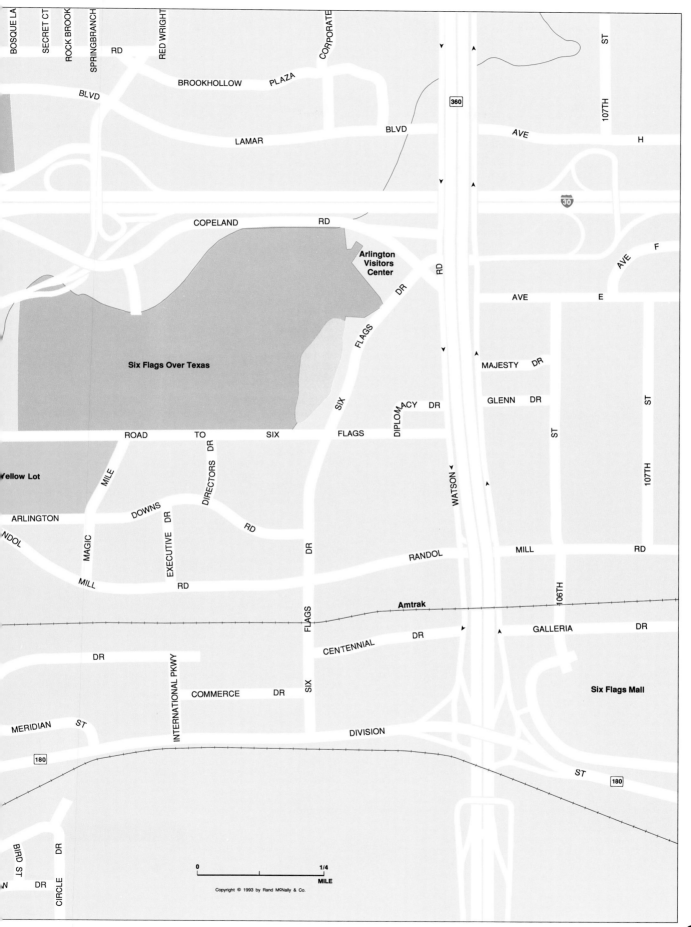

BOSQUE LA

SECRET CT

ROCK BROOK

SPRINGBRANCH

RD

RED WRIGHT

CORPORATE

BROOKHOLLOW   PLAZA

BLVD

LAMAR   BLVD

COPELAND   RD

Arlington
Visitors
Center

ST

107TH

AVE   H

30

AVE   F

Six Flags Over Texas

DR

FLAGS

SIX

ROAD   TO   SIX   FLAGS

DIPLOMACY   DR

FLAGS

RD

AVE   E

MAJESTY   DR

GLENN   DR

ST

ST

107TH

ellow Lot

MILE

DIRECTORS   DR

DOWNS   DR

ARLINGTON

NDOL

MAGIC

MILL

EXECUTIVE

RD

RD

DR

WATSON

RANDOL

MILL   RD

106TH

Amtrak

FLAGS

DR

CENTENNIAL   DR

GALLERIA   DR

DR

INTERNATIONAL PKWY

COMMERCE   DR

SIX

Six Flags Mall

MERIDIAN   ST

DIVISION

180

ST

180

BIRD ST

CIRCLE   DR

N   DR

0   1/4
                                    MILE

Copyright © 1993 by Rand M?Nally & Co.

137

Arlington

Arlington is the state's seventh largest city. Hotels and restaurants listed are primarily located in Arlington, just minutes from the stadium.

Sports Spots

Bachman Lake Park
2750 Bachman Blvd., Dallas
Near Love Field Airport, this small lake offers paved trails for jogging and biking. Paddle boat rentals.

Bobby Valentine's Sports Gallery Cafe
715 Ryan Plaza
817/261-1000
4301 S. Bowen
817/467-9922
Sports bar/restaurant ($)

Mesquite Championship Rodeo
1818 Rodeo Drive, I-635 at Military Parkway, Mesquite
214/285-8777
Texas-style rodeo action every Friday and Saturday night with BBQ and live C & W music.

Sandy Lake Amusement Park
1800 Sandy Lake Road, Carrollton
214/242-7449
Paddle boats, miniature golf, giant swimming pool, rides.

Wet 'N' Wild, Arlington
1800 Lamar Blvd.
817/265-3013, 817/265-3356
47-acre water park.

White Rock Lake and Greenbelt Park
8300 Garland Road, Dallas
Large in-city lake with paddle boat, bike rentals, fishing, paved bike and jogging trail.

Prairie moon over Dallas.

Restaurants

Atchafalaya River Cafe
1520 Pennant Drive
817/261-4696
Cajun-Creole cuisine ($-$$)

Bay Street
2501 E. Lamar Blvd.
817/640-1178
Seafood, pasta, steak ($$)

Black-Eyed Pea
1400 N. Collins St.
817/275-8973
Southern cooking ($)

Texas barbecue is a main attraction.

Chili's
924 Copeland Road
817/261-3891
Ribs, chicken, fajitas ($)

Colter's Barbecue and Grill
1322 N. Collins St.
817/261-1444
Barbecue, sandwiches ($)

Jason's Deli
780 Road to Six Flags
817/860-2888
Sandwiches, salad bar ($)

Key West Grill
919 Six Flags Drive
817/640-3157
Seafood, steak, ribs ($-$$)

On the Border
2011 Copeland Road E.
817/460-8000
Tex-Mex cuisine ($-$$)

Sports Spots & Restaurants (Dinner for two without beverage or tip):
$ Under $20
$$ $20-$40
$$$ More than $40

Accommodations

Arlington Hilton
2401 E. Lamar Blvd.
817/640-3322 ($$)

Arlington Motor Inn
818 E. Division
817/277-1395 ($)

Best Western—Great Southwest Inn
3501 E. Division
817/640-7722, 800/346-BEST ($)

Charlie Hotel and Fitness Club
117 S. Watson Rd.
817/633-4000, 800/4-CHARLIE ($)

Comfort Inn
1601 E. Division
817/261-2300 ($)

Days Inn—Downtown
910 N. Collins
817/261-8444 ($)

Flagship Inn Resort
601 E. Avenue H
817/640-1666 ($)

Holiday Inn Arlington
Highway 360 at Brown Boulevard
817/640-7712 ($$)

La Quinta Inn
825 N. Watson Road
817/640-4142 ($)

Price ranges: Double room during the week (lower rates are often available on weekends)
$ Under $75
$$ $75-$125
$$$ More than $125

Attractions

Air Combat School
1912 E. Randol Mill Road
817/640-1886
Put on a G-suit and crash helmet, get into an actual fighter plane cockpit, and engage in simulated combat.

Dallas Alley
2019 N. Lamar St., Dallas
214/720-0170
Renovated historic buildings with nightclubs.

The thrills, the chills: Six Flags Over Texas.

Fort Worth Museum of Science and History
1501 Montgomery, Fort Worth
817/732-1631
Five exhibit halls, Omni Theatre, Noble Planetarium.

Fort Worth Stockyards
130 E. Exchange Ave., Fort Worth
817/625-9715
Western-style town, shopping, dining, Western activities.

Fort Worth Zoological Park
1989 Colonial Parkway, Fort Worth
817/871-7050, ext. 7051
Native Texas animals and other species.

Ripley's Believe It or Not
601 E. Safari Parkway, Grand Prairie
214/263-2391
Oddities of life. In same complex with Palace of Wax.

Six Flags Over Texas
I-30 at Hwy. 360
817/640-8900
Theme park with rides, entertainment.

Traders Village
2602 W. Mayfield Road, Grand Prairie
214/647-2331
Texas-sized flea market with 1,600 dealers, plus rodeos, children's rides.

West End MarketPlace
603 Munger Ave. at Market Street, Dallas
214/954-4350
Entertainment, specialty stores.

For More Information

Fort Worth Convention & Visitors Bureau
415 Throckmorton
Fort Worth, TX 76102
817/336-8791

Welcome to SkyDome — home of the 1992 World Champions — an untraditional home for a winning team.

The Toronto Blue Jays began playing in 1977 as an AL expansion team. The team landed in this architectural marvel in 1989; it is a park of innovations in action.

SkyDome is baseball's only domed stadium with a fully retractable roof. It takes about 20 minutes to open or shut. The roof (modeled after a turtle's shell) covers eight acres when closed, and rises to the height equivalent of a 31-story building.

The $500-million high-tech stadium, located in downtown Toronto just west of the soaring CN Tower, seats 51,000 on five levels for baseball. That doesn't include the 70 rooms with a view at the 348-room luxury hotel adjacent to the ballpark. There's also a McDonald's (the official food of SkyDome); a Hard Rock Cafe; Windows on SkyDome, a 550-seat buffet restaurant; and Sightlines, a 300-foot-long refreshment area, both of which overlook the field.

Continuing its high-tech approach to the traditions of baseball, the stadium's $17-million video scoreboard is the largest in the world at 33-by-115 feet, and requires 420,000 bulbs.

The Blue Jays team is a real fan favorite. In fact, it was the first Major League team to have 4 million people purchase tickets in a single season, doing so in 1991 (4,001,526). The Blue Jays and SkyDome are hard at work creating many new baseball traditions.

Toronto Blue Jays

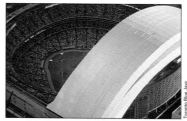

The SkyDome.

Toronto Blue Jays

- ☐ Esplanade Level 100A
- ■ Esplanade Level 100B
- ☐ Skyclub Level 200
- ☐ Lower Skyboxes Level 300
- ☐ Upper Skyboxes Level 400
- ☐ Skydeck Level 500A
- ■ Skydeck Level 500B
- ■ Skydeck Level 500C

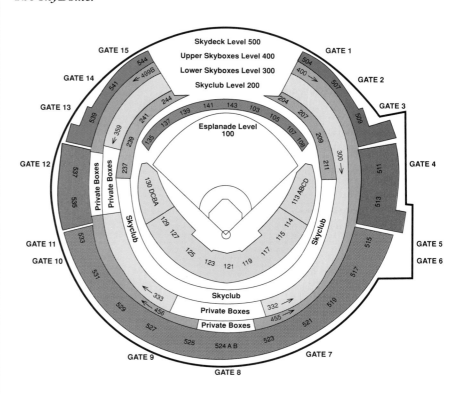

Purchasing Tickets

By mail:
Toronto Blue Jays
300 Bremner Blvd., Suite 3200
Toronto, Ontario M5V 3B3
Include in your request the date of the game you want
to see, the number of tickets you want and the price.
For ticket information, phone 416/341-1111.

In person:
Ticket Office near Gate 9
SkyDome
Ticket office hours: Daily 9 a.m. - 6 p.m. and until
9 p.m. when night games are played. Tickets may also
be purchased downtown at the Commerce Court
Shopping Center, King and Bay streets, Monday -
Friday 9 a.m. - 6 p.m.

By phone:
416/341-1234

Directions to the Stadium

Because the SkyDome is located in a congested area
of downtown Toronto, it is advisable to take public
transportation or walk from a nearby hotel rather than
drive to the stadium.

Public Transportation

For TTC (Toronto Transit Commission) subway, street-
car, and bus information, call 416/393-4636. To reach
the SkyDome by subway, take the Yonge-University-
Spadina line to Union Station at Front and Bay streets
in downtown Toronto. A skywalk connects the station
with the SkyDome. The Yonge-University line connects with the Bloor-Danforth line at both the St.
George and Yonge stations.

Buses and streetcars require a ticket, token, or exact
change. Drivers carry no change and issue no tickets.
Tickets and tokens are available at subway stations
from TTC guides or from a network of more than 1,300
authorized agents throughout the city.

GO (Government of Ontario) commuter trains operate
from the eastern and western borders of the metro
area along the lake shore to Union Station in downtown Toronto at Front and Bay streets, which is a
short walk from the SkyDome. The trains run seven
days a week until midnight. For information, call
416/665-0022.

Parking

The SkyDome has no general parking available, and
parking in the immediate vicinity is limited to about
5,000 spaces within a 20-minute walk to the stadium.
Parking is prohibited on most major downtown streets
during peak hours (7 a.m. - 9 a.m. and 3:30 p.m. - 6:30
p.m.). The city has a strict tow-away policy for illegally
parked cars. If you must drive, your best bet is to look
for event-parking signs north of Front Street or south
of Lake Shore Boulevard.

The SkyDome makes available 50 underground parking
spots on a first-come, first-served basis during home
games. Parking reservations should be made well in
advance by calling 416/341-3004.

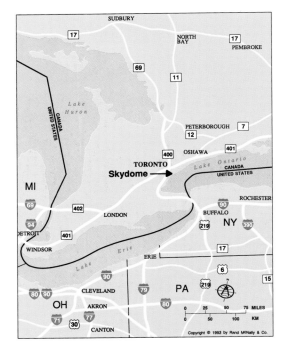

Profile

Team Address
Toronto Blue Jays
SkyDome
300 Bremner Blvd., Suite 3200
Toronto, Ontario M5V 3B3
416/341-1000

Franchise History
Toronto Blue Jays 1977-

World Series Title
1992 vs. Atlanta Braves

American League Pennant
1992

East Division Titles
1985, 1989, 1991, 1992

Award Winners
Most Valuable Player
George Bell, 1987

Rookie of the Year
Alfredo Griffin, 1979

Toronto

The SkyDome is right near the center of downtown. Hotels and restaurants listed are convenient to the stadium and offer a variety of styles and prices.

Sports Spots

Canada's Sports Hall of Fame
Located in the center of Exhibition Place, Lake Shore Boulevard and Bathurst Street
416/595-1046
Three large exhibit halls featuring Canada's greatest athletes and all major sports.

Hard Rock Cafe—SkyDome
300 Bremner Blvd.
416/341-2388
Specializes in rock 'n' roll memorabilia and casual American fare ($-$$)

Hockey Hall of Fame
Exhibition Place, Lake Shore Boulevard and Bathurst Street (before June '93)
Front and Yonge streets (after June '93)
416/595-1345
History and study of hockey.

Klancy's Charters
1001 Bay St., Suite 718
416/866-8489
Sportfishing charter boat.

Lionhead Golf and Country Club
8525 Mississauga Road, Brampton
416/455-4900
Public 27-hole championship course.

Skyfront Bar and Grill
151 Front St. W.
416/367-5790
Sports bar/restaurant ($)

A waterfront cafe in scenic Toronto.

Wild Water Kingdom
On Finch Avenue one mile west of Highway 427 in Brampton
416/794-0468
20,000-square-foot wave pool, slides, hot tubs. Batting cages and miniature golf are nearby.

Whistling Oyster
11 Duncan St.
416/598-7707
Informal seafood restaurant located downstairs of the Filet of Sole ($$)

Sports Spots &
Restaurants (Dinner for two
without beverage or tip in
$Canadian):
$ Under $20
$$ $20-$40
$$$ More than $40

Shops and services abound in Eaton Centre.

Accommodations

Four Seasons Hotel Toronto
21 Avenue Road
416/964-0411 ($$$)

Holiday Inn on King
370 King St. W.
416/599-4000, 800/HOLIDAY ($$)

L'Hotel
225 Front St. W.
416/597-1400, 800/828-7447
(U.S.), 800/268-9411 (Canada)
($$$)

Radisson Hotel Plaza
249 Queens Quay West
416/364-5444, 800/333-3333 ($$)

Royal York Hotel
100 Front St. W.
416/368-2511, 800/828-7447
(U.S.), 800/268-9411 (Canada)
($$$)

SkyDome Hotel
45 Peter St. S.
416/360-7100 ($$$)

Westin Harbour Castle
1 Harbour Square
416/869-1600, 800/228-3000 ($$$)

Price ranges: Double room
during the week (lower rates
are often available on
weekends). Prices are in
$Canadian.
$ Under $75
$$ $75-$125
$$$ More than $125

Ontario Parliament buildings: the seat of legislative power.

Attractions

CN Tower
301 Front St. W.
416/360-8500
Tallest free-standing structure in the world.

Casa Loma
1 Austin Terrace
416/923-1171
Medieval-style castle complete with towers, tunnels, and secret staircases.

The Eaton Centre Shopping Galleria
220 Yonge St.
416/598-8700
This enclosed mall is one of the world's largest shopping centers with more than 340 shops and services.

Harbourfront Centre
235 Queens Quay West
416/973-3000
Shopping, dining, arts and crafts, performing arts, marine events.

Metro Toronto Zoo
Meadowvale Road, Highway 401 in Scarborough, Ontario
416/392-5900
This 710-acre park is home for more than 4,000 animals.

Ontario Parliament Buildings
Legislative Building, half block north of College Street and University Avenue
416/325-7500
Free tours of legislative chambers, historical displays.

Ontario Place
955 Lake Shore Blvd. W.
416/314-9900
Entertainment complex located on three man-made islands in Lake Ontario.

Ontario Science Centre
770 Don Mills Road
416/696-3127
Demonstrations, films, hands-on exhibits.

Royal Ontario Museum
100 Queen's Park Crescent
416/586-5549
Museum of fine and decorative art, archeology, and natural history.

For More Information

Metro Toronto Convention
& Visitors Association
Queens Quay Terminal,
Harbourfront
P.O. Box 126
207 Queens Quay West
Toronto, Ontario, Canada M5J1A7
416/368-9821, 800/363-1990

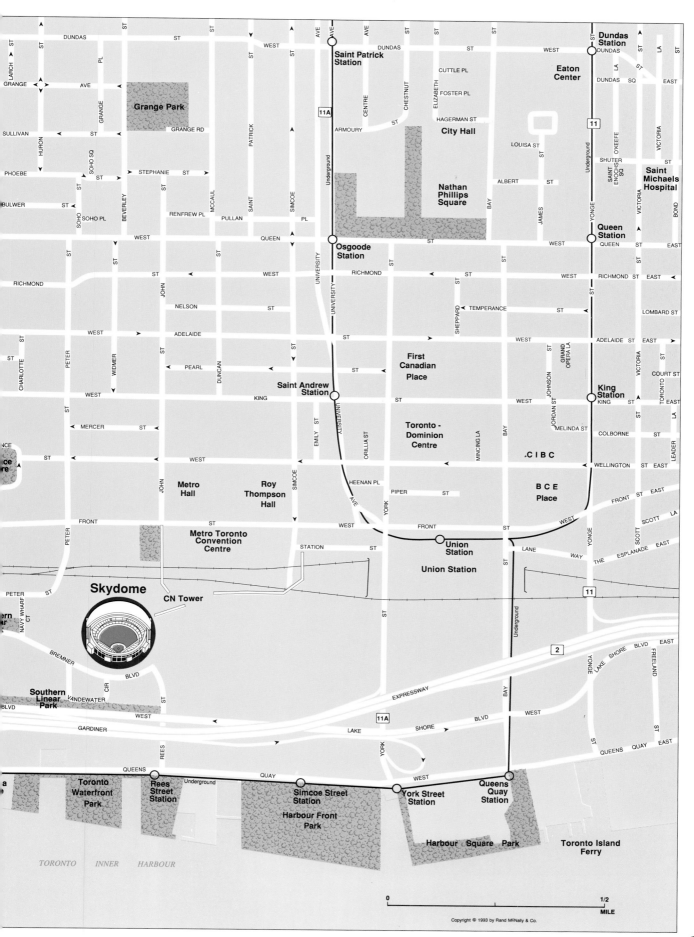

LARCH ST
DUNDAS ST
GRANGE
GRANGE PL
AVE
GRANGE RD
Grange Park
SULLIVAN
HURON
SOHO SQ
STEPHANIE ST
PHOEBE
BEVERLEY
SOHO PL
BULWER ST
RENFREW PL
MCCAUL
PULLAN
PATRICK
SAINT
SIMCOE
PL
WEST
QUEEN ST
RICHMOND
JOHN
ST
NELSON
ST
ADELAIDE
CHARLOTTE
PETER
WIDMER
DUNCAN
PEARL
WEST
ST
ST
MERCER
ST
WEST

DUNDAS ST
WEST
Saint Patrick
Station
11A
ARMOURY
Osgoode
Station
University
Underground

CUTTLE PL
Eaton
Center
ELIZABETH
FOSTER PL
HAGERMAN ST
City Hall
Nathan
Phillips
Square

Dundas
Station
DUNDAS
WEST
DUNDAS
LA
ST
EAST
DUNDAS
SQ
LOUISA ST
ALBERT
ST
JAMES
ST
BAY
11
Underground
YONGE
SAINT
ENOCHS
SQ
SHUTER
Saint
Michaels
Hospital
VICTORIA
VICTORIA
BOND
Queen
Station
QUEEN
WEST
QUEEN
ST
EAST

RICHMOND
WEST
ST
RICHMOND ST
EAST
SHEPPARD
TEMPERANCE
ST
LOMBARD ST
WEST
ADELAIDE ST
EAST
First
Canadian
Place
GRAND
OPERA LA
VICTORIA
COURT ST
TORONTO
King
Station
KING
ST
KING
WEST
JORDAN ST
JOHNSON
MELINDA ST
LA
LEADER

Saint Andrew
Station
KING
EMILY ST
ORILLIA ST

Toronto -
Dominion
Centre
BAY
MINCING LA
.CIBC
COLBORNE
ST
WELLINGTON
ST
EAST

Metro
Hall
Roy
Thompson
Hall
SIMCOE
HEENAN PL
PIPER
ST
AVE
YORK
BCE
Place
FRONT
ST
EAST
SCOTT
LA
FRONT
ST
WEST
YONGE
THE
ESPLANADE
EAST
SCOTT
WAY

FRONT
ST
Metro Toronto
Convention
Centre
STATION
ST
WEST
Union
Station
Union Station
LANE
LANE
WAY
11

PETER
ST
Skydome
CN Tower
ST

NAVY WHARF CT
BREMNER
BLVD
CIR
VANDEWATER
Southern
Linear
Park
WEST
BLVD
GARDINER

EXPRESSWAY
11A
LAKE
Underground
2
BAY
WEST
SHORE
BLVD
YONGE
LAKE SHORE BLVD
EAST
FREELAND
QUEENS QUAY EAST
ST

REES
QUEENS
QUAY
Underground
QUAY
WEST
YORK
Toronto
Waterfront
Park
Rees Street
Station
Simcoe Street
Station
Harbour Front
Park
York Street
Station
Queens
Quay Station
Harbour Square Park
Toronto Island
Ferry

TORONTO   INNER   HARBOUR

0   1/2
MILE

Copyright © 1993 by Rand McNally & Co.

143

The History of Baseball

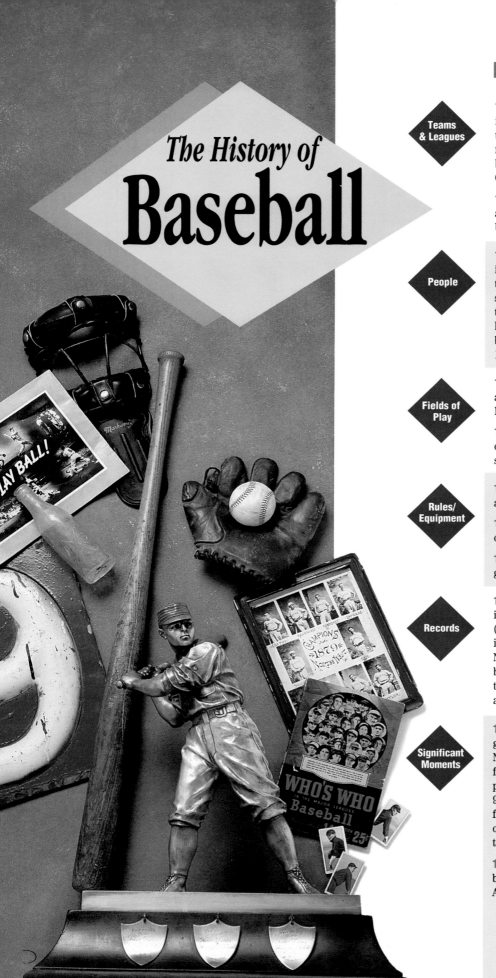

Teams & Leagues

1845 Alexander Cartwright introduces a game similar to today's baseball and forms the Knickerbocker Base Ball Club in New York.

Alexander Cartwright.

1854 Baseball expands in New York area as clubs like the Empires, Eckfords, Unions, and Atlantics spring up.

People

1839 As legend has it, Abner Doubleday introduces game of baseball in Cooperstown, New York. Marked a diamond-shaped field in the dirt and added bases to modify the game of "Town Ball." One hundred years later, Major League Baseball honors Doubleday by celebrating 1939 as its centennial year.

Fields of Play

1845 Cartwright's team plays rivals at a vacant spot of land in Manhattan near Madison Avenue and 27th Street.

1858 First admission is charged to an organized baseball game—an all-star series between New York and Brooklyn.

Rules/Equipment

1849 First baseball uniform style is adopted by the New York Knickerbockers.

1850s Bats are handcrafted from sticks or other wooden objects.

1857 New rule specifies nine innings to a game and nine players to a team.

Records

1854 First extra-inning game (16 innings) is played in New York; between the Knicks and the Gothams.

Line-up card.

Significant Moments

1846 First officially recorded baseball game is played under Cartwright's rules in New York. Under these rules: the team to first reach 21 runs wins the game; teams play on a diamond bounded by four bases 90 feet apart; fair and foul areas are defined; the concepts of pitcher's balk, tag-outs, and force-outs are outlined; and there are three outs to a side.

1856 The *New York Clipper* calls baseball the "national game amongst Americans."

1865 4,000 people attend a "Championship of the U.S." in Hoboken, New Jersey, where the Brooklyn Atlantics defeat the New York Mutuals.

1869 Harry Wright, "Father of Professional Baseball," organizes, manages, and plays centerfield for Cincinnati Red Stockings, baseball's first all-pro team.

The Reds of 1869.

1862 Premier baseballer of the era Jim Creighton of the Excelsiors of Brooklyn dies of internal injuries suffered, as reported at the time, by the strain of hitting a home run.

1867 William "Candy" Cummings, a National Association pitcher, introduces the curve ball, saying he discovered the pitch tossing clamshells in the water. In 1872, Cummings goes 34-19.

"Candy" Cummings.

1862 Union Grounds, Brooklyn, New York, opens. First enclosed baseball field.

1864 Capitoline Grounds, Brooklyn, New York, opens.

1860 Called strikes introduced.

1861 East Coast baseball groups set specifications for balls and bats.

1867 Pitchers restricted to a box 6-feet by 6-feet; hence the origin of the phrase, "hit one back through the box."

1860 First shut-out recorded.

1861-1865 New Yorkers who fight in Civil War spread the game of baseball throughout the country.

1869 First all-pro team, Cincinnati Red Stockings, completes its season undefeated at 57-0; start of trend toward professionalism in baseball.

1871 National Association of Professional Base Ball Players, the first major league, is formed including the Philadelphia Athletics, Troy (NY) Haymakers, Washington Olympics, New York Mutuals, Boston Red Stockings, Rockford Forest Cities, Cleveland Forest Cities, Chicago White Stockings, and Ft. Wayne (Iowa) Kekiongas. Entry fee is $10; James Kerns is elected president. The league survives five years.

1872-1875 Boston Red Stockings are baseball's first dynasty, winning the NA pennant from 1872 through 1875. Players included Al Spalding, Harry Wright, Cal McVey, Harry Shaer, Ross Barnes, Dave Birdsall, Fred Cone, and Charlie Gould.

1876 Chicago manager Al Spalding hurls the new league's first shut-out. In the next outing, he hurls another shut-out. Spalding, with a great fast-ball and change-up, earlier starred for Boston, compiling a 207-56 record in five years.

1870 Chicago White Stockings are first team to train in the spring.

1871 South End Grounds, Boston, opens.

1876 Sportsman's Park, St. Louis, opens May 5. Seating capacity for 30,500.

1870s Base stealing becomes a more important offensive strategy.

1870s Baseball uniforms include knickers with knee socks and short-brimmed pillbox hats.

1872 Minimum number of games comprising a season is raised to 50.

1875 Charlie Waitt uses a street-dress leather glove on his fielding hand.

1871 First batting champion is Long Levi Meyerle, who hit .492 for the NA Philadelphia Athletics.

1876 George Bradley pitches first no-hit game, leading St. Louis to a 2-0 win over Hartford July 15.

1871 Term "pennant" is used by NA to refer to championship.

1871 Charlie Gould hits a "home run with the bases full" against Chicago; home runs were a rarity, grand slams were even rarer.

1876 First doubleheader played; games are played in the morning and afternoon.

1876 National League is born. The eight-team league includes franchises in Chicago, Hartford, Louisville, Cincinnati, St. Louis, Boston, New York (Mutuals), and Philadelphia. Hartford, the Mutuals, and Louisville survive one year, although Louisville does field another team from 1892-99. The Philadelphia franchise doesn't last the season. Morgan G. Bulkeley named league president. Chicago White Stockings win first championship with a 52-14 record.

1877 William A. Hulbert named NL president; holds post through 1882 season.

William A. Hulbert.

1878 John Montgomery Ward makes his NL debut on July 15 pitching for Providence. The 18-year-old rookie goes on to pitch every inning of every league game for Providence for the rest of the season.

1875 Catcher's masks and chest protectors appear. This allows catchers to remain closer to home plate and reduce the number of unearned runs.

1877 "Fair-foul" hit rule is changed; prior to then, any ball that bounced first in fair territory was fair, no matter where it went afterward.

1878 New rules include: pitcher's box narrowed to 4 feet wide; fines are established for pitchers who hit batsmen; batting order rules make it mandatory for the first batter in a new inning to follow last batter from previous inning; nine balls required for a walk (old rule had every third bad pitch called a ball and three called balls constituted a walk).

1878 Paul Hines is the first player to win triple crown, hitting just four home runs, driving in 50 runs, and averaging .358.

1879 Boston's Charlie Jones hits an amazing nine home runs on the season—high mark for the decade. Cincinnati pitcher Will White pitches 75 complete games (680 innings) in season, a ML record.

Mike "King" Kelly

Teams & Leagues

1881 Detroit joins the NL until 1888, then drops out of the majors until 1901 when it becomes a charter member of the American League.

1882 American Association formed.

1883 A.G. Mills named NL president; holds post through 1884 season.

1883 The Philadelphia Phillies franchise rejoins the NL, playing its first game May 1 before 1,000 people at Recreation Park. The name Phillies is the oldest team name in the league.

1883 Forerunner of New York Giants, the New York Gothams, joins the NL.

1885 Nicholas Young named NL president. Holds post through 1902 season.

People

1880s Buck Ewing is the best catcher of the decade; hits .300 in six of seven seasons with the Giants—10 seasons overall. Career .455 slugger and great defensive player— threw baserunners out from a crouch.

1881 Cap Anson hits .399 with 82 RBI for Chicago White Stockings of NL. He batted under .300 only twice in his 22-year career. First player to total 3,000 hits. As player-manager, Anson led the White Stockings to 15 first-division finishes. Called "the symbol of all that was strong and good in baseball."

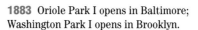

Cap Anson.

1882 Original "Louisville Slugger," after whom bat was named, Pete Browning joins A.A. Louisville team. Through 1889, he is top power hitter in league.

1886 King Kelly hits .388 for the White Stockings, then is sold to Boston. Believed to be one of first players idolized so much he was asked for his autograph. The subject of a popular song, "Slide, Kelly, Slide," he often rode to the park in a carriage drawn by white horses. One of the first to perfect the hit-and-run, he also was one of the first catchers to give signals by hand to the pitcher.

Fields of Play

1883 Oriole Park I opens in Baltimore; Washington Park I opens in Brooklyn.

1887 Philadelphia Phillies move into a "magnificent park" at Broad and Huntington Streets, later named Baker Bowl. Some 20,000 jam into the park for the first game, April 30.

Rules/ Equipment

1880s Number of balls required for a walk reduced throughout decade from nine in 1880 to four in 1889.

1881 Pitchers are allowed to throw sidearm rather than underhand.

1881 Four strikes required for a strike-out.

1882 Three strikes reinstated for a strike-out.

1884 Pitchers are allowed to throw overhand.

Records

1884 Charles Radbourn strikes out 411 batters in 679 innings over 72 games for Providence of the NL.

1886 Matthew Kilroy whiffs 505 batters in 570 innings over 65 games for Baltimore.

Significant Moments

1880 Concessionaire Harry M. Stevens introduces hot dogs, peanuts, and soda pop to the game.

1886 First baseball trading cards issued.

1887 Stolen base stats officially tallied for first time.

1889 Two million fans attend baseball games in the United States.

1885 The Chicago White Stockings post an 87-25 record and win fourth pennant in five years. Pitcher John Clarkson is 53-16 with a 1.85 ERA; Jim McCormick wins 20 games, but Stockings' star is King Kelly. The mustachioed outfielder hits .228, driving in 74 runs and scoring a league-leading 124.

1887 Forerunner of Pittsburgh Pirates, the Innocents, joins the NL.

1889 Brooklyn transfers to NL from American Association.

1888 Timothy Keefe, one of the first great changeup pitchers, wins 19 straight games. The right-hander would eventually win 344 games in 14 seasons. On July 4, 1883, he threw a one-hitter in the first game of a double header, and a two-hitter in the second to win both.

Timothy Keefe.

1888 South End Grounds II opens in Boston.

1888 Washington Senators are first team to train in Florida in the spring.

1887 Batters are no longer allowed to call for a "high" ball or "low" ball pitch; modern strike zone introduced.

1888 A. G. Spalding founds his sporting goods company.

Period ad.

1887 Roger Connor hits 17 home runs to lead league. Connor would total 132 home runs in his career, tops in baseball until Babe Ruth started swinging.

1891 American Association folds at end of season.

1897 Honus Wagner breaks into the majors batting .344. One of baseball's greatest all-around players, the Pittsburgh shortstop batted .300 in 17 consecutive seasons, winning the NL batting title eight times. Nicknamed the "Flying Dutchman."

Honus Wagner.

1891 League Park opens in Cleveland; home to the Indians until 1947.

1893 Distance from pitcher's mound to home plate increased to current length of 60 feet, 6 inches. Pitching rubber introduced to eliminate pitchers' practice of running up or stepping up to deliver pitches. Jeremiah Denny, last of the barehanded players, retires.

1894 Foul bunt ruled a strike.

1895 Rules limit glove weight to 10 ounces and size to 14 inches in circumference except for catcher's mitts and first baseman's gloves. Foul tips held by the catcher are ruled a strike.

1899 Home plate becomes pentagon-shaped.

1891 Billy Hamilton steals 115 bases. His 937 career thefts stands as ML mark until Lou Brock betters it almost 80 years later.

1892 Pitcher Kid Nichols goes 35-19 and finishes with seven straight seasons of 30 wins, a feat never matched.

1893 Amos Rusie starts 52 games, finishing all but two.

1894 Hugh Duffy bats .438 for Boston, still the major league record for the highest average in a 100-game season.

Hugh Duffy.

1892 Bumpus Jones throws the first major league no-hitter on Oct. 15, leading Cincinnati to a 7-1 win over Pittsburgh in his only appearance of the season for the Reds.

1895 Cy Young wins 35 games.

Cy Young

1897 Cap Anson collects his 3,000th career hit, the first to reach the magical figure.

1898 Thomas Edison produces a movie, "The Ball Game."

Nap Lajoie

Teams & Leagues

1901 American League is formed, led by Byron Bancroft "Ban" Johnson and Charles Comiskey. Initial teams: Boston, Milwaukee (moves to St. Louis in 1902), Chicago, Cleveland, Detroit, Baltimore (moves to New York in 1903), Philadelphia (moves to Kansas City in 1955), and Washington (moves to Minnesota in 1961).

1905 New York Giants, led by Christy Mathewson, win World Series for manager and motivator John McGraw. The Giants finish 105-48.

Christy Mathewson.

People

1901 Cy Young throws first perfect game in modern major league history. The right-hander is a 20-game winner 16 times, and wins 30 games five times. Baseball's most prestigious pitching award is named for him. Rookie Christy Mathewson wins 20 games for the New York Giants. In 17 seasons, "Matty" wins 373 games, a NL record. Famous for his fadeaway, or screwball, pitch. Connie Mack takes over as manager of Philadelphia Athletics, beginning 50-year stretch at the helm. Wins four pennants in five years (1910-1914) and three in a row (1929-31).

1902 Left-handed pitcher Rube Waddell joins Athletics; leads AL in strikeouts six straight years.

1905 Bill Klem's first year behind the plate. The umpire, known as "The Old Arbitrator," is assigned to 18 WS. Originated arm signals to coincide with his calls. Famous for saying, "It ain't nothin' 'til I call it."

1906 Eddie Collins signs with Athletics. The second baseman plays 25 major league seasons, a 20th century record equaled by pitcher Jim Kaat in 1983. Umpire Billy Evans, credited for bringing diplomacy to the game, begins his 21-year career.

Umpire Billy Evans

Fields of Play

1900 Organized baseball first played at Bennett Park in Detroit, site of current Tiger Stadium. Name of ballpark changed to Navin Field in 1912, to Briggs Stadium in 1938, and to Tiger Stadium in 1961.

1903 Twelve people are killed and 232 injured when the leftfield bleachers at Baker Bowl in Philadelphia collapse. Fans had climbed to the top row to get a better view of a nearby fire, and the weight was too much.

Rules/ Equipment

1900s Gloves get larger, improving defense. Teams adopt style of home (white) and road (gray) uniforms.

Early equipment made defense tough.

1901 Foul balls are counted as strikes in NL (in 1903 in AL); batting averages and ERAs tumble.

Records

1900 At age 30, Kid Nichols becomes the youngest pitcher to achieve 300 wins.

1901 Cy Young is first AL pitcher to win triple crown: 33 wins, 158 strikeouts, and 1.62 ERA.

1904 Rube Waddell strikes out 349 batters in the season. Spitballer Jack Chesbro starts 51 games, completes 48, and wins 41.

Significant Moments

1901 Nap Lajoie wins triple crown in AL's first year.

1903 First World Series won by AL Boston Pilgrims vs. Pittsburgh.

1904 Cubs win 116 games in regular season but lose WS to Chicago White Sox in first Series with two teams from same city.

Tinker-to-Evers-to-Chance, the Cubs' famous double-play combination.

1907 The Chicago Cubs manager/first baseman Frank Chance leads the team to the pennant. Tinker-to-Evers-to-Chance double-play combo shines. Beat Detroit and Ty Cobb 4-0 in the World Series.

1907 Walter Johnson strikes out 68 in 14 games in his first season. The first hit he gives up is to Ty Cobb. "Big Train" would total 3,508 whiffs with his sweeping sidearm delivery. His 110 shutouts are a ML record. He posts 416 career wins.

Walter Johnson.

1909 Shibe Park, Philadelphia, opens. Forbes Field, Pittsburgh, opens. Cleveland's League Park and St. Louis' Sportsman's Park renovated in steel and concrete.

1907 Shin-guards introduced by New York catcher Roger Bresnahan. It takes a few more years for guards to become easily detachable.

1906 Mordecai "Three Finger" Brown leads baseball with a 1.04 ERA. Nickname derived from accident when he lost parts of two fingers in a farm accident.

1908 "Take Me Out to the Ballgame" introduced and becomes a hit for singing sensation Billy Murray.

TAKE ME OUT TO THE BALL GAME

1913 New York Highlanders re-named Yankees; move to Polo Grounds, home of the New York Giants.

1910 Andrew "Rube" Foster joins with son-in-law of Charles Comiskey to form the Chicago American Giants, recognized as the leading black team of the decade. "The Father of Black Baseball," Foster is a standout pitcher in his playing days.

1911 Ty Cobb hits .420. The "Georgia Peach" finishes with 4,191 hits, a lifetime .367 average, and 12 batting titles.

Ty Cobb.

1913 Ray Schalk catches 129 games in first of 12 seasons with Chicago White Sox. Leads the league in fielding at his position for eight years.

1910 Comiskey Park opens in Chicago on the South Side at 35th and Shields.

1911 National Park opens in Washington, D.C.

1912 Fenway Park opens in Boston. The story of the ballpark's first game is pushed off the front page by the sinking of the *Titanic*. Crosley Field opens in Cincinnati, Ohio.

Boston's Fenway Park on Opening Day.

1911 Baseballs convert from rubber centers to livelier, cushioned cork centers.

1911 Grover Alexander strikes out 277 batters and wins 28 games in his rookie season. Total victories his freshman year still stand as a ML record. Cy Young wins 511th career game, Sept. 22.

1912 Cleveland's Joe Jackson steals home twice in one game. Eddie Collins steals six bases in a single game, September 11. Eleven days later, Collins does it again. Rube Marquard, New York Giants pitcher, wins 19 consecutive games.

1910 First official MVP awarded to top hitter, Nap Lajoie of Cleveland.

1914 The "Miracle" Boston Braves climb from last place in July to win 43 of last 57 games and take the pennant by 10-1/2 games over the New York Giants.

1914 George Herman "Babe" Ruth makes ML debut as a Boston Red Sox pitcher. He is 19 years old.

1915 First full ML season for Babe Ruth. As a left-handed pitcher, wins 18 games, loses eight. Hits .315 with four homers. Ty Cobb, Tris Speaker, and Walter Johnson—the superstars of their era—earn nearly $20,000 each.

1916 Boston Red Sox Tris Speaker, the "Grey Eagle," bats .386 to lead league. Positions himself in shallow centerfield, resulting in more assists than any other outfielder. Revolutionizes outfield play.

1919 New York Yankees pay $125,000 for Babe Ruth and convert him to outfield to take advantage of his power.

1916 Wrigley Field opens in Chicago on the North Side at Clark and Addison Streets. Site of the first permanent concession stand.

1915 Pinstripes first appear on Yankee uniforms.

1915 Ty Cobb steals 96 bases.

1916 Tris Speaker wins batting title with .386 average. Grover Alexander throws 16 shutouts, a ML single-season record. Also holds ML mark for most shutouts by a right-handed pitcher (90). Establishes NL record for lowest ERA (2.56) at 300 or more wins.

1912 Cubs' Tinker-to-Evers-to-Chance double-play combination plays last game together.

1919 Black Sox scandal.

Lou Gehrig

Teams & Leagues

1927 The New York Yankees, led by awesome "Murderers Row" of Ruth, Gehrig, Lazzeri, Combs, and Meusel, never give up first place entire season. Manager Miller Huggins cruises to pennant with 110 wins and a sweep of Pittsburgh in WS.

1929 Connie Mack, in 29th season as manager of the Philadelphia Athletics, unseats the Yankees in the AL. Jimmie Foxx and Al Simmons provide the punch with 33 and 34 homers, respectively.

People

1920 Judge Kenesaw Mountain Landis elected first baseball commissioner; dies in office Nov. 25, 1944. Credited with restoring credibility in game after Black Sox scandal of 1919. Rogers Hornsby, the "Rajah," wins first of six straight batting titles with .370 average. In 1922, he becomes baseball's first .400-40 man, batting .401 with 42 homers.

1922 Philadelphia's Eddie Rommel, "father of modern knuckleball," wins 19 games as starter, 8 in relief for club with only 65 season victories. At the age of 19, James "Cool Papa" Bell begins his baseball career with the St. Louis Stars of the Negro League.

1925 Bill McKechnie guides Pittsburgh to first of four pennants he will win as manager, and first of two WS. Only NL manager to win pennants with three different teams: Pittsburgh (1925), St. Louis (1928), and Cincinnati (1939-40).

1928 Burleigh Grimes wins 25 games for Pittsburgh. Last of the legal spitballers.

1929 Mel Ott hits 42 homers and leads league with 113 RBI.

James "Cool Papa" Bell of the Negro Leagues.

Fields of Play

1923 Yankee Stadium, the "House That Ruth Built," opens; Babe Ruth hits the first home run.

Rules/Equipment

1920s Larger, better-padded gloves introduced, improving defense. Revolutionary Bill Doak glove introduced by Rawlings. Bats become thicker-barreled with thinner handles to generate more speed and power.

1920 Spitball, emery ball, shine ball, and other "trick" deliveries are outlawed. Also, league officials stipulate use of only clean baseballs, which eliminates scuffed, softened, "deadened" balls.

1921 Dead-ball era ends when new "lively" ball is introduced. In 1919, before lively ball, Ruth hits just 29 homers; but in 1920, he hits 54; in 1921, 59.

1929 Yankees uniforms appear with numbers; first team to do so on a permanent basis. Players' numbers were based on position in batting order; hence, Ruth is #3, Gehrig #4.

Records

1920 George Sisler collects 257 hits, a major league record. Sisler bats over .400 twice, and has a 41-game hitting streak in 1922.

1921 Babe Ruth hits 59 home runs, leading the Yankees with a .846 slugging average and 171 RBI.

George Herman "Babe" Ruth.

1922 George Sisler, St. Louis Browns, wins first Most Valuable Player award in AL.

1924 "Sunny Jim" Bottomley drives in 12 runs in a single game on two homers, a double, and three singles.

1925 Lou Gehrig begins "The Streak" June 1.

1927 Babe Ruth hits 60 home runs.

Significant Moments

1920 Cleveland Indians shortstop Ray Chapman is fatally beaned by New York Yankees pitcher Carl Mays. It is the only death in ML history from a playing-field accident. Clevelander Bill Wambsganss turns an unassisted triple play in the WS vs. Brooklyn.

1921 First baseball game is broadcast on radio; Aug. 21, between Pirates and Phillies.

1924 Earl McNeely's ground ball hits a pebble and bounces over Fred Lindstrom's head in the 12th inning of Game 7 of the Series, winning the championship for Washington.

1934 The "Gashouse Gang," led by Dizzy Dean, Frankie Frisch, Leo Durocher, and Pepper Martin, lead the St. Louis Cardinals to WS victory over Detroit Tigers.

1930 Joe Cronin wins MVP award, batting .346 with 125 RBI. A seven-time All-Star shortstop.

1931 Lefty Grove, one of the greatest southpaw pitchers in AL history, posts a 31-4 record for the Athletics.

1932 Dizzy Dean's first season. The fireballer averages 24 wins in his first five seasons, and leads the league in strikeouts four times.

Dizzy Dean.

1932 Municipal Stadium, Cleveland, opens. Indians play here through 1933 season; then return to old League Park until 1947.

1930s Caps feature a rounder crown and a larger brim; collars on uniform shirts disappear.

1930 The Cubs' Hack Wilson drives in a ML record 190 runs in 155 games. Hits .356 with 56 home runs.

1933 Carl Hubbell posts 46-inning scoreless streak. He wins 16 straight games in 1936.

Johnny Vander Meer of back-to-back no-hit fame.

1931 MVP award, determined by vote of Baseball Writers Association of America, inaugurated.

1932 "The Call"— where Babe Ruth appears to point to the spot in the Wrigley Field bleachers where he hits a home run on the next pitch.

1933 First All-Star Game; Babe Ruth hits first home run in All-Star history. Squads are managed by two legends: Connie Mack (AL) and John McGraw (NL). World Series is first broadcast on radio. Baseball trading cards are first packed with gum.

Jimmie Foxx.

1933 Jimmie Foxx wins second straight MVP award. Has back-to-back seasons of 58 and 48 homers, 169 and 163 RBIs, and .364 and .356 averages. "Double-x" wins the triple crown in '33.

1934 Female athlete Babe Didrickson pitches in spring training games for the Philadelphia Athletics and the St. Louis Cardinals. Lefty Gomez is 26-5 for Yankees, with 6 shutouts and 25 complete games.

1934 A four-alarm, four-hour blaze Jan. 5 virtually destroys construction underway to refurbish Fenway Park. The new Fenway still opens April 17.

1935 First night baseball game played at Crosley Field, Cincinnati.

1930 Rules state gloves must be made of leather.

1932 NL rules that numbers must be worn on uniforms.

1935 Babe Ruth finishes career with 714 home runs, still a ML record for a left-handed hitter.

1938 Johnny Vander Meer throws consecutive no-hitters for Cincinnati, beating Boston on June 11 and Brooklyn on June 15.

1934 In the All-Star Game, Carl Hubbell strikes out Babe Ruth, Lou Gehrig, Jimmie Foxx, Al Simmons, and Joe Cronin in succession.

1936 Ruth, Johnson, Wagner, Cobb, and Mathewson elected in first Hall of Fame balloting.

Lou Gehrig's farewell at Yankee Stadium with Joe McCarthy (right).

1939 Celebrated as baseball's centennial year.

1936 Luke Appling leads league with .388 average. Known as "Old Aches and Pains" because of imaginary ailments. Jocko Conlan's umpiring debut; known for trademark polka-dot ties.

1938 Hank Greenberg slugs 58 home runs for Detroit.

1939 Lou Gehrig retires when he is diagnosed with a degenerative disease, amyotrophic lateral sclerosis—now also called Lou Gehrig's Disease. Is elected to Hall of Fame the same year and dies two years later at age 37. His uniform number, 4, is the first ever retired in baseball.

1938 The Phillies move permanently to Shibe Park after 51 years at Baker Bowl. First electric scoreboard installed at Sportsman's Park in St. Louis.

1939 Rules outlaw use of netting on gloves, limit webbing to four inches from thumb to palm, and restrict size of first baseman's glove.

1939 The Streak ends; Lou Gehrig plays in 2,130th consecutive, and final game April 30.

Gabby Hartnett.

1938 Gabby Hartnett hits his famous "Homer in the Gloamin'," slugging a home run in the bottom of the ninth inning at Wrigley Field to give the Cubs a 6-5 win over Pittsburgh and the NL pennant.

1939 Lou Gehrig bids farewell to baseball July 4 in front of 61,808 fans at Yankee Stadium, calling himself "the luckiest man on the face of the earth." National Baseball Hall of Fame in Cooperstown, NY, opens. First ballgame telecast between Brooklyn Dodgers and Cincinnati Reds from Ebbetts Field, Aug. 26.

Larry Doby

Teams & Leagues

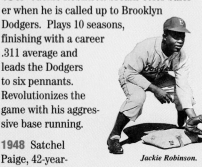

Ted Williams.

1942 St. Louis Cardinals win the NL pennant. Playing his first major league season, Stan Musial bats .315 and is part of NL's premier outfield with Enos Slaughter in right and Terry Moore in center.

People

1941 Ted Williams bats .406. The "Splendid Splinter" wins two triple crowns, two MVP awards, six AL batting championships, totals 521 home runs, a lifetime .344 average, and 18 All-Star Game appearances.

1943 Stan "The Man" Musial wins first of seven batting titles with a .357 average. Also garners first of three MVP awards. He once hits five home runs in a double header, although his most famous was a blast that won the 1955 All-Star Game in the 12th inning.

1944 Ray Dandridge bats .370 in the Negro National League. Dandridge is called the best third baseman to never play in the all-white major leagues.

Stan "The Man" Musial.

1947 Jackie Robinson breaks color barrier when he is called up to Brooklyn Dodgers. Plays 10 seasons, finishing with a career .311 average and leads the Dodgers to six pennants. Revolutionizes the game with his aggressive base running.

Jackie Robinson.

1948 Satchel Paige, 42-year-old legendary pitcher from the Negro Leagues, is signed to ML contract by Cleveland Indians.

1949 Casey Stengel wins first of seven world titles with New York Yankees. Guides the team to 10 pennants in a 12-year span. In his 25-year career, the "Ol' Perfesser" compiles a 1,905-1,842 record and .508 winning percentage.

Fields of Play

Rules/ Equipment

1943 Switch to balata ball because of rubber shortage; switched back before end of the season due to lack of resilience in ball.

1948 New three-finger Playmaker gloves introduced by Rawlings.

1941 Joe DiMaggio hits in 56 consecutive games (May 15 to July 16). Ted Williams bats .406, baseball's last .400 hitter.

1946 Bob Feller strikes out 348 batters.

1949 Bobby Shantz pitches nine no-hit innings in relief of Carl Scheib.

Dorothy Kamenshek of the All American Girls Professional Baseball League

Records

1940 Bob Feller throws a no-hitter on opening day. Lou Boudreau wins first Rookie of the Year award.

Significant Moments

1941 Mickey Owens' dropped third strike in Game 4 of WS opens the door for a Yankees comeback.

1943 First season for All American Girls Professional Baseball League.

1945 Hank Greenberg hits a ninth-inning grand slam on the final day of the season to lift Detroit Tigers to the pennant.

1946 Ted Williams homers off Rip Sewell's famed blooper pitch in All-Star Game.

1947 Start of regular televising of WS.

1948 Cleveland beats Boston in first AL playoff.

1949 First black All-Stars are Jackie Robinson, Roy Campanella, Don Newcombe, and Larry Doby.

Willie Mays.

1953 New York Yankees win fifth straight pennant and WS under manager Casey Stengel. Edge Brooklyn 4-2 in the WS.

1954 St. Louis Browns move to Baltimore and are renamed the Orioles; the first inter-city shift of an AL club in 52 seasons. Willie Mays, who serves 21 months in the Army, returns to the New York Giants to lead them to pennant. Giants beat Cleveland in the Series, 4-0, known for "The Catch" by Mays.

1955 Arnold Johnson buys Philadelphia Athletics, moves franchise to Kansas City.

1957 Brooklyn Dodgers' last season in New York. Owner Walter O'Malley moves the Dodgers west to Los Angeles for the '58 season, where they play in Memorial Coliseum, a converted football stadium. New York Giants' final year at Polo Grounds. Owner Horace Stoneham moves the team to San Francisco, playing at Seals Stadium, which has a capacity of less than half of the Polo Grounds. Yet the Giants draw 1.27 million in their first year (1958) on the West Coast, nearly double the gate of the previous season.

Yogi Berra.

1953 Yogi Berra drives in 108 runs, the first of four straight 100 RBI seasons as the Yankees catcher. Best known today for his Yogiisms, such as, "It ain't over 'til it's over."

1956 Mickey Mantle wins triple crown, hitting 52 homers, driving in 130 runs, and averaging .353. Overcomes numerous injuries and bad knees, belting 536 homers in 18 seasons in pinstripes.

1957 Roy Campanella's last season. An auto accident in '58 cuts short his career. Began playing in the Negro Leagues with the Baltimore Elite Giants as a teenager. Warren Spahn, winningest left-handed pitcher in baseball history, captures Cy Young Award. The southpaw totals 363 victories in 21 seasons. Holds NL career record for most innings pitched (5,246). Tosses two no-hitters. Spahn said: "Hitting is timing. Pitching is upsetting timing."

1958-59 Ernie Banks, "Mr. Cub," wins consecutive MVP honors, first to do so in the NL.

1959 Bill Veeck's Chicago White Sox win first pennant in 40 years.

Warren Spahn.

Ernie Banks, "Mr. Cub."

1953 Memorial Stadium, Baltimore, opens. County Stadium, Milwaukee, opens.

1959 Major League Baseball rules that any park built after 1959 must conform to minimum distances of 325 feet from home plate to right and leftfield fences.

Some exceptions apply, including Oriole Park at Camden Yards and the Kingdome.

1955 Batting helmets adopted in NL.

1956 Batting helmets adopted in AL.

1959 New six-finger fielder's glove introduced by Rawlings.

1952 Larry Doby becomes first black player to lead either league in homers, hitting 32 for Cleveland.

1953 Mickey Mantle hits a 565-foot home run at Griffith Stadium, April 17.

1954 Cleveland Indians win 111 games under manager Al Lopez.

1956 Don Larsen pitches perfect game Oct. 8 in Game 5 of the WS, leading New York Yankees to 2-0 victory over Brooklyn Dodgers. Don Newcombe of Brooklyn is first recipient of Cy Young Award.

1959 Pittsburgh Pirates pitcher Harvey Haddix throws 12 perfect innings against the Milwaukee Braves only to lose the game in the 13th on a Joe Adcock home run.

1950 Start of regular televising of All-Star Game. Dick Sisler's homer in the 10th inning of final game of season wins NL pennant for Philadelphia.

1951 "The shot heard 'round the world." Bobby Thomson hits a ninth-inning home run in Game 3 of the tie-breaker playoff series to lead the New York Giants to victory over the Brooklyn Dodgers.

1954 "The Catch"—Game 1 of the WS between the New York Giants and Cleveland Indians. Indian Vic Wertz drives a ball toward the centerfield bleachers. Willie Mays streaks after the ball. The ball disappears over Mays' shoulder, and into his glove. Mays wheels and throws back to the infield. The Indians lose that game and the next three.

1955 Brooklyn Dodgers, known as "The Boys of Summer," finally win pennant over archrival New York Giants, then defeat New York Yankees in WS after losing in seven other tries.

1957 Gold Glove award first awarded.

Teams & Leagues

1961 Washington club moves to Minnesota and is renamed the Minnesota Twins. New Washington Senators and Los Angeles Angels teams added to AL schedule in first modern-day expansion. The New York Yankees starring the "M & M Boys," Mickey Mantle and Roger Maris, win WS.

1962 New York Mets and Houston join the NL. Houston franchise known as Colt .45s until it moves into new Astrodome, when the team is renamed the Astros.

1965 Los Angeles Angels move to Anaheim; become California Angels.

1966 Milwaukee Braves move to Atlanta. Major League Baseball Players Association is formed.

1968 Athletics move to Oakland, CA.

Mickey Mantle

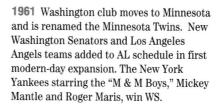

People

1961 Whitey Ford wins the Cy Young Award. The "Chairman of the Board," Ford leads the AL in victories three times, and ERA and shutouts twice. Billy Williams, sweet-swinging outfielder for Chicago Cubs, wins Rookie of the Year. He eventually plays in a NL-record 1,117 consecutive games.

1963 Brothers Matty, Felipe, and Jesus Alou play simultaneously in the same San Francisco outfield.

1964 Brooks Robinson wins MVP. Orioles third baseman leads the AL in fielding 10 times; wins 16 consecutive Gold Gloves.

1965 Satchel Paige makes his final appearance at age 59 pitching for the Kansas City A's.

1966 Frank Robinson wins AL triple crown and MVP. He also wins MVP in 1961 when with Cincinnati, becoming first player to win honor in both leagues. The first black to manage a big league team. Roberto Clemente wins NL MVP. Finishes with a .317 career average, 3,000 hits, 1,416 runs scored, and 1,305 RBI; leads NL in assists five times and wins 12 Gold Gloves.

Roberto Clemente.

The Alou Brothers: Jesus, Matty, and Felipe.

Fields of Play

1960 Candlestick Park, San Francisco, opens.

1961 Metropolitan Stadium in suburban Bloomington hosts first Minnesota Twins game. The Twins lead the league in total attendance for the first 10 years there with an overall draw of 13,264,656. Last game played in Griffith Stadium.

1962 Dodger Stadium, Los Angeles, opens.

1964 Shea Stadium, New York, opens.

1965 Astrodome, Houston, opens.

Rules/ Equipment

1960 Baltimore manager Paul Richards devises catcher's mitt nearly 50 inches in circumference to handle Hoyt Wilhelm's knuckleball. Shortly after the mitt appears, rules amended to set a 38-inch circumference standard.

1969 Adoption of "save" statistic to measure effectiveness of relief pitchers.

Records

1961 Roger Maris hits record 61 home runs.

1962 Maury Wills steals 104 bases.

1965 Sandy Koufax strikes out 382 in 336 innings over 43 games for the Los Angeles Dodgers. The southpaw still holds the post-1900 NL single-season strikeout record.

1968 Don Drysdale pitches 58-consecutive scoreless innings, throwing six straight shutouts. Tiger Denny McLain wins 31 games, earning him the AL MVP and Cy Young awards.

Significant Moments

1960 Bill Mazeroski's home run wins the 1960 WS.

1966 Sandy Koufax wins fifth straight ERA title.

1969 Both leagues expand to 12 teams, split into divisions, and play first League Championship Series. Montreal Expos and San Diego Padres join the NL. Seattle Pilots and Kansas City Royals join the AL. The "amazing" New York Mets, who had never finished higher than ninth, win first NL pennant.

Johnny Bench.

1967 Carl Yastrzemski wins triple crown in the Red Sox's "impossible dream" season. Hits 44 home runs (after just 16 the year before), bats .326, and drives in 121 runs.

1968 Bob Gibson wins NL MVP, posting the lowest ERA in league history at 1.12. The powerful Gibson also wins two Cy Young Awards in his career.

1966 Anaheim Stadium, Anaheim, opens. Fulton County Stadium, Atlanta, opens. Busch Stadium, St. Louis, opens; Sportsman's Park closes.

1968 San Diego Jack Murphy Stadium opens; Padres begin play here in 1969. Oakland-Alameda County Coliseum, Oakland, opens.

1969 Bobby Bonds becomes only the fourth player to hit 30 home runs and steal 30 bases, a feat he repeats four more times.

1969 Curt Flood challenges baseball's reserve clause, refusing to be traded from St. Louis to Philadelphia after the '69 season. Saying he did not want to feel like a piece of property, Flood rejects a $100,000 contract. The case goes all the way to the U.S. Supreme Court, where his plea is rejected, 5-3. But baseball's owners agree to an arbitration system, ending the reserve clause. Flood sits out 1970 and returns for a brief stay with Washington in 1971 before retiring.

1970 First season in Milwaukee for transplanted Seattle Pilots—now Brewers—franchise. Pilots last only one season in Seattle. Baltimore Orioles win 108 games and the WS with a 4-1 win over Cincinnati. Pitching is their hallmark as Mike Cuellar, Dave McNally, and Jim Palmer total 54 complete games.

1972 Washington Senators move to Texas, become the Rangers. First players' strike cancels first 10 days of the season.

1970 Johnny Bench wins MVP by hitting 45 home runs and driving in 148 runs. Betters Berra's career mark of home runs by a catcher (325 to 313).

1972 Roberto Clemente dies in a plane crash on a flight carrying supplies to earthquake victims in Nicaragua. Is elected to Hall of Fame the next year.

1970 Riverfront Stadium, Cincinnati, opens. Three Rivers Stadium, Pittsburgh, opens.

1971 Veterans Stadium, Philadelphia, opens.

1972 Arlington Stadium, Arlington, opens to Major League Texas Rangers.

1972 Rules committee drafts 13-point system for measuring a glove.

1973 AL adopts designated-hitter rule.

1970 Mets pitcher Tom Seaver strikes out a record 10 batters in a row and 19 in one game.

1972 Phillie Steve Carlton wins the Cy Young Award, the only pitcher to do so from a last-place team. The lefthander also wins triple crown that year with 27 wins, 1.97 ERA, and 310 strike outs. Wins 329 career games, second only to Warren Spahn among southpaws.

1973 Nolan Ryan strikes out 383 batters in 41 games for California, an AL record. "Save" statistic for relief pitchers is changed to tighten requirements.

1975 Baseball's reserve clause is struck down, opening the way for free agency. Carlton Fisk hits memorable 12th-inning home run in Game 6 of the WS.

1974 Flamboyant owner Charles O. Finley and his Oakland A's win third straight WS. Roster includes Reggie Jackson, Bert Campaneris, Joe Rudi, Sal Bando, Catfish Hunter, Rollie Fingers, John "Blue Moon" Odom, and Vida Blue.

1975 The "Big Red Machine," the Cincinnati Reds, win 108 games under Sparky Anderson. All-Star lineup includes George Foster, Pete Rose, Dave Concepcion, Johnny Bench, and Joe Morgan. Beat Boston 4-3 to win WS.

1977 Toronto Blue Jays and Seattle Mariners added to AL.

1974 Ten years after starting his big league career, Catfish Hunter wins the Cy Young Award. Hunter is 25-12 with a league-leading 2.49 ERA.

1977 Rod Carew wins MVP with .388. Finishes with seven batting titles.

1979 Willie Stargell, the only man to hit a ball out of Dodger Stadium, named MVP for the season, the playoffs, and the WS. Father of "We Are Family" Pirates in '79, he awards "Stargell stars" to players.

1973 Royals Stadium, Kansas City, opens.

1974-75 Yankee Stadium restoration. Team shares Shea Stadium with Mets for two seasons.

1977 Olympic Stadium, Montreal, opens. The Kingdome, Seattle, opens.

1979 Construction begins on Metrodome in downtown Minneapolis.

1974 Change in baseball cover from horsehide to cowhide.

"Hammerin' Hank" – Hank Aaron.

1974 Henry Aaron ties Babe Ruth's career home run mark in his first at-bat, and hits #715 a few days later on April 8. Lou Brock steals 118 bases. Mike Marshall pitches in 106 games.

1976 Henry Aaron finishes career with 755 home runs.

1977 Yankee rightfielder Reggie Jackson hits five home runs in WS against Dodgers.

Teams & Leagues

1990 Spring training opens late because of player-management disagreements, postponing regular season by one week.

1993 Colorado Rockies and Florida Marlins join NL.

People

1990 Ken Griffey Sr. and Jr. are the first father and son to play as teammates. George Brett wins the batting title, his third in three decades.

1991 Ferguson Jenkins is first Canadian elected to Hall of Fame.

Ferguson Jenkins.

1992 Seattle Mariner Bret Boone becomes the first third-generation Major League player, following his dad, Bob, and grandfather, Ray.

1992 Cecil Fielder of the Detroit Tigers wins the AL runs-batted-in crown for the third straight year.

Fields of Play

1982 The Metrodome, Minneapolis, opens.

1988 First night game at Wrigley Field, Chicago, on Aug. 9. Last major league ballpark to install lights.

1989 SkyDome, Toronto, opens.

1991 New Comiskey Park, Chicago, opens.

1992 Oriole Park at Camden Yards, Baltimore, opens.

Rules/ Equipment

George Brett

Records

1980 George Brett bats .390 to win second of three batting titles, and comes within one point of John McGraw's 1899 record for highest average by a third baseman. Brett also wins the batting title in 1976 (.333) and 1990 (.329).

1982 Rickey Henderson steals 130 bases.

1983 Steve Garvey's consecutive game stretch (NL) ends at 1,207 games.

1985 Pete Rose collects his 4,192nd career hit to surpass Ty Cobb. Dwight Gooden claims first pitchers' triple crown in 13 years, going 24-4 with a 1.53 ERA and 268 strikeouts.

1986 Boston's Roger Clemens strikes out 20 on April 29 against Seattle. Dave Righetti saves 46 games.

1988 Dodger Orel Hershiser pitches 59 consecutive scoreless innings, beginning the sixth inning on Aug. 30 to the 10th inning on Sept. 28.

Orel Hershiser.

1990 Pitchers throw a total of nine no-hitters. Nolan Ryan's 12th career one-hitter ties him with Bob Feller. Cub second baseman Ryne Sandberg sets ML record for errorless games at second base at 123 and 584 chances. Cal Ripken Jr. sets record at 95 errorless games at shortstop. Chicago White Sox reliever Bobby Thigpen saves 57 games.

1991 At the age of 44, Nolan Ryan throws a record seventh no-hitter. On the same day, Oakland's Rickey Henderson breaks Lou Brock's stolen-base record with his 939th career theft. Henderson then goes on to break Maury Wills' record by stealing 130 bases in one season.

Nolan Ryan.

1992 Bip Roberts of the Cincinnati Reds gets 10 straight hits, tying a 95-year old NL record.

Significant Moments

1983 Fred Lynn hits first All-Star Game grand slam.

1988 Injured Dodger Kirk Gibson comes off the bench to pinch hit a game-winning ninth-inning homer to win Game 1 in the series against Oakland.

1990 Dave Stewart and Fernando Valenzuela toss no-hitters on the same day.

1992 Second baseman Mickey Morandini of the Phillies makes an unassisted triple play, the ninth in Major League history.

1992 Robin Yount and George Brett become the 17th and 18th players to record 3,000 career hits.

No matter where you travel across the United States, you will encounter reminders of America's favorite pastime.

From small memorabilia halls honoring local heroes to the National Baseball Hall of Fame in Cooperstown, New York, America is filled with homage to the game, the teams, and the players.

From Alabama to Alaska, from Maine to Mississippi, from Ohio to Oregon, discover and celebrate baseball as you travel.

The following is a sampling of things to do, places to see, and teams to watch. Although the information offered here was accurate at presstime, please check locally to verify information, hours, and admission policies.

About minor league teams: If the team's Major League affiliation is part of the team name (e.g., Dodgers), no affiliation is indicated. However, if affiliation is not part of the team name (e.g., Arkansas Travelers), the Major League team affiliation is indicated in parentheses: (St. Louis Cardinals).

Affiliations of minor league teams with Major League teams change frequently. If you wish to see a farm club of a particular Major League team, double check to make sure team affiliation has not changed before you order tickets.

Baseball & Travel

Attractions & Minor League Clubs

Alabama

Anniston
Sports Wearhouse
Anniston Shopping Plaza
3122 McClellan Blvd.
205/237-7678
MLB-licensed team apparel.

Birmingham
Alabama Sports Hall of Fame Museum
1 Civic Center Plaza
205/323-6665
Few states have produced as many stars as Alabama, and the home-state heroes are all represented here: Willie Mays, Hank Aaron, Billy Williams, Willie McCovey, and more.

Birmingham Barons, Southern League-AA (Chicago White Sox)
Hoover Metropolitan Stadium
I-65 near U.S. 31
205/988-3200
This 10,000-seat park was built in 1988, complete with 12 skyboxes.

Boaz
Sports Wearhouse
Boaz Outlet Mall
100 Elizabeth St.
205/593-5990
Outlet store offers MLB-licensed team apparel.

ASHOF

Alabama Sports Hall of Fame & Museum, Birmingham, Alabama.

Huntsville
Huntsville Stars, Southern League-AA (Oakland A's)
Joe W. Davis Stadium
3125 Leeman/Ferry Rd.
205/882-2562
The road outside the outfield fence is nicknamed "Jose Parkway" for Jose Canseco, who slugged many minor league homers into it.

Alaska

Fairbanks
Gold Panners Baseball
Fairbanks Park
907/451-0095
The Gold Panners play the ultimate night game—without lights. The game starts at midnight on June 21—the summer solstice. The midnight sun does all the illuminating.

Arizona

Chandler
Brewers & Cardinals, Arizona State League-Rookie
Chandler Sports Complex
4500 S. Alma School Rd.
602/895-1412

Padres, Arizona State League-Rookie
Compadre Stadium
1425 W. Ocotillo Rd.
602/895-1200

Mesa
Angels, Arizona State League-Rookie
Gene Autry Park
4125 E. McKellips east of Mesa Drive
602/830-4137

Cubs & Rockies, Arizona State League-Rookie
Fitch Park
655 N. Center St.
602/844-2391

Randy Hundley's Official Big League Baseball Camp
Mailing Address:
675 North Court, Suite 160
Palatine, IL 60067
708/991-9595

Fantasy camps in Arizona feature Cubs, Cardinals, and Angels; sessions are usually held in January and April.

Phoenix
Phoenix Firebirds, Pacific Coast League-AAA (San Francisco Giants)
Scottsdale Stadium
7402 E. Osborn Rd.
602/275-0500 (information);
602/678-2222 (tickets)
The $7-million, 10,000-seat facility opened in 1991.

Scottsdale
Athletics Arizona State League-Rookie
Scottsdale Community College
9000 E. Chaparral at Pima
602/949-5951

Tempe
Mariners, Arizona State League-Rookie
Diablo Stadium
2200 W. Alameda near 48th Street
602/350-5205
Diablo Stadium was closed during the 1992 season; check locally for information on the Mariners 1993 season.

Tucson
Tucson Toros, Pacific Coast League-AAA (Houston Astros)
Hi Corbett Field
3400 E. Camino Campestre at Randolph Park
602/325-2621
The park is also scheduled to host the Colorado Rockies' first spring training season in 1993.

Arkansas

Little Rock
Arkansas Travelers, Texas League-AA (St. Louis Cardinals)
Ray Winder Field
Fair Park Boulevard north of I-630 at War Memorial Park
501/664-1555
Ray Winder is one of the oldest ballparks in the country, built in the early 1930s.

California

Adelanto
High Desert Mavericks, California League-A (San Diego Padres)
Maverick Stadium
12,000 Stadium Way off U.S. 395 in the Mojave Desert
619/246-6287

Bakersfield
Bakersfield Dodgers, California League-A
Sam Lynn Ballpark
4009 Chester Ave. east of U.S. 99
805/322-1363

Escondido
San Diego Padres Clubhouse Shop
North County Fair Mall
200 E. Via Rancho Pkwy.
619/745-9656
Licensed memorabilia store.

Glendale
Forest Lawn Cemetery
Burial site of Casey Stengel.

Hayward
Oakland A's Clubhouse Shop
Southland Mall
510/732-5995
Licensed memorabilia store.

Hollywood
UCLA Film and TV Archives/Research Center
1015 N. Cahuenga Blvd.
310/206-8013
Tapes of radio broadcasts; movies; a Sports Dynasty collection; baseball clips from the Hearst News Reel Collection.

Los Angeles
Rosedale Cemetery
Burial site of Frank Chance.

Ziffren Sports Library
2141 W. Adams Blvd.
213/730-9600
Books, videos, and photographs covering sports from 1932 to the present. Memorabilia includes trophies, Olympic medals, and uniforms from various sporting events.

Modesto
Modesto A's, California League-A
John Thurman Field
501 Neece Drive west of U.S. 99
209/529-7368

Palm Springs
Palm Springs Angels, California League-A
Angels Stadium
Sunrise Way at Baristo Road
619/325-4487

Richmond
Oakland A's Clubhouse Shop
Hilltop Mall
2248 Hilltop Mall Road
510/758-1229
Official Major League Baseball licensed memorabilia store.

Scottsdale Stadium, home of the Phoenix Firebirds.

San Diego Hall of Champions Sports Museum, San Diego, California.

Salinas Spurs, California League-A (Independent)
Salinas Municipal Stadium
175 Maryal Drive at Laurel Street
East Exit off U.S. 101
408/422-3812

San Bernardino
San Bernardino Spirit, California League-A (Seattle Mariners)
Fiscalini Field
1007 E. Highland east of I-215
714/881-1836

San Diego
The San Diego Hall of Champions and Sports Museum
1649 El Prado, Balboa Park
619/234-2544
Exhibits include "History of Baseball in San Diego" and a computer display that lists statistics for every Major League Padres player.

San Jose
San Jose Giants, California League-A
San Jose Municipal Stadium
588 E. Alma, near Tully west of U.S. 101
408/297-1435

Stockton
Stockton Ports, California League-A (Milwaukee Brewers)
Billy Hebert Field
Sutter and Alpine between I-5 and U.S. 99
209/944-5943

Visalia
Visalia Oaks, California League-A (Minnesota Twins)
Recreation Park
440 N. Giddings, one mile north of California Hwy. 198
209/625-0480

Colorado

Colorado Springs
Colorado Springs Sky Sox, Pacific Coast League-AAA (Cleveland Indians)
Sky Sox Stadium
4385 Tutt near Barnes on the northeast side of town
719/597-1449
At 6,800 feet above sea level, this is the country's highest ball park.

Denver
Denver Zephyrs, American Association-AAA (Milwaukee Brewers)
303/433-2032

Connecticut

Hartford
Cedar Hill Cemetery
Burial site of Morgan Buckeley.

New Britain
New Britain Red Sox, Eastern League-AA
Beehive Field, in the Willowbrook Park Complex off Connecticut Hwy. 72, east of I-84
203/224-8383

New Haven
First Pick Starters
Outlet Store
370 James St.
203/776-2571
MLB-licensed merchandise.

Delaware

Newark
University Archives
U. of Delaware
78 E. Delaware Ave.
302/831-2750
The archives offer a collection of photographs of former University baseball teams.

District of Columbia

Library of Congress
101 Independence Ave., S.E.
202/707-5000
Baseball-related photographs, newspapers, recordings, and periodicals.

National B'nai B'rith Headquarters
1640 Rhode Island Ave. N.W.
202/857-6583
Houses Jewish Sports Hall of Fame. Has photos, exhibits, memorabilia, and information.

National Museum of American History
Smithsonian Institution
14th Street and Constitution Avenue
202/357-2700
The museum features displays on Major Leagues, Little Leagues, Negro Leagues, and the All-American Girls Professional Baseball League.

Florida

Bradenton
Pirates, Gulf Coast League-Rookie
Pirate City
27th Street east of U.S. 301
813/747-3031

Clearwater
Clearwater Phillies, Florida State League-A
Jack Russell Stadium
800 Phillies Drive
813/441-8638

Daytona Beach
Cedar Hill Cemetery
Burial site of Nap Lajoie.

Dunedin
Dunedin Blue Jays, Florida State League-A;
Gulf Coast League-Rookie
Grant Field
Douglas Avenue near Main Street
813/733-9302

Haines City
Baseball City Royals, Florida State League-A;
Gulf Coast League-Rookie
Baseball City Stadium
I-4 at U.S. 27
813/424-2424

Ft. Lauderdale
Ft. Lauderdale Yankees, Florida State League-A
Ft. Lauderdale Yankee Stadium
5301 Yankee Blvd.
305/776-1921

Fort Myers
Miracle Professional Baseball Club, Florida State League-A;
Gulf Coast League-Rookie (Independent)
Lee County Sports Complex
Daniels Road east of U.S. 41
813/768-4210

Fort Myers Twins, Gulf Coast League-Rookie
Lee County Sports Complex
14200 Six Mile Cypress Parkway
813/768-4289

Homosassa Springs
Stage Stand Cemetery
Burial site of Dazzy Vance.

Colorado Springs Sky Sox, Colorado Springs, Colorado.

Texas/Charlotte Rangers, Port Charlotte, Florida.

Jacksonville
Jacksonville Suns, Southern League-AA (Seattle Mariners)
Wolfson Park, near Gator Bowl off I-10
904/358-2846
Wolfson is a bandbox park built in 1955 in a town that's had pro ball since 1904.

Kissimmee
Osceola Astros, Florida State League-A;
Gulf Coast League-Rookie
Osceola Stadium
1000 Bill Beck Blvd. near U.S. 192
407/933-5500

Lakeland
Lakeland Tigers, Florida State League-A
Joker Marchant Stadium
Lakeland Hills Boulevard, Exit 19 off I-4
813/682-1401 (for tickets)

Miami
Flagler Memorial Park
Burial site of Hall of Famer Jimmie Foxx.

Graceland Memorial Park
Burial site of Hall of Fame umpire Bill Klem.

Oneco
Manasota Cemetery
Burial site of Paul Waner and Bill McKechnie.

Orlando
Greenwood Cemetery
Burial site of Hall of Famer Joe Tinker.

Orlando SunRays, Southern League-AA (Minnesota Twins)
Tinker Field
287 Tampa Ave. South
407/872-7593

Port Charlotte
Charlotte Rangers, Florida State League-A;
Gulf Coast League-Rookie
Charlotte County Stadium
2300 El Jobean Rd., west of U.S. 41 on Florida Hwy. 776
813/625-9500

Port St. Lucie
St. Lucie Mets, Florida State League-A (New York Mets);
Gulf Coast League-Rookie (Los Angeles Dodgers)
Thomas J. White Stadium
525 N.W. Peacock Blvd. east of I-95
407/871-2100; 407/871-2114 (for tickets)

St. Petersburg
St. Petersburg Cardinals, Florida State League-A
Al Lang Stadium
180 Second Ave. at Bayshore Drive
813/822-3384

Sarasota
Memorial Cemetery
Burial site of Heinie Manush.

Randy Hundley's Official Big League Baseball Camp
Mailing Address:
675 North Court, Suite 160
Palatine, IL 60067
708/991-9595
Held at Ed Smith Stadium.

Sarasota White Sox, Florida State League-A;
Gulf Coast League-Rookie
Ed Smith Stadium
1090 N. Euclid at 12th Street
813/954-7699

Tampa
Tampa Yankees, Gulf Coast League-Rookie
Yankees Complex
3102 Himes
813/875-7753

Vero Beach
Los Angeles Dodgers Adult Baseball Camp
Mailing Address:
P.O. Box 2887
800/334-7529
Fantasy camps, in February and November.

Vero Beach Dodgers, Florida State League-A
Holman Stadium
4001 26th St. east of 43rd Avenue
407/569-4900

West Palm Beach
West Palm Beach Expos, Florida State League-A;
Gulf Coast League-Rookie
Municipal Stadium
715 Hank Aaron Drive east of I-95 at the Palm Beach Lakes exit
407/684-6801

Winter Haven
Winter Haven Red Sox, Florida State League-A;
Gulf Coast League-Rookie
Chain O'Lakes Park
813/293-3900

Georgia

Albany
Albany Polecats, South Atlantic League-A (Montreal Expos)
1130 Ball Park Lane
912/435-6444

Atlanta
Georgia Sports Hall of Fame
1455 Tullie Circle, Suite 317
404/875-8509
Two hundred home-state heroes—baseball and otherwise—are honored here.

Augusta
Augusta Pirates, South Atlantic League-A
Heaton Stadium
78 Milledge Rd., east of I-20 off Broad Street
706/736-7889

Columbus
Columbus Redstixx South Atlantic League-A (Cleveland Indians)
Golden Park
100 4th St. (U.S. 27)
706/571-8866
A "Wall of Fame" details notables who have played here since 1909, including Ruth, Aaron, Banks, and Mays.

Macon
Macon Braves, South Atlantic League-A
Luther Williams Field
Central City Park
End of Riverside Drive
912/745-8943

Royston
Village Cemetery
Burial site of Ty Cobb.

Savannah
Savannah Cardinals, South Atlantic League-A
Grayson Stadium
1401 E. Victory Drive (U.S. 80), east of I-516
912/351-9150

Hawaii

Honolulu
Nuuanu Cemetery
Burial site of Alexander Cartwright.

William Hulbert Gravesite, Graceland Cemetery, Chicago, Illinois.

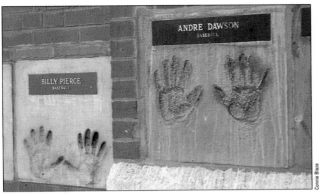

MC Mages Sports Wall of Fame, Chicago, Illinois

Idaho

Boise

Boise Hawks, Northwest League-A (California Angels)
Memorial Stadium
5600 N. Glenwood north of U.S.
20-26 in the Fairgrounds
208/322-5000

Idaho Falls

Idaho Falls Gems, Pioneer League-Rookie (Atlanta Braves)
McDermott Field
568 W. Elva east of I-15 and south of U.S. 20
208/522-8363

Illinois

Chicago

Calvary Cemetery
Burial site of Charles Comiskey.

Chicago Historical Society
1601 N. Clark St.
312/642-4600
The collection includes the 1873 personal papers and ledger books of Al Spalding and William Hulbert.

Graceland Cemetery
A large baseball marks the grave of National League founder William Hulbert.

Italian-American Sports Hall of Fame
2625 Clearbrook Dr. (Arlington Heights)
708/437-3077
Top ball players of Italian heritage.

MC Mages Sports Wall of Fame
620 N. LaSalle St.
312/337-6151
Cement handprints of local sports heroes appear on this wall.

Oakwood Cemetery
Burial site of Hall of Famer Cap Anson.

Randy Hundley's Official Big League Baseball Camp
Mailing Address:
675 North Court, Suite 160
Palatine, IL 60067
708/991-9595
A three-day fantasy camp is held at Wrigley Field.

Des Plaines

All Saints Cemetery
Burial site of Gabby Hartnett.

Geneva

Kane County Cougars Midwest League-A (Baltimore Orioles)
Elfstrom Stadium
34W002 Cherry Lane, six miles north of I-88 near Farnsworth Road
708/232-8811

Oak Brook

Chicago White Sox Clubhouse Shop
Oak Brook Center
708/990-0459
Licensed memorabilia store.

Peoria

Peoria Chiefs, Midwest League-A (Chicago Cubs)
Pete Vonachen Field
1524 W. Nebraska, west of I-74
309/688-1622

Rockford

Rockford Expos, Midwest League-A
Marinelli Field
101 15th Ave., north of U.S. 20 at Blackhawk Park
815/964-5400

Hillerich & Bradsby Company
Home of the Louisville Slugger

The first Louisville Slugger was born from the splinters of a bat used by a Major Leaguer in a slump.

In 1884 Pete "the Old Gladiator" Browning, star of the Louisville Eclipse, was battling a slump that only seemed to get worse after he broke his favorite bat. John Andrew "Bud" Hillerich happened to be watching the game that day. When it was over, Bud invited Browning to his father's woodworking shop. They chose a piece of white ash, and young Hillerich began fashioning the new bat according to Browning's direction. The two worked through the night, with Browning taking periodic practice swings until he pronounced the bat "just right."

The next day, Browning went three-for-three—pulling himself out of his slump. It was a fateful day for both men: Browning went on to a career batting average of .341. And the bat Bud Hillerich built—the ancestor of the Louisville Slugger— elevated the Hillerichs to eminence in the world of sporting goods. Today, Hillerich & Bradsby Company, makers of baseball gloves, hockey sticks, golf clubs, aluminum bats, and its crown-jewel, the Louisville Slugger, is the oldest and largest such business in the world.

The Plant Tour

Tour the plant where Louisville Sluggers and PowerBilt golf clubs are made. The free, one-hour tour begins in the Tour Center, which includes a small museum with photos, memorabilia, and legendary bats.

The Slugger Theater then welcomes fans to H&B with a 12-minute film presentation on the company's history.

Throughout the plant, visitors can see the machines that turn and brand the bats, and the areas where master craftsmen turn bats built to order for the Major League stars of today.

At the close of the tour, visitors receive 16-inch Louisville Sluggers to commemorate their trip to Slugger Park.

Hillerich & Bradsby Co., Jeffersonville, Indiana

Directions

Hillerich & Bradsby Co. is located at 1525 Charlestown-New Albany Road in Jeffersonville, Indiana.

From Louisville: Take I-65 north (follow signs toward Indianapolis) to Exit 4 (Clarksville-Cementville). At the bottom of the ramp, proceed through the first light. H&B is on the left just after the train tracks.

From Indianapolis: Take I-65 south, then take Exit 4. At the bottom of the ramp, turn left at the traffic light. Proceed to next light and turn right. H&B is on the left just after the train tracks.

From St. Louis: Take I-265 east to I-65 south and then follow directions from Indianapolis (above).

Call ahead for reservations: 502/585-5226, extension 201. Private tours for groups of 25 are more are scheduled in advance, subject to availability. Contact Tour Director: 502/585-5226, extension 201.

South Bend White Sox, South Bend, Indiana.

Springfield
Springfield Cardinals, Midwest League-A
Lanphier Park
1351 N. Grand Ave. E., north of Clear Lake Avenue
217/525-6570

Indiana

Fort Wayne
Fort Wayne Wizards, Midwest League-A
Memorial Stadium (April '93)
4000 Parnell Ave.
219/482-9502

Indianapolis
Indianapolis Indians, American Association-AAA (Montreal Expos)
Owen J. Bush Stadium
1501 W. 16th St., west of I-65
317/269-3545
Built in 1931, the 12,000-seat park has the league's closest centerfield (395 feet).

International Baseball Association
Pan American Plaza, Suite 490
201 S. Capitol Ave.
317/237-5757
Documents available pertain to international baseball federations and some statistics from international amateur games.

Logo 7 Inc. Factory
I-70 and Post Road
317/895-7000
Groups of 25 or more can tour the plant where licensed apparel is manufactured. By reservation only.

Logo 7 Inc. Outlet Store
8677 Logo 7 Court
Offers licensed apparel.

National Art Museum of Sports
Bank One Tower, Mezzanine
317/687-1715
Colorful collection of prints, sculpture, and lithographs.

Jeffersonville
Hillerich & Bradsby Company
1525 Charlestown-New Albany Pike, across the river from Louisville
800/282-BATS
Tour of plant and museum is available. (See article, this section.)

South Bend
South Bend White Sox, Midwest League-A
Stanley Coveleski Regional Stadium
501 W. South St., just west of U.S. Business Hwy. 31-33
219/284-9988

Sports Research Collection, Hesburgh Library
University of Notre Dame
219/239-6506
Archives include books, artifacts, and magazines, and a special Red Smith Collection.

Terre Haute
Roselawn Memorial Cemetery
Burial site of Mordecai "Three-Finger" Brown.

Iowa

Burlington
Burlington Astros, Midwest League-A
Community Field
2712 Mt. Pleasant
P.O. Box 824, near U.S. 61
319/754-5705

Cedar Rapids
Cedar Rapids Reds, Midwest League-A
Veterans Memorial Stadium
950 Rockford Rd. S.W., west of I-380
319/363-3887

Clinton
Clinton Giants, Midwest League-A
Riverview Stadium
6th Avenue North and 1st Street
319/242-0727

Davenport
Quad City River Bandits, Midwest League-A
John O'Donnell Stadium
209 S. Gaines, U.S. 61 at the Mississippi River
319/324-2032

Des Moines
Iowa Cubs, American Association-AAA
Taylor Stadium
350 S.W. First St., south of I-235
515/243-6111
Taylor underwent $11.5 million in renovations before the 1992 season. Located on the Des Moines River.

Dyersville
"Field of Dreams" Site
Lansing Road, 25 miles west of Dubuque
319/875-8404
The ball field carved from a cornfield for the movie has been kept as it was. Locals put on exhibition games.

Van Meter
Bob Feller Museum
Brenton Bank, downtown off I-80 west of Des Moines
515/996-2255
Uniforms, gloves, bats, trophies represent the career of the famed fireballer. Hours vary (banking hours). The museum's permanent home is under construction.

Waterloo
Waterloo Diamonds, Midwest League-A (San Diego Padres)
Municipal Stadium
850 Park Rd., off U.S. 57
319/233-8146

Kansas

Wichita
Wichita Wranglers, Texas League-AA (San Diego Padres)
Lawrence-DuMont Stadium
300 S. Sycamore, west of I-135

on Kellogg, then north at Sycamore exit
316/267-3372
The club spent $5.1 million to upgrade the park on the banks of the Arkansas River.

Winfield
St. Mary's Cemetery
Burial site of Fred Clarke.

Kentucky

Louisville
Louisville Redbirds, American Association-AAA (St. Louis Cardinals)
Cardinal Stadium
Freedom Way at Phillips Lane in the state fairgrounds, off I-264
502/367-9121

Richmond
City Cemetery
Burial site of Earle Combs.

Louisiana

New Orleans
Metairie Cemetery
Burial site of Mel Ott.

Shreveport
Shreveport Captains, Texas League-AA (San Francisco Giants)
Fair Grounds Field
2901 Pershing Blvd., in the fairgrounds off I-20 at Herne Avenue
318/636-5555
Air conditioned skyboxes are available on a per-game basis at this park, which opened in 1986.

Shreveport Captains, Shreveport, Louisiana.

Indian Island
Penobscot Indian Reservation
The New Cemetery
Gravesite of Louis Sockalexis. Sockalexis was one of the first Native Americans in organized baseball; Cleveland Indians were named in honor of him.

Maryland

Baltimore
Babe Ruth Birthplace and Baseball Center
216 Emory St.
301/727-1539
The museum features memorabilia of the Babe in the house where he was born, plus material on the Orioles. (See article this section.)

Hebrew Cemetery
Burial site of Rube Marquard, a Hall of Famer.

New Cathedral Cemetery
Burial site of Hall of Famers John McGraw, Joe Kelley, and Wilbert Robinson.

Chester
Sports Wearhouse
Kent Narrows Factory Stores
13 Piney Narrows Road
410/643-3975
Outlet store offers MLB-licensed apparel.

Frederick
Frederick Keys, Carolina League-A (Baltimore Orioles)
Harry Grove Stadium
6201 New Design Rd., near Market Street exit off I-70
301/662-0013

Frostburg
Memorial Cemetery
Burial site of Lefty Grove.

Hagerstown
Hagerstown Suns, Southern Atlantic League-A (Toronto Blue Jays)
Municipal Stadium
274 E. Memorial Blvd. near I-70 and U.S. 40 junction
A large outdoor grill on the main concourse offers great cube steak sandwiches and quarter-pound hot dogs. Top the latter with sauerkraut.

Rockville
Union Cemetery
Burial site of pitcher Walter Johnson.

Suitland
Ft. Lincoln Cemetery
Burial site of Clark Griffith.

Massachusetts

Boston
Boston Public Library
666 Boylston St.
617/536-5400
Offerings feature the McGreevey Baseball Collection, which includes rare photos and paintings from 1870 to 1914.

Burlington
Boston Red Sox Clubhouse Shop
Burlington Mall
Middlesex Road at Rt. 128
617/273-0883
Licensed memorabilia store.

Cambridge
City Cemetery
Burial site of Tim Keefe.

The Sports Museum of New England
Cambridgeside Galleria
100 Cambridgeside Place
617/621-0520
Artifacts, photos, paintings, and equipment showcase baseball and other New England sporting traditions. Look for the life-size wooden sculpture of Carl Yastrzemski.

Mattapan
Old Calvery Cemetery
Burial site of Hugh Duffy and Tom McCarthy.

Pittsfield
Pittsfield Mets, New York-Penn League-A
Wahconah Park
105 Wahconah at U.S. 7
413/499-6387

Springfield
St. Michael's Cemetery
Burial site of Rabbit Maranville.

Ware
Ware Cemetery
Burial site of "Candy" Cummings.

Babe Ruth Birthplace and Baseball Center
Home of One of Baseball's Biggest Legends

George Herman "Babe" Ruth.

From his heyday to today, millions of fans have idolized The Babe. The Babe Ruth Birthplace and Baseball Center in Baltimore, Maryland, addresses the facts and legends about Babe Ruth.

Founded in 1974 to preserve the birthplace of George Herman "Babe" Ruth, the museum is a major sports and cultural center. The site is also a national historic landmark, the only birthplace of an American athlete with such a designation. Babe Ruth is indeed an historic figure in American sports and popular culture.

Remembering The Babe
The museum's Birthplace Room is decorated with period pieces. An adjoining room displays photos dating from Ruth's childhood to his death in 1948. Many more exhibits honor Ruth, including a Slugger's Alcove, which displays 714 plaques, one for each of Ruth's career home runs. Also, the 500 Home Run Club exhibit displays artifacts and photos of the 14 players who have hit 500 home runs or more.

A Trip through Orioles' History
The Orioles Museum, housed here since 1983, focuses on three eras: 1882-1902, 1903-1953, and 1954-present.

The center also offers the Maryland Baseball Hall of Fame; a display of memorabilia from Orioles owner Jack Dunn; and changing displays of Maryland baseball memorabilia.

During 1993, the birthplace is scheduled to move into a new, larger facility, just two blocks from Oriole Park at Camden Yards.

Directions
The Babe Ruth Birthplace and Baseball Center is located at 216 Emory St. in Baltimore. Take I-95 to 395 to Martin Luther King Jr. Boulevard; take a right onto Pratt Street and then a right onto Emory Street. Call 301/727-1539 for more information.

National Baseball Hall of Fame and Museum
Cooperstown — Celebrating the Heroes of Our Youth

Cooperstown Room, National Baseball Hall of Fame, Cooperstown, New York.

The National Baseball Hall of Fame and Museum in Cooperstown, New York, spotlights the history, the people, and the events of baseball—America's national pastime. Here you'll see baseball evolve through an impressive assemblage of more than 1,000 artifacts and photographs chronicling the past 150 years.

First and foremost, the Hall of Fame honors the game's immortals: bronze plaques in the majestic Hall of Fame Gallery depict the more than 200 baseball greats who, by their talent and dedication to the game, enhanced the sport. Each year, the Baseball Writers Association and the Veterans Committee vote to choose the game's "immortals" and induct them into the Hall of Fame. Individuals must have played for at least 10 years and been retired for at least five years before they are considered for the honor. (Roberto Clemente was an exception. The year after he died in a plane crash while on a mission to deliver relief supplies to Managua, Nicaragua, he was voted into the Hall.)

Travel Through Time

Each room in The Hall of Fame uncovers another chapter in baseball's colorful history: the Cooperstown Room traces the origin of the game; the Records Room provides up-to-date statistics on baseball's many significant records and the players who hold those records; the World Series Room recreates magic Octobers with photographs, programs, tickets, and a collection of World Series rings.

Other attractions include continuous showings of Abbott and Costello's "Who's on First" routine; a memory-laden exhibition of baseball's golden moments—from Carl Hubbell's pitching tour-de-force in the 1934 All-Star Game to Fred Lynn's '83 All-Star grand-slam; a collection of historic baseball cards, including the rare Honus Wagner T-206 tobacco card; and tributes to the Negro leagues, the All-American Girls Professional Baseball League, and legendary ball players.

Directions

The National Baseball Hall of Fame and the National Baseball Library are on Main Street in Cooperstown.

From the west or north: Thruway Exit 30 at Herkimer, south on Route 28 to Cooperstown. Or from Exit 30, south on Route 28 to Route 20, east on 20 to Route 80, south to Cooperstown.

From the east or north: Thruway Exit 25A, I-88 to Duanesburg, west on Route 20 to Route 80, south on 80.

From the south: I-88 from Binghamton, Exit 17, Route 28 north to Cooperstown.

From the southeast: Thruway Exit 21 at Catskill, Route 23 west, Route 145 north, Route 20 west, Route 80 south to Cooperstown. Or, Thruway Exit 21, Route 23 west, I-88 east, Exit 17, Route 28 north to Cooperstown.

Pine Hills Trailways provides twice-daily round-trip bus service between Cooperstown and New York City's Port Authority Bus Terminal.

For more information, contact the Cooperstown Chamber of Commerce, 31 Chestnut St., P.O. Box 46, Cooperstown, NY 13326, 607/547-9983.

Origins of Baseball

Just as some of baseball's World Series titles have been hotly contested, so has the title of the founder of baseball. Questions about the game's origin began surfacing early in baseball's history.

In 1905, the Mills Commission set about to determine the origin of the game. During its three-year study, the commission was deluged with theories.

According to the testimony of Abner Graves, Cooperstown resident Abner Doubleday adapted the then-popular game of "town ball," limiting the number of players and adding bases, pitchers, catchers, and a diamond-shaped field. The committee favored this theory and, on Dec. 30, 1907, ruled that "the first scheme for playing baseball, according to the best evidence available to date, was devised by Abner Doubleday at Cooperstown, New York, in 1839."

Since then, Graves' credibility as a reliable witness has been questioned. Also, surprisingly, Doubleday's diaries made no mention of baseball. Thus emerged Alexander J. Cartwright, a surveyor and amateur athlete. Many baseball historians now believe that Cartwright envisioned the field and created the rules of the game we play today as baseball.

In 1846, Cartwright introduced a game similar to today's baseball and formed the Knickerbocker Base Ball Club. According to Cartwright's rules, the first team to reach 21 runs was declared the winner; the playing field was diamond-shaped with four bases 90 feet apart; three outs constituted half an inning; and foul areas, pitcher's balk, tag-outs, and force-outs were all defined.

Though some fans continue to debate the game's origin, one fact remains true. From its humble beginnings, some 150 years ago, baseball has grown into America's national pastime.

Women in Baseball Exhibit, National Baseball Hall of Fame, Cooperstown, New York.

Michigan

Birch Run
Sports Wearhouse
Manufacturer's Marketplace
12373 S. Beyer Road
517/624-5504
MLB-licensed apparel.

Detroit
Detroit Public Library
5201 Woodward Ave.
Detroit, MI 48202
313/833-1000
The Burton Historical and Ernie Harwell collections trace the history of the Detroit Tigers.

Monroe
Sports Wearhouse
Manufacturer's Marketplace
14750 LaPlaisance Road
313/457-2580
MLB-licensed apparel.

Minnesota

Minneapolis
Baseball Hall of Fame
406 Chicago Ave. South
612/375-9707
Exhibits include All-Star and World Series bats, autographed baseballs, and jerseys from earlier Twins uniforms.

Mississippi

Jackson
Dizzy Dean Museum
1202 Lakeland Drive
601/960-2404
Trophies, gloves, balls, and other artifacts of the pitcher's glory days with the Cardinals and Cubs are all on display.

Jackson Generals, Texas League-AA (Houston Astros)
Smith-Wills Stadium
1200 Lakeland Drive, east of I-55
601/981-4664
A $2.1 million renovation improved concessions and fan accommodations at the park.

Wiggins
Bond Cemetery
Burial site of Dizzy Dean.

Missouri

Kansas City
Forest Hill Cemetery
Burial site of Hall of Famers Satchel Paige and Zack Wheat.

Mt. Moriah Cemetery
Burial site of Kid Nichols.

Negro Leagues Baseball Museum
1601 E. 18th St.
816/221-1920
The museum pays homage to African-American ballplayers who never got the opportunity to play in the Major Leagues. Until the museum moves into its new 20,000-square-foot building at 18th and Vine in the Culture District in 1994, artifacts and memorabilia on display at location indicated.

Milan
Milan Cemetery
Burial site of Cal Hubbard.

St. Louis
Randy Hundley's Official Big League Baseball Camp
Mailing Address:
675 North Court, Suite 160
Palatine, IL 60067
708/991-9595
Three-day fantasy camps are held every summer at Busch Stadium.

St. Louis Cardinals Hall of Fame
Busch Memorial Stadium
314/421-3263
Displays honor St. Louis baseball greats: Stan Musial, Dizzy Dean, Rogers Hornsby, August A. Busch, Jr., Jack Buck, and others.

Montana

Billings
Billings Mustangs, Pioneer League-Rookie (Cincinnati Reds)
Cobb Field
27th Street at 9th Avenue, north of I-90
406/252-1241

Butte
Butte Copper Kings, Pioneer League-Rookie (Texas Rangers)
Alumni Coliseum
Montana Tech College
Montana Street north of I-90-15
406/723-8206.

Great Falls
Great Falls Dodgers, Pioneer League-Rookie
Legion Park
2600 River Drive North, east of U.S. 87
406/452-5311

Helena
Helena Brewers, Pioneer League-Rookie
Kindrick Legion Field
Memorial and Warren streets
406/449-7616

Nebraska

Omaha
Omaha Royals, American Association-AAA
Rosenblatt Stadium
1202 Burt Murphy Drive, south of I-80 and 13th Street
402/734-2550
Site of the College World Series since 1950.

St. Paul
Elmwood Cemetery
Burial site of Grover Alexander.

Nevada

Las Vegas
Las Vegas Club
Main and Fremont streets in downtown casino center
702/385-1664
The club boasts Dodger memorabilia, including a pair of Maury Wills' spikes.

Las Vegas Stars, Pacific Coast League-AAA (San Diego Padres)
Cashman Field
850 Las Vegas Blvd. N., one mile north of downtown casino center
702/386-7200

Reno
Reno Silver Sox, California League-A (Oakland Athletics)
Moana Municipal Stadium
240 W. Moana Lane, five blocks west of U.S. 395
702/825-0678

New Hampshire

Hanover
Baker Library
Dartmouth College
603/646-2560
Dartmouth baseball uniforms are on display; write to the Chief Archivist for an appointment to see collection.

New Jersey

Atlantic City
City Cemetery
Burial site of John Lloyd.

Menlo Park
New York Mets Clubhouse Shop
Menlo Park Mall
414 Menlo Park, Edison
908/548-1955
Licensed memorabilia store.

Princeton
University Archives
Princeton University
65 Olden St.
609/258-3213
Early photographs, scorecards, programs, and newspaper clippings of Princeton teams.

Salem
Baptist Cemetery
Burial site of Leon "Goose" Goslin.

New Mexico

Albuquerque
Albuquerque Dukes, Pacific Coast League-AAA (Los Angeles Dodgers)
Albuquerque Sports Stadium
1601 Stadium Blvd. S.E., east of I-25
505/243-1791
A beautiful setting with a drive-in, park-and-watch area beyond the outfield walls that can handle up to 300 cars.

Albuquerque Dukes, Albuquerque, New Mexico.

Albany
Albany-Colonie Yankees, Eastern League-AA (New York Yankees)
Heritage Park
Watervliet-Shaker Road north of I-87
518/869-9236

Auburn
Auburn Astros, New York-Penn League-A
Falcon Park
108 N. Division
315/255-2489

Batavia
Batavia Clippers, New York-Penn League-A (Philadelphia Phillies)
Dwyer Stadium
Denio and Banks streets
716/343-7531

Binghamton
Binghamton Mets, Eastern League-AA
Binghamton Municipal Stadium
P.O. Box 598
607/723-6387

Brooklyn
Brooklyn Historical Society
128 Pierrepont St.
718/624-0890
Dodger memorabilia include uniforms, Jackie Robinson mementos, and Ebbets Field bleachers.

Cypress Hills Cemetery
Burial site of Jackie Robinson.

Greenwood Cemetery
Burial site of Henry Chadwick.

Buffalo
Buffalo Bisons, American Association-AAA (Pittsburgh Pirates)
Pilot Field
Swan and Washington streets, north of I-190
716/846-2000

Holy Cross Cemetery
Burial site of Jimmy Collins.

Mt. Olivet Cemetery
Burial site of Joe McCarthy.

Trench Manufacturing Outlet Stores
2495 Main St./ 716/837-5894
1312 Main St./ 716/883-7868
Licensed apparel.

Durham Bulls, Durham, North Carolina.

Cooperstown
National Baseball Hall of Fame & Museum
P.O. Box 590, Main St.
607/547-9988
Mecca for baseball fans. (See article, this section.)

National Baseball Library
P.O. Box 590
Cooper Park
607/547-9988
(See article on National Baseball Hall of Fame, this section.)

Elmira
Elmira Pioneers, New York-Penn League-A (Boston Red Sox)
Dunn Field
Luce Street near Maple Avenue
607/734-1811

Geneva
Geneva Cubs, New York-Penn League-A
McDonough Park
Nursery Avenue near Lyceum Street
315/789-2827

Hawthorne
Gate of Heaven Cemetery
Burial site of Hall of Famer Babe Ruth.

Jamestown
Jamestown Expos, New York-Penn League-A
College Stadium
485 Falconer on the Jamestown Community College campus
716/665-4092

Lake George
Sports Wearhouse
Log Jam Outlet Center
Route 9
518/792-9154
MLB-licensed apparel.

Long Island City
New York Mets Clubhouse Shop
30-93 Steinway St.
718/204-0927
MLB-licensed memorabilia..

New York City
New York Mets Clubhouse Shop
575 Fifth Ave.
212/986-4887
MLB-licensed memorabilia..

New York Yankees Clubhouse Shops
110 E. 59th St.
212/758-7844
393 Fifth Ave.
212/685-4693
MLB-licensed memorabilia.

Niagara Falls
Niagara Falls Rapids, New York Penn League-A (Detroit Tigers)
Sal Maglie Stadium
1201 Hyde Park Blvd., off I-190
716/298-5400

Trench Manufacturing Outlet Stores
Niagara Factory Outlet Mall
Military Road at Niagara Falls Blvd./ 716/298-5998
Rainbow Center Mall
Rainbow Blvd. and Rt. 62
716/284-6601
MLB-licensed apparel.

Oneonta
Oneonta Yankees, New York-Penn League-A
Damaschke Field
Neahwa Park, just off I-88
607/432-6326

Queens
Calvary Cemetery
Burial site of Willie Keeler and Mickey Welch.

Rochester
Rochester Red Wings, International League-AAA (Baltimore Orioles)
Silver Stadium
500 Norton St., just south of New York Hwy. 104
716/467-3000
This older ballpark (1928) comes complete with triple-deck outfield billboards.

Syracuse
Syracuse Chiefs, International League-AAA (Toronto Blue Jays)
MacArthur Stadium, near the junction of I-81 and I-90
315/474-7833
The stadium is a pitcher's dream. Only seven players have hit a ball over the 434-foot centerfield fence.

Utica
Utica Blue Sox, New York-Penn League-A (Chicago White Sox)
Donovan Stadium
Genessee Street south of the New York State Thruway
315/738-0999

Valhalla

Kensico Cemetery
Burial site of Lou Gehrig and Ed Barrow.

Watertown

Watertown Indians, New York-Penn League-A
Duffy Fairgrounds
900 Coffeen St., off I-81
315/788-8747

Williamsville

Trench Manufacturing Outlet Store
Transitown Plaza
Transit Road and Main Street
716/626-1463
Major League and Buffalo Bisons apparel and memorabilia.

North Carolina

Asheville

Asheville Tourists, South Atlantic League-A (Houston Astros)
McCormick Field
Charlotte Street, just south of I-240
704/258-0428

Burlington

Burlington Indians, Appalachian League-Rookie
Burlington Athletic Stadium
Beaumont Street at Grahm
919/222-0223

Charlotte

Charlotte Knights, Southern League-AA (Chicago Cubs)
Knights Castle
2280 Deerfield Drive
Fort Mills, S.C., off I-77 south of the state line
803/548-8051

Durham

Durham Bulls, Carolina League-A (Atlanta Braves)
Durham Athletic Park
Washington Street (take Gregson Street off I-85 to Trinity and turn left to Washington, turns into Moris Street)
919/688-8211

Fayetteville

Fayetteville Generals, South Atlantic League-A (Detroit Tigers)
J.P. Riddle Stadium
2823 Legion Rd.
919/424-6500

Gastonia

Gastonia Rangers, South Atlantic League-A
Sims Legion Park
1001 N. Marietta, just south of I-85
704/867-3721

Greensboro

Greensboro Hornets, South Atlantic League-A (New York Yankees)
War Memorial Stadium
510 Yanceyville St. at Lindsay
919/275-1641

Kinston

Kinston Indians, Carolina League-A
Grainger Stadium
400 E. Grainger Ave.
919/527-9111

Salisbury

National Sportscasters and Sportswriters Hall of Fame
322 E. Innes St.
704/633-4275
Scheduled to open in 1993, the Hall will feature pressbox memorabilia spanning all sports.

Winston-Salem

Winston-Salem Spirits, Carolina League-A (Chicago Cubs)
Ernie Shore Field
401 W. 30th St.
919/759-2233

Zebulon

Carolina Mudcats, Southern League-AA (Pittsburgh Pirates)
Five County Stadium
U.S. 264 at North Carolina Hwy. 39
919/269-2287

North Dakota

Fargo

Roger Maris Museum
West Acres Shopping Mall
I-29 at 13th Avenue S.
A free-standing permanent exhibit in the mall honors the hometown hero who hit 61 in '61.

Ohio

Aurora

Sports Wearhouse
Aurora Farms Outlet Complex
549 S. Chillicothe
216/562-6802
MLB-licensed apparel.

Character, Courage, and Loyalty Live On at the Peter J. McGovern Little League Museum

In 1939, the same year the Baseball Hall of Fame opened in Cooperstown, New York, Little League Baseball was born as a three-team neighborhood activity in Williamsport, Pennsylvania. In just over 50 years, Little League has evolved from its original three teams to the world's largest organized youth sports program, with more than 2.6 million children, 180,000 teams, and 750,000 adult volunteers participating in 60 countries worldwide.

The Peter J. McGovern Little League Museum, named for the organization's first full-time president, combines exhibits, hands-on displays, photographs, memorabilia, batting and pitching facilities, and video footage in a "hall of delights" for everyone who has ever swung a bat or caught a ball.

The Theme Rooms

The museum is divided into several theme rooms.

In the Founders Room, for example, a time-line display exhibit escorts visitors through Little League history, from its early days in Williamsport to its national and international expansion.

Special film presentations on the history of Little League welcome visitors to the Diamond Theater, which hosts several showings throughout the day.

For many visitors, the pitching and batting cages in the Play Ball Room are the museum's star attractions. Players of all ages can test their slugging and pitching prowess and analyze their form in instant video replays.

Lamade Stadium

Adjacent to the Little League Baseball Museum is Lamade Stadium, site of the annual Little League World Series held each August. The stadium holds 12,000 fans, and the surrounding natural grass embankment makes room for 30,000 more.

Directions

The Peter J. McGovern Little League Baseball Museum and Lamade Stadium are located on U.S.15 in South Williamsport, Pennsylvania.

Take U.S.180/220 into Williamsport; exit at Route 15. Take Route 15 across the Susquehanna River into South Williamsport. Proceed 1-1/2 miles to the Little League complex.

Call ahead for museum hours and admission, World Series schedules, or camp information, 717/326-3607.

Little League Museum, Williamsport, Pennsylvania.

The All-Star FanFest
A New Chapter in Baseball History

The Upper Deck All-Star FanFest, a baseball "theme park" presented by Major League Baseball, takes to the Baltimore Convention Center from July 9-13, 1993. Fest-goers will feast on ballpark fare, meet a hero or two, and visit the baseball-related attractions that will trans-form the Center into an All-Star tribute to America's favorite pastime.

Pitching Booth at FanFest.

All-Star FanFest, now in its third year, was introduced at the 1991 All-Star Game in Toronto. The 1992 FanFest, held at the San Diego Convention Center, lured an estimated 85,000 fans, who enjoyed the more than 28 attractions. Among the more popular attractions:

- The largest Hall of Fame exhibit on loan outside of Cooperstown
- Free autographs from baseball legends
- Bat and glove-making demonstrations
- A baseball collectibles show and swap meet
- A simulated Major League clubhouse and dugout
- Radar pitching booths
- Interactive video batting cages where fans of all ages batted against images of pitching stars

Fans sampled the variety of foods served at Major League parks, like Philly cheese steak sandwiches made famous in Philadelphia, hot pretzels from New York, bratwurst from Milwaukee, and nachos from San Diego.

Similar attractions and more are planned for FanFest 1993. In addition, the Inner Harbor/downtown area will come alive with entertainment, decorations, food, and lots of great fireworks.

FanFest exhibits and attractions.

Blue Ash
Crosley Field
Blue Ash Sports Center
11540 Grooms Rd., west of I-71, northeast of Cincinnati
513/745-8586
The field is complete with the original scoreboard, same dimensions, terraced outfield, and some seats from the former home of the Reds.

Canton
Canton-Akron Indians, Eastern League-AA
Thurman Munson Memorial Stadium
I-77, south of U.S. 30/62
216/456-5100

Cincinnati
Mt. Washington Cemetery
Burial site of Buck Ewing.

Spring Grove Cemetery
Burial site of Miller Huggins.

Columbus
Columbus Clippers, International League-AAA (New York Yankees)
Cooper Stadium
1155 W. Mound St., just south of I-70
614/462-5250

Peoli
Methodist Church Cemetery
Burial site of Cy Young.

Toledo
Calvary Cemetery
Burial site of Roger Bresnahan.

Ohio Baseball Hall of Fame
Lucas County Recreation Center
2901 Key St., Maumee (south of the Ohio Turnpike)
419/893-9481
Collection features Cy Young and other home-state Hall of Famers.

Toledo Mud Hens, International League-AAA (Detroit Tigers)
Ned Skeldon Stadium
2901 Key St. (Maumee, south of the Ohio Turnpike)
419/893-9483

Woodlawn Cemetery
Burial site of Addie Joss.

Twinsburg
Crown Hill Cemetery
Burial site of Elmer Flick.

Oklahoma

McAllister
Oak Hill Cemetery
Burial site of Joe McGinnity.

Oklahoma City
Oklahoma Amateur Softball Association Hall of Fame
2801 N.E. 50th St.
405/424-5266
The Hall honors the game and the national champions of the American Softball Association. Research Center includes rule books, guides, videotapes, and books.

Oklahoma City 89ers, American Association-AAA (Texas Rangers)
All Sports Stadium
89er Drive at the State Fairgrounds
405/946-8989

Rosehill Cemetery
Burial site of Lloyd Waner.

Tulsa
Tulsa Drillers, Texas League-AA (Texas Rangers)
Drillers Stadium
4802 E. 15th St., at the Tulsa County Fairgrounds
918/744-5901

Yale
Jim Thorpe House
706 E. Boston, Oklahoma Hwy. 51, east of Stillwater
918/387-2815
Thorpe lived in this house during his days as a baseball player with Cincinnati, the Giants, and the Braves.

Oregon

Bend
Bend Rockies, Northwest League-A
Vince Genna Stadium, one block east of U.S. 97
503/382-8011

Eugene
Eugene Emeralds, Northwest League-A (Kansas City Royals)
Civic Stadium
2077 Willamette St., near Amazon Park
503/342-5367

Medford
Southern Oregon Athletics, Northwest League-A
Miles Field
1801 South Pacific Hwy.
503/770-5364

Portland

Oregon Sports Hall of Fame
900 S.W. 5th
503/227-7466
Commemorates almost 200 inductees, including Johnny Pesky, Bobby Doerr, Rick Wise, Ed Basinski, and Larry Jansen. Special exhibits include Dale Murphy's Gold Glove, Rick Wise's bat, Portland Beavers uniforms.

Portland Beavers, Pacific Coast League-AAA (Minnesota Twins)
Civic Stadium
1844 S.W. Morrison Street at 18th Avenue
503/223-2837

Pennsylvania

Erie

Erie Sailors, New York-Penn League-A (Florida Marlins)
Ainsworth Field
24th and Washington Streets, north of U.S. 20
814/459-7245

Harrisburg

Harrisburg Senators, Eastern League-AA (Montreal Expos)
RiverSide Stadium on City Island in the Susquehanna River
717/231-4444
The Senators play in the only ballpark on an island.

Lancaster

Sports Wearhouse
Rockvale Square
Willowdale Drive and Rt. 30
717/299-4473
MLB-licensed apparel.

Lewisburg

City Cemetery
Burial site of Christy Mathewson.

Monroeville

Pittsburgh Pirates Clubhouse Shop
Monroeville Mall
300 Monroeville Mall Blvd.
412/856-7610
Offical MLB memorabilia.

Morgantown

Sports Wearhouse
Mall of Morgantown
Exit 22 off Penn. Turnpike
215/286-7320
MLB-licensed apparel.

Greenville Braves, Greenville, South Carolina.

Philadelphia

African-American Historical and Cultural Museum
7th and Arch Streets
215/574-0380
Museum and research archives include oral histories, tapes, and other materials on the Hilldales and the Philadelphia Stars, as well as photos, clippings, and files on African-American players from 1912 to 1950.

Ardsley Cemetery
Burial site of Chief Bender.

Holy Sepulchre Cemetery
Burial site of Connie Mack.

Pittsburgh

Forbes Field site
University of Pittsburgh campus off Forbes Avenue (near the Carnegie Museum)
A remnant of the centerfield wall still stands, and inlaid bricks trace the path of the leftfield wall made immortal by Bill Mazeroski's homer in the 1960 World Series. The exact spot is marked by a plaque. Home plate rests in a glass case in the school library.

Homewood Cemetery
Burial site of Pie Traynor.

Jefferson Memorial Park
Burial site of Honus Wagner.

Reading

Reading Phillies, Eastern League-AA
Municipal Memorial Stadium
Pennsylvania Hwy. 61 south of U.S. 222
215/375-8469

Sports Wearhouse
The Big Mill
8th and Oley streets
215/373-6884
MLB-licensed apparel.

Scranton

St. Catherine Cemetery
Burial site of Hugh Jennings.

Scranton/Wilkes-Barre Red Barons, International League-AAA (Philadelphia Phillies)
Lackawanna County Multipurpose Stadium
P.O. Box 3449
235 Montage Mountain Rd., off I-81 in Moosic
717/963-6556

South Williamsport

Little League Baseball Museum
U.S. Hwy. 15, adjacent to Howard J. Lamade Stadium
717/326-3607
More than 50 years of memorabilia, plus batting and pitching cages. (See article, this section.)

Tannersville

Sports Wearhouse
Crossing Outlet Square
Rts. 715 and 611
717/620-2573
MLB-licensed apparel.

Rhode Island

Pawtucket

Pawtucket Red Sox, International League-AAA
McCoy Stadium
1 Columbus Ave.
401/724-7300

South Carolina

Charleston

Charleston Rainbows, South Atlantic League-A (San Diego Padres)
College Park
701 Rutledge Ave., off I-26
803/723-7241

Columbia

Columbia Mets, South Atlantic League-A
Capital City Stadium
301 South Assembly St., half mile south of University of South Carolina football stadium
803/256-4110

Fort Mill

Charlotte Knights, Southern League-AA (Chicago Cubs)
Knights Castle Stadium
2280 Deerfield Drive
803/548-8051
704/332-3746 (Charlotte)

Greenville

Greenville Braves, Southern League-AA
Greenville Municipal Stadium
One Braves Ave., two miles east of I-85, Exit 46
803/299-3456

Myrtle Beach

Sports Wearhouse
Waccamaw Mall
3301 Outlet Blvd.
803/236-2200
MLB-licensed apparel.

Spartanburg

Spartanburg Phillies, South Atlantic League-A
Duncan Park Stadium
1000 Duncan Park Drive
803/585-6279

South Dakota

Sioux Falls

Pettigrew Museum Library
Siouxland Heritage Museums
131 N. Duluth Ave.
605/339-7097
Historical data on the Northern League, a minor league which covered the Dakotas, Wisconsin, Minnesota, and part of Canada from 1902 to 1971.

Tennessee

Chattanooga

Chattanooga Lookouts, Southern League-AA (Cincinnati Reds)
Engel Stadium
1131 E. 3rd St.
615/267-2208

Elizabethton

Elizabethton Twins, Appalachian League-Rookie
Joe O'Brien Field
Holly Lane, Tennessee Hwy. 67
615/543-4395

Johnson City

Johnson City Cardinals, Appalachian League-Rookie
Howard Johnson Field, off I-181
615/461-4850

Kingsport

Kingsport Mets, Appalachian League-Rookie
J. Fred Johnson Stadium
Fort Henry Drive at Dobyns Bennett High School
615/246-6464

Knoxville

Knoxville Smokies, Southern League-AA (Toronto Blue Jays)
Bill Meyer Stadium
I-40 at Exit 388
615/637-9494

Memphis

Memphis Chicks, Southern League-AA (Kansas City Royals)
Tim McCarver Stadium, next to the Liberty Bowl in the state fairgrounds (best entrance is off Central)
901/272-1687

Millington

USA Stadium
Biloxi Road, off Hwy. 51 North
901/872-8326
The training site of the U.S.A. Olympic team hosts games from mid June through early August.

Nashville

Nashville Sounds, American Association-AAA (Cincinnati Reds)
Herschel Greer Stadium, off I-65 at Wedgewood exit
615/242-4371

Pigeon Forge

Sports Wearhouse
Zbuda Mall
2828 Parkway
615/428-4829
Outlet store offers MLB-licensed apparel.

Tullahoma

Worth Sports Company
U.S. Hwy. 41A between Nashville and Chattanooga
615/455-0691
Tour baseball- and bat-making plants. Reservations are recommended.

El Paso

El Paso Diablos, Texas League-AA (Milwaukee Brewers)
Cohen Stadium
U.S. 54 near Diana Drive, north of the city
915/755-2000

Hornsby's Bend

City Cemetery
Burial site of Hall of Famer Rogers Hornsby.

Houston

Houston Sports Museum
4001 Gulf Freeway in the Fingers Furniture Store
713/221-4441
The museum features much baseball memorabilia, particularly of the minor league Houston Buffalos.

Hubbard

Fairview Cemetery
Burial site of Tris Speaker.

Midland

Midland Angels, Texas League-AA
Angels Stadium
4300 N. LaMesa Rd., at Loop 250
915/683-4251

San Antonio

Mission Burial Park
Burial site of Rube Waddell and Ross Youngs.

San Antonio Missions, Texas League-AA (Los Angeles Dodgers)
V.J. Keefe Stadium
36th Street at Culebra Road
St. Mary's University
512/434-9311

Waco

Texas Sports Museum and Hall of Fame
I-35 and University Parks Drive
817/756-2307
Collection includes a Hall of Fame of outstanding home-state players and coaches.

Salt Lake City

Salt Lake Trappers, Pioneer League-Rookie (Independent)
Derks Field
1301 Southwest Temple off I-15
801/484-9900

Burlington

Sports Hall of Fame
University of Vermont Campus
Patrick Gymnasium off Speer Street
802/656-2005
Memorabilia of U. of V. Catamount greats who played baseball and other sports.

Bristol

Bristol Tigers, Appalachian League-Rookie
DeVault Stadium
1501 Euclid, off I-81, just north of the Tennessee state line
703/669-6859

Hampton

Peninsula Pilots, Carolina League-A (Seattle Mariners)
War Memorial Stadium, off I-664, Powhattan Parkway exit
804/244-2255

Lynchburg

Lynchburg Red Sox, Carolina League-A
City Stadium
Fort Avenue and Wythe Road
804/528-1144

Martinsville

Martinsville Phillies, Appalachian League-Rookie
Hooker Field
Chatham Heights at Commonwealth Boulevard
703/666-2000

Norfolk

Tidewater Tides, International League-AAA (New York Mets)
Metropolitan Memorial Park
Military Road and Northhampton Blvd.
804-461-5600

The Diamond, home of the Richmond Braves, Richmond, Virginia.

Richmond Braves

Burleigh Grimes Room, Clear Lake Historical Museum, Clear Lake, Wisconsin.

Pulaski
Pulaski Braves, Appalachian League-Rookie
Calfee Park, corner of 5th and Pierce streets, U.S. 11 north of I-81
703/980-8200

Richmond
Richmond Braves, International League-AAA
The Diamond
Boulevard exit of I-64/95
804/359-4444

Salem
Salem Buccaneers, Carolina League-A (Pittsburgh Pirates)
Salem Municipal Field
620 Florida St., near downtown, two miles south of I-81
703/389-3333

Woodbridge
Prince William Cannons, Carolina League-A (New York Yankees)
Prince William County Stadium
Davis Ford Road, off I-95 at Exit 156
703/590-2311

Washington

Bellingham
Bellingham Mariners, Northwest League-A
Joe Martin Stadium
1500 Orleans
206/671-6347

Everett
Everett Giants, Northwest League-A
Everett Memorial Stadium
Broadway and 39th Street, off I-5
206/258-3673

Seattle
Acadia Memorial Park
Burial site of Amos Rusie.

Spokane
Spokane Indians, Northwest League-A
Interstate Fairgrounds, north of I-90 at Havana exit
509/535-2922

Tacoma
Tacoma Tigers, Pacific Coast League-AAA (Oakland Athletics)
Cheney Stadium
2502 S. Tyler St.
206/752-7707

Yakima
Yakima Bears, Northwest League-A (Los Angeles Dodgers)
Parker Field, west on 16th Street from I-82
509/457-5151

West Virginia

Bluefield
Bluefield Orioles, Appalachian League-Rookie
Bowen Field
U.S. 460 near the Westgate Shopping Center
703/322-5734

Charleston
Charleston Wheelers, South Atlantic League-A (Cincinnati Reds)
Watt Powell Park
3403 MacCorkle
304/925-8222

Huntington
Huntington Cubs, Appalachian League-Rookie
St. Cloud Commons
1901 Jackson Ave.
304/429-1700

Martinsburg
Rosehill Cemetery
Burial site of Hack Wilson.

Princeton
Princeton Reds, Appalachian League-Rookie
Hunnicutt Field
Three miles west of U.S. 460 — I-77 junction
304/487-2000

Wisconsin

Appleton
Appleton Foxes, Midwest League-A (Kansas City Royals)
Goodland Field
Spencer Street, south of College Avenue east of U.S. 41
414/733-4152

Beloit
Beloit Brewers, Midwest League-A
Pohlman Field
Cranston Road west of I-90
608/362-2272

Brookfield
Milwaukee Brewers Clubhouse Shop
Brookfield Square Mall
95 N. Moorland Rd.
414/789-1148
Offical MLB memorabilia.

Clear Lake
Clear Lake Area Historical Museum/Burleigh Grimes Museum
540 Fifth Ave.
Clear Lake, WI 54005
715/263-3050
The last legal spitballer is honored.

Madison
Madison Muskies, Midwest League-A (Oakland A's)
Warner Park
1617 Northport Drive
608/241-0010

Milwaukee
St. Adalbert's Cemetery
Burial site of Al Simmons.

Wyoming

Cheyenne
Wyoming State Museum
2301 Central
307/777-7022
A major exhibit runs April through October 1993: "Wyoming Baseball." Traces the history of the sport from the days it was played at cavalry posts like Ft. Laramie to World War II.

Alberta, Canada

Calgary Cannons, Pacific Coast League-AAA (Seattle Mariners)
Foothills Stadium
Crowchild Trail & 24th Ave., NW
403/284-1111

Edmonton Trappers, Pacific Coast League-AAA (California Angels)
John Ducey Park
10233 96th Ave.
403/429-2934

Lethbridge Mounties, Pioneer League-Rookie (Co-op)
Henderson Stadium
2601 Parkside Drive South
403/327-7975

Medicine Hat Blue Jays, Pioneer League-Rookie
Athletic Park
361 First St., S.E.
403/526-0404

British Columbia

Vancouver Canadians, Pacific Coast League-AAA (Chicago White Sox)
Nat Bailey Stadium
4601 Ontario St.
604/872-5232

Ontario

Hamilton Redbirds, New York-Pennsylvania League-A (St. Louis Cardinals)
Bernie Arbour Stadium
Mohawk East & Upper Kenilworth
416/527-3000

London Tigers, Eastern League-AA
Labatt Park
93 Wharncliffe Rd. North
519/645-2255

St. Catherines Blue Jays, New York-Pennsylvania League-A
Community Park
426 Merrit St.
416/641-5297

Welland Pirates, New York-Pennsylvania League-A
Welland Sports Complex Stadium
90 Quaker Rd.
416/735-7634

Arizona and Florida are synonymous with warmth, sunshine, and palm trees. For baseball fans, the attraction of spring training is hope. It's a chance to start over, to see if that phenomenal shortstop really does have good range, or if the left-handed pitcher can throw a forkball.

In Arizona, the majority of teams are clustered in the Phoenix area. If you stay for one week in nearby Scottsdale, you can see almost every Arizona-based team play at least once with a minimum amount of time driving.

Florida's teams can be grouped into regions — the Gulf Coast, Central Florida, and South Florida. You can either drive to see games at the various locales around the state, or stay in one city and wait for the teams to come to you. Traffic can be sluggish on either coast because of spring-break tourist crowds, and Interstate 4 may be clogged with cars and vans headed for Walt Disney World.

Bring plenty of suntan lotion, a camera, and an autograph book. Spring training is a great way to get up close and personal with the players. Almost all the teams' training complexes are adjacent to their respective parks; exceptions are noted.

Baseball & Travel

Spring Training

Arizona

Chandler
Milwaukee Brewers
Compadre Stadium
(capacity 5,000)
Three miles south of downtown Chandler via Alma School Road or Country Club Drive at Ocotillo Road
602/895-1200
This clean, modern ballpark is sunken, which can make things extra hot as April approaches. Seating on the grass down the lines and in the outfield can swell the crowds to 9,000, particularly for Brewers-Cubs games. Autograph possibilities are excellent as players walk from adjacent batting cages and practice fields.

Mesa
Chicago Cubs
HoHoKam Park (capacity 8,937)
1235 N. Center St., near Brown Road, about a half-mile north of Main Street
602/964-4467; 800/366-DBOX

The Cubs have long been the top-drawing club in Arizona, which makes advance ticket purchases a good idea. The open parking lot is the best place for autographs before and after games. South of the park, Harry and Steve's Chicago Grill, a sports bar/burger emporium named for broadcasters Harry Caray and Steve Stone, is a popular gathering spot for fans.

HoHoKam Park, Chicago Cubs spring training site, Mesa, Arizona.

Peoria
Seattle Mariners
Facility is under construction. The Mariners plan to play all spring training games at other Cactus League stadiums in 1993. Ticket and other stadium information not available at presstime.

Los Angeles Dodgers spring training, Vero Beach, Florida.

Phoenix
Oakland Athletics
Phoenix Municipal Stadium
(capacity 8,500)
5999 E. Van Buren St., just west
of Papago Park
602/392-0074
Nicely set, with desert rocks
beyond the fence in leftfield.
Tickets can be difficult to
secure. Best chance for autographs is in the players' parking
lot near the leftfield corner.

Scottsdale
San Francisco Giants
Scottsdale Stadium
(capacity 7,000)
7402 E. Osborn, two blocks east
of Scottsdale Road
602/230-9112 (TicketMaster)
A brand new park (1992) on the
site of old 5,000-seat Scottsdale
Stadium. Grassy outfield berms,
perfect for picnics, swell capacity to 9,500. The nearby Pink
Pony restaurant draws a sports
crowd.

Tempe
California Angels
Diablo Stadium (capacity 5,600)
West on Broadway to 48th
Street, then left a half mile
602/350-5205
The Angels replace the Seattle
Mariners here in 1993. For auto-
graphs, try the bullpens.

Tucson
Colorado Rockies
Hi Corbett Field (capacity 9,500)
East from I-10 on Broadway to
Randolph Way, right on
Randolph Way to park
602/325-2621
The Rockies will hold its first
spring training here, which was
home to the Cleveland Indians
for 45 years. Low fences and
tight confines make autographs
easy.

Yuma
San Diego Padres
Desert Sun Stadium
(capacity 7,000)
Exit I-8 at 16th Street, go west to
Avenue A, then south two miles
to the park
602/343-1715
Players sign autographs near the
seats by the field.

Bradenton
Pittsburgh Pirates
McKechnie Field
(capacity 5,000)
From I-75, exit Florida Hwy. 64,
continue west to 9th Street and
the park
813/747-3031
This dowager ballpark was
spruced up for 1992 with a new
outfield fence, and seating
improvements are planned for
the '93 season. Players sign
autographs along the fence.

Clearwater
Philadelphia Phillies
Jack Russell Stadium
(capacity 7,350)
Florida Hwy. 60 west to Greenwood Street, right to Seminole
Street, right at Seminole to the
park
Tickets in advance by mail only:
P.O. Box 10336, 34617
A nice old park (1955) in a nice
old town. No wonder Clearwater is filled with retired players
and sportswriters. For autographs, linger around the clubhouse entrance.

Dunedin
Toronto Blue Jays
Dunedin Stadium
(capacity 6,218)
U.S. 19 north to Sunset Point
Road, west to Douglas Avenue,
north to the park
813/733-0429
Tickets can be scarce in this
handsome new park, populated
heavily by Canadians down for
the season.

Fort Myers
Minnesota Twins
Lee County Sport Complex
(capacity 7,500)
West from I-75 on Daniels Road
to Six Mile Cypress Parkway,
then south to the park
800/28-TWINS
Opened in 1991, spring parks
don't get any more elegant than
this. Frost-bitten Minnesotans
flock here, creating sellout
crowds.

Boston Red Sox
(New stadium is scheduled to
open in 1993, additional information not available at presstime)
813/293-3900
The new home of the Boston
Red Sox, who are moving south
after spending 25 springs in Winter Haven.

Port Charlotte
Texas Rangers
Charlotte County Stadium
(capacity 6,026)
U.S. Hwy. 41, then west 2 miles
on Florida Hwy. 776
813/625-9500
Autographs are easiest near the
Texas clubhouse and the nearby
bullpen.

St. Petersburg
St. Louis Cardinals & Balti-
more Orioles
Al Lang Field (capacity 7,227)
From I-275, east on First Avenue
to Bayshore Drive
813/822-3384
One of the best spring parks in
baseball. Yachts bob in Tampa
Bay beyond the outfield walls.
Known for singing hot dog ven-
dor Tommy Walton. You'll see
lots of red when Cardinals are
home.

Sarasota
Chicago White Sox
Ed Smith Stadium
(capacity 7,500)
Tuttle and 12th Street
Tickets by mail: P.O. Box 1702,
34930, or 813/366-8451
Player's parking is fenced off
and guarded, which limits auto-
graphing to the low boxes.

Davenport
Kansas City Royals
Baseball City Stadium
(capacity 8,000)
Off I-4 at U.S. 27
813/424-2424
As with all the ballparks located
along I-4, expect heavy traffic
from both directions at
any time.

Kissimmee
Houston Astros
Osceola County Stadium
(capacity 5,000)
Off I-4 to U.S. 192 east, about 10 miles
405/933-2520

Lakeland
Detroit Tigers
Joker Marchant Stadium
(capacity 7,009)
From I-4, east on Memorial Boulevard to Lakeland Hills Boulevard, left about a mile
813/499-8229
The park was built in 1966, upgraded in 1988, and looks as if it's been there forever, just like Tiger Stadium. It also seems to attract serious fans who don't understand these games don't count. That adds to the fun.

Plant City
Cincinnati Reds
Plant City Stadium
(capacity 6,700)
From I-4, south on Park Road about 2-1/2 miles
Tickets by mail: P.O. Box 2275, 33564, or 813/757-6712
The Reds moved here in 1988.

South Florida

Fort Lauderdale
New York Yankees
Fort Lauderdale Stadium
(capacity 8,340)
From I-95, Commercial Boulevard West to Yankee Boulevard, then right on 12th Avenue
305/776-1921
A tough ticket.

Homestead
Cleveland Indians
City of Homestead Sports Complex (capacity 6,500)
Florida Turnpike to exit at S.W. 312 St., make right at light; travel under underpass and follow signs to stadium
305/247-1801
The complex sustained heavy damage during Hurricane Andrew; the status of spring training at this field in 1993 was not available at presstime.

Port St.Lucie
New York Mets
St. Lucie County Stadium
(capacity 7,347)
I-95 to exit 63C, bear right, then first left onto Peacock Boulevard
407/871-2115
The envy of general managers everywhere when it opened in 1988. Access to players is tough here.

Vero Beach
Los Angeles Dodgers
Holman Stadium
(capacity 6,500)
Take Florida Hwy. 60 to 43rd Avenue., left to 26th Street, right onto 26th. Stadium is the second right off 26th Street.
Tickets by mail: Dodgertown, P.O. Box 2887, Vero Beach, FL 32961-2887, 407/569-4900
In every respect, what the spring training experience should be: activity everywhere and easy access to players. (No real outfield wall, just a token fence.)

Viera
Florida Marlins
New stadium is near Cape Canaveral between Melbourne and Rockledge, FL
Ticket Info: P.O. Box 158, Melbourne, FL 32902
The Marlins' new facility is not scheduled to open until 1994. Until then, the expansion team will play 1993 games at Cocoa Expo, former complex for the Houston Astros, in Cocoa Beach.

West Palm Beach
Atlanta Braves, Montreal Expos
Municipal Stadium (capacity: 7,200) I-95 to Palm Beach Lakes Boulevard exit
Braves: 407/683-6100;
Expos: 407/689-9121
Two clubs sharing the facilities means there's a home game just about every day. Try the parking lot behind first base for autographs.

American League Schedules • 1993 Season

Day Games are in bold type. All-Star Game: July 13, Baltimore/Camden Yards. *All schedules are subject to change.*

Eastern Division

Baltimore

Apr. **5**, 7	TEX
Apr. 9, 10, **11**	at SEA
Apr. 12, 13, 14	at TEX
Apr. 16, **17, 18**	CAL
Apr. 20, 21	CHI
Apr. 23, **24, 25**	at KC
Apr. 26, 27	at CHI
Apr. 28, 29	MIN
Apr. 30, May **1, 2**	KC
May 4, **5**	at MIN
May 6, 7, **8, 9**	at TOR
May 10, 11, 12	BOS
May 14, 15, **16**	at DET
May 17, 18, 19, **20**	CLE
May 21, **22, 23**	MIL
May 24, 25, 26, 27	at NY
May 28, 29, **30**	at CAL
May **31**, June 1, **2**	at OAK
June 4, 5, **6**	SEA
June 7, 8, 9	OAK
June 10, 11, **12, 13**	at BOS
June 14, 15, **16**	at MIL
June 18, **19, 20**	at CLE
June 22, 23, 24	DET
June 25, 26, **27**	NY
June 28, 29, 30	TOR
July 1, 2, 3, **4**	at CHI
July 5, 6, 7	at KC
July 8, 9, **10, 11**	CHI
July 15, 16, 17, **18**	MIN
July 19, 20, **21**	KC
July 22, 23, **24, 25**	at MIN
July 27, 28	at TOR
July 30, 31, Aug. **1**	BOS
Aug. 2, 3, 4, 5	MIL
Aug. 6, 7, **8**	CLE
Aug. 9, 10, 11, **12**	at DET
Aug. 13, **14, 15**	at NY
Aug. 16, 17, **18**	at SEA
Aug. 20, 21, **22**, 23	TEX
Aug. 24, 25, **26**	CAL
Aug. 27, 28, **29**	at TEX
Aug. 31, Sept. 1, 2	at CAL
Sept. 3, **4, 5**	at OAK
Sept. 6, 7, 8	SEA
Sept. 10, 11, 12	OAK
Sept. 13, 14, 15	at BOS
Sept. 17, 18, **19**	at MIL
Sept. 20, 21, 22	at CLE
Sept. 24, 25, **26**	DET
Sept. 27, 28, 29	NY
Sept. 30, Oct. 1, 2, **3**	TOR

Boston

Apr. **5**, 7, 8	at KC
Apr. 9, 10, **11**	at TEX
Apr. **12, 14**, 15	CLE
Apr. 16, **17, 18, 19**	CHI
Apr. 20, 21, 22	at SEA
Apr. 23, 24, 25	at CAL
Apr. 27, **28**	at OAK
Apr. 30, May **1, 2**	CAL
May 3, 4	SEA
May 5, **6**	OAK
May 7, **8, 9**	at MIL
May 10, 11, 12	at BAL
May 14, **15, 16**	at MIN
May 17, 18, 19	TOR
May 21, **22**, 23	NY
May 24, 25, **26**	at DET
May 28, **29, 30**	TEX
May 31, June 1, 2	KC
June 4, 5, **6**	at CHI
June 7, 8, 9	at CLE
June 10, 11, **12, 13**	BAL
June 14, 15, 16	at NY
June 17, 18, **19, 20**	at TOR
June 21, 22, 23	MIN
June 25, **26, 27**	DET
June 28, 29, 30	MIL
July 2, 3, 4	at SEA
July 5, 6, **7**	at CAL
July **8**, 9, **10, 11**	at OAK
July 15, 16, **17, 18**	SEA
July 19, 20, **21**	CAL
July 22, 23, **24, 25**	OAK
July 26, 27, 28, **29**	at MIL
July 30, 31, Aug. **1**	at BAL
Aug. 3, 4, **5**	at MIN
Aug. 6, **7, 8**	at DET
Aug. 10, 11, 12	NY
Aug. 13, **14, 15**	TOR
Aug. 17, 18	CHI
Aug. 19, 20, **21, 22**	CLE
Aug. 24, 25, 26	at TEX
Aug. 27, **28, 29**	at KC
Aug. 30, 31, Sept. 1	TEX
Sept. 3, **4, 5**	KC
Sept. 6, 7, 8	at CHI
Sept. 10, **11, 12**	at CLE
Sept. 13, 14, 15	BAL
Sept. 16, 17, **18, 19**	at NY
Sept. 21, 22, 23	at TOR
Sept. 24, **25, 26**	MIN
Sept. 27, 28, 29, 30	DET
Oct. 1, **2, 3**	MIL

Cleveland

Apr. **5**, 7, 8	NY
Apr. **9, 10, 11**	at TOR
Apr. **12, 14**, 15	at BOS
Apr. 16, **17, 18, 19**	TOR
Apr. 20, 21, 22	at CAL
Apr. 23, **24, 25**	at OAK
Apr. 26, 27, 28	at SEA
Apr. 30, May **1, 2**	OAK
May 3, 4	CAL
May 5, **6**	SEA
May 7, 8, **9**	at CHI
May 11, 12, **13**	KC
May 14, **15, 16**	at MIL
May 17, 18, 19, **20**	at BAL
May 21, **22, 23**	DET
May 24, 25, 26	TEX
May 28, 29, **30**	at MIN
May **31**, June 1, 2	at NY
June 4, **5, 6**	MIN
June 7, 8, 9	BOS
June 11, 12, 13	at TEX
June 14, 15, 16, **17**	at DET
June 18, **19, 20**	BAL
June 21, 22, 23, 24	MIL
June 25, 26, 27	KC
June 28, 29, 30	CHI
July 2, 3, 4	at CAL
July **5**, 6, **7**	at OAK
July 9, 10, **11**	at SEA
July 15, 16, **17, 18**	CAL
July 19, 20, 21	OAK
July 22, 23, 24, **25**	SEA
July 26, 27, **28**	at CHI
July 30, 31, Aug. **1**	at KC
Aug. 3, 4, **5**	DET
Aug. 6, 7, **8**	at BAL
Aug. 10, 11, **12**	at MIL
Aug. 13, 14, **15**	TEX
Aug. 16, 17, 18	TOR
Aug. 19, 20, **21, 22**	at BOS
Aug. 23, 24, **25**	at TOR
Aug. 26, 27, **28, 29**	NY
Aug. 31, Sept. 1, **2**	at MIN
Sept. 3, **4, 5**	at NY
Sept. 7, 8, 9	MIN
Sept. 10, **11, 12**	BOS
Sept. 13, 14, 15	at TEX
Sept. 17, **18, 19**	at DET
Sept. 20, 21, 22	BAL
Sept. 24, **25, 26**	MIL
Sept. 27, 28, 29	at KC
Oct. 1, **2, 3**	CHI

Detroit

Apr. 5, 7, **8**	at OAK
Apr. 9, 10, **11**	at CAL
Apr. **13, 15**	OAK
Apr. 16, **17, 18, 19**	SEA
Apr. 20, **21**	TEX
Apr. 23, 24, **25**	at MIN
Apr. 26, 27	at KC
Apr. 28, 29	at TEX
Apr. 30, May **1, 2**	MIN
May 4, **5**	KC
May 7, 8, **9**, 10	NY
May 11, 12, 13	at TOR
May 14, 15, **16**	BAL
May 17, 18, 19, **20**	at MIL
May 21, **22, 23**	at CLE
May 24, 25, **26**	BOS
May 28, 29, 30	at SEA
June 1, 2, 3	CHI
June 4, **5, 6**	CAL
June 7, 8, 9	at CHI
June 10, 11, 12, **13**	TOR
June 14, 15, 16, **17**	CLE
June 18, **19, 20**	MIL
June 22, 23, 24	at BAL
June 25, **26, 27**	at BOS
June 28, 29, **30**	at NY
July 1, 2, **3, 4**	TEX
July 5, 6, **7**	at MIN
July 8, 9, 10, **11**	at KC
July 15, 16, 17, 18	at TEX
July 19, 20, **21**	MIN
July 22, 23, 24, **25**	KC
July 26, 27, **28**	NY
July 29,30,**31**,Aug.**1**	at TOR
Aug. 3, 4, **5**	at CLE
Aug. 6, **7, 8**	BOS
Aug. 9, 10, 11, **12**	BAL
Aug. 13, 14, **15**	at MIL
Aug. 16, 17, 18	at CAL
Aug. 20, 21, **22**, 23	OAK
Aug. 24, **25**	SEA
Aug. 27, **28, 29**	at OAK
Aug. 30, 31, Sept. **1**	at SEA
Sept. 3, **4, 5**	CHI
Sept. 7, 8, 9	CAL
Sept. 10, 11, **12**	at CHI
Sept. 14, 15	TOR
Sept. 17, **18, 19**	CLE
Sept. 20, 21, **22**	MIL
Sept. 24, 25, **26**	at BAL
Sept. 27, 28, 29, 30	at BOS
Oct. 1, **2, 3**	at NY

Milwaukee

Apr. **6**, 7	at CAL
Apr. 9, **10, 11**	at OAK
Apr. **12**, 14, **15**	CAL
Apr. 16, **17, 18**	OAK
Apr. 20, 21, **22**	at MIN
Apr. 23, **24, 25**	TEX
Apr. 26, **27**	MIN
Apr. 28, 29	at CHI
Apr. 30, May **1, 2**, 3	at TEX
May 4, **5**	CHI
May 7, **8, 9**	BOS
May 11, 12, 13	at NY
May 14, **15, 16**	CLE
May 17, 18, 19, **20**	DET
May 21, **22, 23**	at BAL
May **24**, 25, 26, **27**	at TOR
May 28, 29, **30**	KC
June 1, **2**	at SEA
June 3, 4, 5, **6**	at KC
June 7, 8, **9**	SEA
June 10, 11, 12, 13	NY
June 14, 15, **16**	BAL
June 18, **19, 20**	at DET
June 21, 22, 23, 24	at CLE
June 25, 26, **27**	TOR
June 28, 29, 30	at BOS
July 2, **3, 4**	at MIN
July **5**, 6, **7**	TEX
July 8, 9, 10, **11**	MIN
July 15, 16, 17, **18**	CHI
July 19, 20	at TEX
July 22, 23, 24, **25**	at CHI
July 26, 27, 28, **29**	BOS
July 30, **31**, Aug. **1**	at NY
Aug. 2, 3, 4, 5	at BAL
Aug. 6, **7**, 8	at TOR
Aug. 10, 11, **12**	CLE
Aug. 13, 14, **15**	DET
Aug. 16, 17, **18**	at OAK
Aug. 19, 20, 21, **22**	at CAL
Aug. 24, 25, **26**	OAK
Aug. 27, **28, 29**	CAL
Aug. 30, 31, Sept. **1**	KC
Sept. 2, 3, 4, **5**	at SEA
Sept. 6, 8	at KC
Sept. 10, **11, 12**	SEA
Sept. 13, 14, **15**	NY
Sept. 17, 18, **19**	BAL
Sept. 20, 21, **22**	at DET
Sept. 24, **25, 26**	at CLE
Sept. 27, 28, 29	TOR
Oct. 1, **2, 3**	at BOS

New York

Apr. **5**, 7, 8	at CLE
Apr. **9**, 10, **11**	at CHI
Apr. **12, 14**, 15	KC
Apr. 16, **17, 18**	TEX
Apr. 20, 21, **22**	at OAK
Apr. 23, 24, **25**	at SEA
Apr. 27, 28	at CAL
Apr. 30, May **1, 2**	SEA
May 3, 4	OAK
May 5, **6**	CAL
May 7, 8, **9**, 10	at DET
May 11, 12, 13	MIL
May 14, **15, 16**	TOR
May 17, 18, **19**	at MIN
May 21, **22**, 23	at BOS
May 24, 25, 26, 27	BAL
May 28, **29, 30**	CHI
May **31**, June 1, 2	CLE
June 4, 5, 6	at TEX
June 7, 8, 9	at KC
June 10, 11, 12, 13	at MIL
June 14, 15, 16	BOS
June 17, 18, **19, 20**	MIN
June 22, 23, 24	at TOR
June 25, 26, **27**	at BAL
June 28, 29, **30**	DET
July 2, **3**, 4	at OAK
July 5, 6, **7**	at SEA
July 8, 9, **10, 11**	at CAL
July 15, 16, **17**, 18	OAK
July 19, 20, **21**	SEA
July 22, 23, **24, 25**	CAL
July 26, 27, **28**	at DET
July 30, **31**, Aug. **1**	MIL
Aug. 2, 3, 4, **5**	TOR
Aug. 6, 7, **8**	at MIN
Aug. 10, 11, 12	at BOS
Aug. 13, **14, 15**	BAL
Aug. 16, 17, **18**	TEX
Aug. 20, **21, 22**	KC
Aug. 23, 24, 25	at CHI
Aug. 26, 27, **28, 29**	at CLE
Aug. 31, Sept. 1, 2	CHI
Sept. 3, **4, 5**	CLE
Sept. 6, 7, 8	at TEX
Sept. 10, 11, **12**	at KC
Sept. 13, 14, **15**	at MIL
Sept. 16, 17, **18, 19**	BOS
Sept. 21, 22	MIN
Sept. 24, **25, 26**	at TOR
Sept. 27, 28, 29	at BAL
Oct. 1, **2, 3**	DET

Toronto

Apr. 6, **7**	at SEA
Apr. 9, **10, 11**	CLE
Apr. 13, 14, **15**	SEA
Apr. 16, **17, 18, 19**	at CLE
Apr. 20, 21, 22	at KC
Apr. 23, **24, 25**	CHI
Apr. 26, 27	TEX
Apr. 28, **29**	KC
Apr. 30, May 1, **2**	at CHI
May 4, 5	at TEX
May 6, 7, **8, 9**	BAL
May 11, 12, 13	DET
May 14, **15, 16**	at NY
May 17, 18, 19	at BOS
May 21, **22, 23**	MIN
May **24**, 25, 26, **27**	MIL
May 28, **29, 30**	at OAK
May **31**, June 1, 2	at CAL
June 4, **5, 6**	OAK
June 7, 8, 9	CAL
June 10, 11, 12, **13**	at DET
June 14, 15, **16**	at MIN
June 17, 18, **19, 20**	BOS
June 22, 23, 24	NY
June 25, 26, **27**	at MIL
June 28, 29, 30	at BAL
July 2, 3, 4	at KC
July 5, 6, 7	CHI
July 8, 9, **10, 11**	TEX
July 15, 16, **17, 18**	KC
July 19, 20, 21	at CHI
July 22, 23, 24, 25	at TEX
July 27, 28	BAL
July 29, 30, **31**, Aug. **1**	DET
Aug. 2, 3, 4, **5**	at NY
Aug. 6, **7**, 8	MIL
Aug. 10, 11, **12**	MIN
Aug. 13, **14, 15**	at BOS
Aug. 16, 17, 18	at CLE
Aug. 20, **21, 22**	SEA
Aug. 23, 24, **25**	CLE
Aug. 26, 27, 28, **29**	at SEA
Aug. 30, 31, Sept. **1**	at OAK
Sept. 3, 4, **5**	at CAL
Sept. 7, 8, 9	OAK
Sept. 10, **11, 12**	CAL
Sept. 14, 15	at DET
Sept. 17, **18, 19**	at MIN
Sept. 21, 22, 23	BOS
Sept. 24, **25, 26**	NY
Sept. 27, 28, 29	at MIL
Sept. 30, Oct.1,2,**3**	at BAL

Western Division

California

Apr. **6**, 7	MIL
Apr. 9, 10, **11**	DET
Apr. **12**, 14, **15**	at MIL
Apr. 16, **17, 18**	at BAL
Apr. 20, 21, 22	CLE
Apr. 23, 24, 25	BOS
Apr. 27, 28	NY
Apr. 30, May **1, 2**	at BOS
May 3, 4	at CLE
May 5, **6**	at NY
May 7, 8, **9**	OAK
May 10, 11, **12**	MIN
May 14, 15, **16**	KC
May 17, 18, 19	at CHI
May 21, **22, 23**	at TEX
May 24, 25, 26, 27	at SEA
May 28, 29, **30**	BAL
May **31**, June 1, 2	TOR
June 4, **5, 6**	at DET
June 7, 8, 9	at TOR
June 11, 12, **13**	SEA
June 14, 15, 16, 17	TEX
June 18, 19, **20**	CHI
June 21, 22, 23, **24**	at KC
June 25, 26, **27**	at MIN
June 29, **30**, July **1**	at OAK
July 2, 3, 4	CLE
July 5, 6, **7**	BOS
July 8, 9, **10, 11**	NY
July 15, 16, **17, 18**	at CLE
July 19, 20, **21**	at BOS
July 22, 23, **24, 25**	at NY
July 26, 27, 28, 29	OAK
July 30, 31, Aug. **1**	MIN
Aug. 3, 4, **5**	KC
Aug. 6, 7, **8**	at CHI
Aug. 10, 11, 12	at TEX
Aug. 13, 14, **15**	at SEA
Aug. 16, 17, 18	DET
Aug. 19, 20, 21, **22**	MIL
Aug. 24, 25, **26**	at BAL
Aug. 27, **28, 29**	at MIL
Aug. 31, Sept. 1, 2	BAL
Sept. 3, 4, **5**	TOR
Sept. 7, 8, 9	at DET
Sept. 10, **11, 12**	at TOR
Sept. 13, 14, 15	SEA
Sept. 17, 18, **19**	TEX
Sept. 20, 21, 22, **23**	CHI
Sept. 24, 25, **26**	at KC
Sept. 27, 28, 29, **30**	at MIN
Oct. 1, **2, 3**	at OAK

Chicago

Apr. 6, 7, **8**	at MIN
Apr. **9**, 10, **11**	NY
Apr. 12, 13, 14	MIN
Apr. 16, **17, 18, 19**	at BOS
Apr. 20, 21	at BAL
Apr. 23, **24, 25**	at TOR
Apr. 26, 27	BAL
Apr. 28, 29	MIL
Apr. 30, May 1, **2**	TOR
May 4, **5**	at MIL
May 7, 8, **9**	CLE
May 10, 11, **12**	at SEA
May 14, 15, 16	at TEX
May 17, 18, 19	CAL
May 21, **22, 23**	OAK
May 25, 26, **27**	KC
May 28, **29, 30**	at NY
June 1, 2, 3	at DET
June 4, 5, **6**	BOS
June 7, 8, 9	DET
June 11, 12, **13**	at KC
June 14, 15, **16, 17**	at OAK
June 18, 19, **20**	at CAL
June 21, 22, **23**	TEX
June 25, 26, **27**	SEA
June 28, 29, 30	at CLE
July 1, 2, 3, **4**	BAL
July 5, 6, 7	at TOR
July 8, 9, **10, 11**	at BAL
July 15, 16, 17, **18**	at MIL
July 19, 20, 21	TOR
July 22, 23, 24, **25**	MIL
July 26, 27, **28**	CLE
July **30**, 31, Aug. 1	at SEA
Aug. 2, 3, 4, 5	at TEX
Aug. 6, 7, **8**	CAL
Aug. 9, 10, **11**	OAK
Aug. 12, 13, 14, **15**	KC
Aug. 17, 18	at BOS
Aug. 20, 21, **22**	at MIN
Aug. 23, 24, 25	NY
Aug. 27, 28, 29, 30	MIN
Aug. 31, Sept. 1, 2	at NY
Sept. 3, **4, 5**	at DET
Sept. 6, 7, 8	BOS
Sept. 10, 11, **12**	DET
Sept. 13, 14, 15	at KC
Sept. 17, **18, 19**	at OAK
Sept. 20, 21, 22, **23**	at CAL
Sept. 24, 25, **26**	TEX
Sept. 27, 28, 29, 30	SEA
Oct. 1, **2, 3**	at CLE

Kansas City

Apr. **5**, 7, 8	BOS
Apr. 9, **10, 11**	MIN
Apr. **12, 14**, 15	at NY
Apr. 16, 17, **18**	at MIN
Apr. 20, 21, 22	TOR
Apr. 23, **24, 25**	BAL
Apr. 26, 27	DET
Apr. 28, **29**	at TOR
Apr. 30, May **1, 2**	at BAL
May 4, **5**	at DET
May 7, 8, **9**	TEX
May 11, 12, **13**	at CLE
May 14, 15, **16**	at CAL
May 18, 19, 20	OAK
May 21, 22, 23	SEA
May 25, 26, **27**	at CHI
May 28, 29, **30**	at MIL
May 31, June 1, 2	at BOS
June 3, 4, 5, **6**	MIL
June 7, 8, 9	NY
June 11, 12, **13**	CHI
June 14, 15, 16	at SEA
June **18, 19, 20**	at OAK
June 21, 22, 23, **24**	CAL
June 25, 26, 27	at CLE
June 28, 29, 30	at TEX
July 2, 3, 4	TOR
July 5, 6, 7	BAL
July 8, 9, 10, **11**	DET
July 15, 16, **17, 18**	at TOR
July 19, 20, **21**	at BAL
July 22, 23, 24, **25**	at DET
July 26, 27, 28, **29**	TEX
July 30, 31, Aug. **1**	CLE
Aug. 3, 4, **5**	at CAL
Aug. 6, 7, **8**	OAK
Aug. 9, 10, 11	SEA
Aug. 12, 13, 14, **15**	at CHI
Aug. 17, 18, **19**	at MIN
Aug. 20, **21, 22**	at NY
Aug. 23, 24, 25, 26	MIN
Aug. 27, **28, 29**	BOS
Aug. 30, 31, Sept. **1**	at MIL
Sept. 3, **4, 5**	at BOS
Sept. 6, 8	MIL
Sept. 10, 11, **12**	NY
Sept. 13, 14, 15	CHI
Sept. 16, 17, 18, **19**	at SEA
Sept. 20, 21, 22, **23**	at OAK
Sept. 24, 25, **26**	CAL
Sept. 27, 28, 29	CLE
Oct. 1, 2, **3**	at TEX

Minnesota

Apr. 6, 7, **8**	CHI
Apr. 9, **10, 11**	at KC
Apr. 12, 13, 14	at CHI
Apr. 16, 17, **18**	KC
Apr. 20, 21, **22**	MIL
Apr. 23, 24, **25**	DET
Apr. 26, **27**	at MIL
Apr. 28, 29	at BAL
Apr. 30, May **1, 2**	at DET
May 4, **5**	BAL
May 7, 8, **9**	at SEA
May 10, 11, **12**	at CAL
May 14, **15, 16**	BOS
May 17, 18, **19**	NY
May 21, **22, 23**	at TOR
May 25, **26, 27**	at OAK
May 28, 29, **30**	CLE
May **31**, June 1, 2	TEX
June 4, **5, 6**	at CLE
June 7, 8, 9, 10	at TEX
June 11, 12, **13**	OAK
June 14, 15, **16**	TOR
June 17, 18, **19, 20**	at NY
June 21, 22, 23	at BOS
June 25, 26, **27**	CAL
June 28, 29, 30, July **1**	SEA
July 2, **3, 4**	MIL
July 5, 6, **7**	DET
July 8, 9, 10, **11**	at MIL
July 15, 16, 17, **18**	at BAL
July 19, 20, **21**	at DET
July 22, 23, **24, 25**	BAL
July 27, 28, 29	at SEA
July 30, 31, Aug. **1**	at CAL
Aug. 3, 4, **5**	BOS
Aug. 6, 7, **8**	NY
Aug. 10, 11, **12**	at TOR
Aug. 13, **14, 15**	at OAK
Aug. 17, 18, **19**	KC
Aug. 20, 21, **22**	CHI
Aug. 23, 24, 25, 26	at KC
Aug. 27, 28, 29, 30	at CHI
Aug. 31, Sept. 1, **2**	CLE
Sept. 3, 4, 5	TEX
Sept. 7, 8, 9	at CLE
Sept. 10, 11, **12**	at TEX
Sept. 13, 14, 15, 16	OAK
Sept. 17, **18, 19**	TOR
Sept. 21, 22	at NY
Sept. 24, **25, 26**	at BOS
Sept. 27, 28, 29, **30**	CAL
Oct. 1, 2, **3**	SEA

Oakland

Apr. 5, 7, **8**	DET
Apr. 9, **10, 11**	MIL
Apr. **13, 15**	at DET
Apr. 16, **17, 18**	at MIL
Apr. 20, 21, **22**	NY
Apr. 23, **24, 25**	CLE
Apr. 27, **28**	BOS
Apr. 30, May **1, 2**	at CLE
May 3, 4	at NY
May 5, **6**	at BOS
May 7, 8, **9**	at CAL
May 10, 11, 12, **13**	TEX
May 14, **15, 16**	SEA
May 18, 19, 20	at KC
May 21, **22, 23**	at CHI
May 25, **26, 27**	MIN
May 28, **29, 30**	TOR
May **31**, June 1, **2**	BAL
June 4, **5, 6**	at TOR
June 7, 8, 9	at BAL
June 11, 12, **13**	at MIN
June 14, 15, **16, 17**	CHI
June **18, 19, 20**	KC
June 21, 22, 23, **24**	at SEA
June 25, 26, 27	at TEX
June 29, **30**, July **1**	CAL
July 2, **3**, 4	NY
July **5**, 6, **7**	CLE
July **8**, 9, **10, 11**	BOS
July 15, 16, **17**, 18	at NY
July 19, 20, 21	at CLE
July 22, 23, **24, 25**	at BOS
July 26, 27, 28, 29	at CAL
July 30, **31**, Aug. 1	TEX
Aug. 3, **4, 5**	SEA
Aug. 6, 7, **8**	at KC
Aug. 9, 10, **11**	at CHI
Aug. 13, **14, 15**	MIN
Aug. 16, 17, **18**	MIL
Aug. 20, 21, **22**, 23	at DET
Aug. 24, 25, **26**	at MIL
Aug. 27, **28, 29**	DET
Aug. 30, 31, Sept. **1**	TOR
Sept. 3, **4, 5**	BAL
Sept. 7, 8, 9	at TOR
Sept. 10, 11, 12	at BAL
Sept. 13, 14, 15, 16	at MIN
Sept. 17, **18, 19**	CHI
Sept. 20, 21, 22, **23**	KC
Sept. 24, 25, **26**	at SEA
Sept. 28, 29, 30	at TEX
Oct. 1, **2, 3**	CAL

Seattle

Apr. 6, **7**	TOR
Apr. 9, 10, **11**	BAL
Apr. 13, 14, **15**	at TOR
Apr. 16, **17, 18, 19**	at DET
Apr. 20, 21, 22	BOS
Apr. 23, 24, **25**	NY
Apr. 26, 27, 28	CLE
Apr. 30, May **1, 2**	at NY
May 3, 4	at BOS
May 5, **6**	at CLE
May 7, 8, **9**	MIN
May 10, 11, **12**	CHI
May 14, **15, 16**	at OAK
May 17, 18, 19, 20	at TEX
May 21, 22, 23	at KC
May 24, 25, 26, 27	CAL
May 28, 29, 30	DET
June 1, **2**	MIL
June 4, 5, **6**	at BAL
June 7, 8, **9**	at MIL
June 11, 12, **13**	at CAL
June 14, 15, 16	KC
June 18, 19, **20**	TEX
June 21, 22, 23, **24**	OAK
June 25, 26, **27**	at CHI
June28,29,30,July**1**	at MIN
July 2, 3, 4	BOS
July 5, 6, **7**	NY
July 9, 10, **11**	CLE
July 15, 16, **17, 18**	at BOS
July 19, 20, **21**	at NY
July 22, 23, 24, **25**	at CLE
July 27, 28, 29	MIN
July **30**, 31, Aug. 1	CHI
Aug. 3, **4, 5**	at OAK
Aug. 6, 7, 8	at TEX
Aug. 9, 10, 11	at KC
Aug. 13, 14, **15**	CAL
Aug. 16, 17, **18**	BAL
Aug. 20, **21, 22**	at TOR
Aug. 24, **25**	at DET
Aug. 26, 27, 28, **29**	TOR
Aug. 30, 31, Sept. **1**	DET
Sept. 2, 3, 4, **5**	MIL
Sept. 6, 7, 8	at BAL
Sept. 10, **11, 12**	at MIL
Sept. 13, 14, 15	at CAL
Sept. 16, 17, 18, **19**	KC
Sept. 20, 21, 22	TEX
Sept. 24, 25, **26**	OAK
Sept. 27, 28, 29, 30	at CHI
Oct. 1, 2, **3**	at MIN

Texas

Apr. **5**, 7	at BAL
Apr. 9, 10, **11**	BOS
Apr. 12, 13, 14	BAL
Apr. 16, **17, 18**	at NY
Apr. 20, **21**	at DET
Apr. 23, **24, 25**	at MIL
Apr. 26, 27	at TOR
Apr. 28, 29	DET
Apr. 30, May **1, 2**, 3	MIL
May 4, 5	TOR
May 7, 8, **9**	at KC
May 10, 11, 12, **13**	at OAK
May 14, 15, 16	CHI
May 17, 18, 19, 20	SEA
May 21, **22, 23**	CAL
May 24, 25, 26	at CLE
May 28, **29, 30**	at BOS
May **31**, June 1, 2	at MIN
June 4, 5, 6	NY
June 7, 8, 9, 10	MIN
June 11, 12, 13	CLE
June 14, 15, 16, 17	at CAL
June 18, 19, **20**	at SEA
June 21, 22, **23**	at CHI
June 25, 26, 27	OAK
June 28, 29, 30	KC
July 1, 2, **3, 4**	at DET
July **5**, 6, **7**	at MIL
July 8, 9, **10, 11**	at TOR
July 15, 16, 17, 18	DET
July 19, 20	MIL
July 22, 23, 24, 25	TOR
July 26, 27, 28, **29**	at KC
July 30, **31**, Aug. 1	at OAK
Aug. 2, 3, 4, 5	CHI
Aug. 6, 7, 8	SEA
Aug. 10, 11, 12	CAL
Aug. 13, 14, **15**	at CLE
Aug. 16, 17, **18**	at NY
Aug. 20, 21, **22**, 23	at BAL
Aug. 24, 25, 26	BOS
Aug. 27, 28, **29**	BAL
Aug. 30, 31, Sept. 1	at BOS
Sept. 3, 4, 5	at MIN
Sept. 6, 7, 8	NY
Sept. 10, 11, **12**	MIN
Sept. 13, 14, 15	CLE
Sept. 17, 18, **19**	at CAL
Sept. 20, 21, 22	at SEA
Sept. 24, 25, **26**	at CHI
Sept. 28, 29, 30	OAK
Oct. 1, 2, **3**	KC

Day Games are in bold type. All-Star Game: July 13, Baltimore/Camden Yards. *All schedules are subject to change.*

Eastern Division

Chicago

Apr. **5, 6, 7**	ATL
Apr. **9**, 10, **11**	at PHI
Apr. 12, 13, 14	at ATL
Apr. **16, 17, 18**	PHI
Apr. 19, 20, **21**	HOU
Apr. **23, 24, 25**	CIN
Apr. 26, 27	at COL
Apr. 28, 29	at HOU
Apr. 30, May **1, 2**	at CIN
May 4, **5**	COL
May **7, 8, 9**	SD
May 10, **11, 12**	LA
May **14**, 15, **16**	PIT
May 18, 19, 20	at STL
May 21, 22, **23**	at FLA
May **25, 26**, 27	SF
May **28, 29, 30**	MON
May **31**, June 1, **2**	NY
June 3, 4, 5, 6	at MON
June 7, 8, 9	at NY
June 11, **12, 13**	at SF
June 14, 15, **16**	FLA
June **17, 18, 19, 20**	STL
June **21**, 22, 23	at PIT
June 25, 26, **27**	at LA
June 28, 29, **30**	at SD
July 2, 3, **4, 5**	at COL
July 6, **7, 8**	CIN
July **9**, 10, **11**	HOU
July 15, **16, 17, 18**	COL
July 19, 20, 21	at CIN
July 22, **23, 24, 25**	at HOU
July 26, **27, 28**	SD
July **30, 31**, Aug. **1**	LA
Aug. **2, 3, 4, 5**	PIT
Aug. 6, **7, 8**	at FLA
Aug. 9, 10, 11, 12	at FLA
Aug. **13, 14, 15**	SF
Aug. **17, 18**, 19	MON
Aug. **20, 21**, 22	ATL
Aug. 23, 24, 25	at MON
Aug. 27, **28, 29**	at ATL
Aug. **30, 31**, Sept. **1**	PHI
Sept. 2, **3, 4, 5**	NY
Sept. 6, 7, 8, 9	at PHI
Sept. 10, **11, 12**	at NY
Sept. 13, 14, **15**	SF
Sept. **17, 18, 19**	FLA
Sept. 20, 21, **22**	STL
Sept. 24, 25, 26	at PIT
Sept. 27, 28, 29	at LA
Oct. 1, 2, **3**	at SD

Florida

Apr. **5**, 6, 7	LA
Apr. 9, 10, **11**	SD
Apr. **12, 13, 14**	at SF
Apr. 16, **17, 18**	at HOU
Apr. 20, 21, **22**	ATL
Apr. 23, **24, 25**	at COL
Apr. 26, 27	at CIN
Apr. 28, 29	at ATL
Apr. 30, May 1, 2	COL
May 4, **5**	CIN
May **7, 8, 9**, 10	at NY
May 11, 12, 13	at MON
May 14, 15, **16**	at STL
May 18, 19	PHI
May 21, 22, **23**	CHI
May **25, 26**, 27	at PIT
May **28, 29, 30**	HOU
May **31**, June 1, 2	SF
June 3, 4, 5, 6	at SD
June 7, 8	at LA
June 10, 11, 12, **13**	PIT
June 14, 15, **16**	at CHI
June **17, 18, 19, 20**	at PIT
June 21, 22, 23	STL
June 25, 26, **27**	at STL
June 29, 30, July 1	NY
July 2, 3, **4, 5**	at COL
July 6, **7, 8**	at COL
July **9**, 10, **11**	at CIN
July 15, 16, 17, **18**	at CIN
July 19, 20, 21	COL
July 22, 23, 24, 25	CIN
July 27, **28, 29**	at NY
July 30, 31, Aug. **1**	at ATL
Aug. 2, 3, 4, **5**	at STL
Aug. 6, **7, 8**	PHI
Aug. 9, 10, 11, 12	CHI
Aug. **13, 14, 15**	at PIT
Aug. **17, 18**, 19	at HOU
Aug. 20, **21, 22**	at SF
Aug. **24, 25, 26**	HOU
Aug. 27, **28, 29**	SF
Aug. **30, 31**, Sept. **1, 2**	SD
Sept. **3, 4, 5**	LA
Sept. 6, **7, 8**	at SD
Sept. 9, 10, 11, **12**	at LA
Sept. 14, 15, 16	PIT
Sept. **17, 18, 19**	at CHI
Sept. 20, 21, 22	at PHI
Sept. 24, 25, **26**	STL
Sept. 27, 28, 29, 30	MON
Oct. 1, 2, **3**	NY

Montreal

Apr. **5, 7, 8**	at CIN
Apr. **9, 10, 11**	at COL
Apr. 12, 13, 14	HOU
Apr. 16, **17, 18**	COL
Apr. 20, 21, 22	LA
Apr. 23, **24, 25**	SF
Apr. 26, 27	at SD
Apr. 28, 29	at LA
Apr. 30, May **1, 2**	at SF
May 4, **5**	SD
May 7, 8, **9**	at PIT
May 11, 12, 13	FLA
May **14, 15, 16**	NY
May 17, 18, **19**	at ATL
May 20, 21, 22, **23**	at PHI
May 24, 25, 26	STL
May **28, 29, 30**	at CHI
May **31**, June 1, **2**	at HOU
June 3, 4, 5	CHI
June 7, 8, 9	CIN
June 10, 11, 12, **13**	at STL
June 14, 15, 16	PHI
June 18, 19, **20**	ATL
June 21, 22, **23**	at NY
June 25, 26, **27**	at PHI
June 29, 30, July **1**	PIT
July 2, 3, **4**	LA
July 5, 6, 7	SF
July 8, 9, 10, **11**	SD
July 15, 16, **17, 18**	at LA
July **19, 20, 21**	at SF
July 22, 23, 24, **25**	at SD
July 27, 28, 29	at PIT
July 30, 31, Aug. **1**	FLA
Aug. 2, 3, 4, **5**	NY
Aug. 6, 7, 8	at ATL
Aug. 10, 11, **12**	at PHI
Aug. 13, 14, **15**	STL
Aug. **17, 18**, 19	at CHI
Aug. 20, 21, **22**	at CIN
Aug. 23, 24, **25**	CHI
Aug. 27, 28, 29	HOU
Aug. 30, 31, Sept. **1** at COL
Sept. 3, 4, **5**	at HOU
Sept. **6, 7, 8**	COL
Sept. 10, 11, **12**	CIN
Sept. 14, 15, 16	at STL
Sept. 17, 18, **19**	PHI
Sept. 21, 22, 23	ATL
Sept. 24, 25, **26**	at NY
Sept. 27, 28, 29, 30	at FLA
Oct. 1, 2, 3	PIT

New York

Apr. **5, 7**	COL
Apr. 9, **10, 11**	HOU
Apr. 12, 13, 14, **15**	at COL
Apr. **16, 17, 18**	at CIN
Apr. 20, 21, 22	SF
Apr. 23, **24, 25**	SD
Apr. 26, **27**	LA
Apr. 28, **29**	at SF
Apr. 30, May 1, **2**	at SD
May 4, **5**	at LA
May 7, **8, 9**, 10	FLA
May 11, 12, **13**	at STL
May 14, **15, 16**	at MON
May 17, 18, 19	PIT
May 21, **22, 23**	ATL
May 24, 25, 26	at PHI
May 28, **29, 30**	CIN
May **31**, June 1, **2**	at HOU
June 3, 4, 5, 6	CHI
June 7, 8, 9	CHI
June 10, 11, 12, **13**	at STL
June 14, 15, 16	at ATL
June **17, 18, 19, 20**	at PHI
June 21, 22, **23**	MON
June 25, 26, **27**	at FLA
June 29, 30, July 1	at FLA
July 2, 3, **4**	SF
July 5, 6, 7	SD
July 8, 9, **10, 11**	LA
July 15, 16, **17, 18**	at SF
July 19, 20, **21**	at SD
July 22, **23, 24, 25**	at LA
July 27, **28, 29**	FLA
July 30, 31, Aug. **1**	HOU
Aug. 2, 3, 4, **5**	at MON
Aug. 6, **7, 8**	PIT
Aug. 10, 11, **12**	ATL
Aug. 13, 14, **15**	STL
Aug. **17, 18**, 19	at CHI
Aug. 20, **22**	at COL
Aug. 23, **24, 25**	COL
Aug. 26, 27, 28, **29**	COL
Aug. 30, 31, Sept. **1**	HOU
Sept. 2, **3, 4, 5**	at CHI
Sept. 6, **7, 8**	at HOU
Sept. 10, 11, **12**	CHI
Sept. 14, 15, 16	STL
Sept. 17, 18, 19	at ATL
Sept. 21, 22, 23	PHI
Sept. 24, 25, **26**	MON
Sept. 27, 28, 29, 30	STL
Oct. 1, 2, **3**	at FLA

Philadelphia

Apr. 5, 6, 7	at HOU
Apr. **9**, 10, **11**	CHI
Apr. 12, 13, 14	SD
Apr. **16, 17, 18**	at CHI
Apr. 20, 21, 22	SD
Apr. 23, **24, 25**	LA
Apr. 26, **27**	SF
Apr. 28, **29**	at SD
Apr. 30, May 1, 2	at LA
May 4, **5**	at SF
May 7, **8, 9**, 10	STL
May 10, **11, 12**	PIT
May 14, **15, 16**	ATL
May 17, 18, 19	at FLA
May 20, 21, 22, **23**	MON
May 24, 25, 26	NY
May **28, 29, 30**	at COL
May **31**, June 1, 2	at ATL
June 4, 5, **6**	COL
June 7, 8, 9	HOU
June 10, 11, 12, **13**	at FLA
June 14, 15, 16	at MON
June **17, 18, 19**	FLA
June 21, 22, **23**	ATL
June 25, 26, **27**	MON
June 28, 29, 30 July**1**	at STL
July 2, 3, **4, 5**	SD
July 6, 7, 8	LA
July 8, 9, **10, 11**	SF
July 15, **16, 17, 18**	at ATL
July 19, 20, 21	at LA
July **22, 23, 24, 25**	at SF
July 27, **28, 29**	STL
July 30, 31, Aug. **1**	PIT
Aug. 3, 4, 5	ATL
Aug. 6, **7, 8**	at FLA
Aug. 10, 11, **12**	MON
Aug. **13, 14, 15**	FLA
Aug. 17, 18, **19**	SF
Aug. 20, 21, **22**	at HOU
Aug. 23, 24, **25**	at COL
Aug. 27, 28, 29	CIN
Aug. 30, 31, Sept. **1** at HOU
Sept. 3, 4, **5**	at CIN
Sept. 6, 7, 8	CHI
Sept. 10, 11, **12**	HOU
Sept. 13, 14, 15	at FLA
Sept. 17, 18, **19**	at MON
Sept. 20, 21, 22	FLA
Sept. 24, 25, **26**	ATL
Sept. 27, 28, 29, 30	at PIT
Oct. 1, 2, **3**	at STL

Pittsburgh

Apr. 6, **8**	SD
Apr. **9, 10, 11**	SF
Apr. 12, 13, 14, **15**	at SD
Apr. 16, 17, 18	at LA
Apr. 20, 21, 22	CIN
Apr. 23, 24, 25	HOU
Apr. 26, **27**	at ATL
Apr. 28, 29	at CIN
Apr. 30, May 1, **2**	at HOU
May 4, **5**	ATL
May **7, 8, 9**	MON
May 10, 11, 12	at PHI
May **14, 15, 16**	at CHI
May 17, 18, 19	at NY
May 21, 22, **23**	STL
May **25, 26**, 27	FLA
May **28, 29, 30**	LA
May **31**, June 1, 2	at COL
June 3, 4, **5, 6**	COL
June 8, 9	COL
June 10, 11, 12, **13**	at FLA
June 14, 15, **16**	STL
June **17, 18, 19, 20**	FLA
June **21**, 22, 23	CHI
June 25, 26, **27**	at STL
June 28,29,30,July**1**at MON
July 2, 3, **4, 5**	at CIN
July 6, **7, 8**	at HOU
July **9**, 10, **11**	CIN
July 15, 16, **17, 18**	at ATL
July 19, 20, 21	HOU
July 22, **23, 24, 25**	at ATL
July 27, **28, 29**	MON
July 30, 31, Aug. **1**	at PHI
Aug. **2, 3, 4, 5**	at CHI
Aug. 6, **7, 8**	at NY
Aug. 9, 10, 11, 12	SD
Aug. **13, 14, 15**	FLA
Aug. 17, 18, **19**	SF
Aug. 20, **22**	at SD
Aug. 23, 24, 25	at LA
Aug. 27, 28, 29	SD
Aug. 31, Sept. 1, 2	at LA
Sept. 3, 4, 5	at COL
Sept. **6, 7**	SF
Sept. 9, 10, 11, **12**	COL
Sept. 14, 15, 16	at FLA
Sept. 17, 18, **19**	at STL
Sept. 20, 21, 22	NY
Sept. 24, 25, 26	CHI
Sept. 27, 28, 29, 30	PHI
Oct. 1, 2, **3**	at MON

St. Louis

Apr. 6, 7, **8**	SF
Apr. 9, 10, 11	CIN
Apr. 12, 13, 14	at LA
Apr. 16, 17, 18	at SD
Apr. 20, 21, 22	COL
Apr. 23, 24, 25	ATL
Apr. 26, 27	at HOU
Apr. 28, **29**	at COL
Apr. 30, May **1, 2**	at ATL
May 4, 5	HOU
May 7, 8, 9	at PHI
May 10, 11, 12, **13**	NY
May 14, 15, **16**	FLA
May 18, 19	CIN
May 21, 22, **23**	at PIT
May 24, 25, 26	at MON
May **28, 29, 30**	SD
May **31**, June 1, 2	LA
June 3, 4, 5, 6	at CIN
June **8, 9**	at SF
June 10, 11, 12, **13**	MON
June 14, 15, **16**	PIT
June **17, 18, 19, 20**	at CHI
June 21, 22, 23	at FLA
June 25, 26, **27**	FLA
June 28, 29, 30, July **1**	PHI
July 2, 3, **4, 5**	at HOU
July 6, 7, 8	ATL
July **9**, 10, **11**	COL
July 15, 16, **17, 18**	HOU
July 19, 20, 21	at ATL
July 22, 23, 24, **25**	at COL
July 27, **28, 29**	at PHI
July 30, 31, Aug. **1**	NY
Aug. 2, 3, 4, 5	FLA
Aug. 6, **7, 8**	CHI
Aug. 9, 10, 11, 12	at PIT
Aug. 13, 14, **15**	at MON
Aug. 17, 18, **19**	SD
Aug. 20, 21, **22**	LA
Aug. 23, 24, 25	at SD
Aug. 27, 28, 29	at LA
Aug. 30, 31, Sept. 1	PIT
Sept. 3, 4, 5	SF
Sept. 7, 8	at CIN
Sept. 10, 11, **12**	at SF
Sept. 14, 15, 16	MON
Sept. 17, 18, **19**	PIT
Sept. 20, 21, 22	at CHI
Sept. 24, 25, 26	at FLA
Sept. 27, 28, 29, 30	at NY
Oct. 1, 2, **3**	PHI

Western Division

Atlanta

Apr. **5, 6, 7**	at CHI
Apr. 8, 9, 10, **11**	at CIN
Apr. 12, 13, 14	CHI
Apr. **15**, 16, **17, 18**	at SF
Apr. 20, 21, **22**	at FLA
Apr. 23, 24, **25**	at STL
Apr. 26, 27	PIT
Apr. 28, 29	FLA
Apr. 30, May **1, 2**	STL
May 4, 5	at PIT
May 6, 7, **8, 9**	at SD
May 10, 11, 12	at HOU
May 14, 15, **16**	PHI
May 17, 18, 19	MON
May 21, **22, 23**	at NY
May 25, 26, 27	at CIN
May **28, 29, 30**	SF
May **31**, June 1, 2, **3**	PHI
June 4, 5, **6**	at LA
June 7	at SF
June 10, 11, 12, **13**	CIN
June 14, 15, 16	NY
June 18, 19, **20**	at MON
June 21, 22, **23**	at PHI
June 25, 26, 27	HOU
June 29, 30, July 1	COL
July 2, 3, **4, 5**	FLA
July 6, 7, 8	at STL
July **9**, 10, 11	at COL
July 15, 16, 17, **18**	PIT
July 19, 20, 21	at NY
July 22, 23, 24, **25**	PIT
July 26, 27, 28	at COL
July 29,30,**31**,Aug.**1**at HOU
Aug. 3, 4, 5	PHI
Aug. 6, 7, 8	MON
Aug. 10, 11, 12	at NY
Aug. 13, 14, 15	at CIN
Aug. 17, 18, 19	LA
Aug. **20, 21**, 22	at CHI
Aug. 23, **24, 25**	at SF
Aug. 27, **28, 29**	CHI
Aug. 31, Sept. 1, 2	SF
Sept. 3, 4, **5**	SD
Sept. 6, **7, 8**	at LA
Sept. 9, 10, 11, **12**	at SD
Sept. 14, 15, 16	LA
Sept. 17, 18, 19	NY
Sept. 21, 22, 23	at MON
Sept. 24, 25, **26**	at PHI
Sept. 28, 29 30	HOU
Oct. 1, 2, **3**	COL

Cincinnati

Apr. **5, 7, 8**	MON
Apr. 9, 10, **11**	at STL
Apr. 12, 13, 14	at PHI
Apr. **16, 17, 18**	NY
Apr. 20, 21, 22	at PIT
Apr. **23, 24, 25**	at CHI
Apr. 26, **27**	FLA
Apr. 28, 29	PIT
Apr. 30, May **1, 2**	CHI
May 4, 5	at FLA
May **6, 7, 8, 9**	at HOU
May 10, 11, 12	SD
May 14, 15, **16**	COL
May 17, 18, 19	at LA
May **20**, 21, 22, **23**	at SF
May 25, 26, 27	ATL
May **28, 29, 30**	at NY
May **31**, June 1, 2	PHI
June 3, 4, 5, **6**	STL
June 7, 8, **9**	at MON
June 10, 11, 12, **13**	at ATL
June 15, 16, **17**	SF
June 18, 19, **20**	LA
June 21, 22, 23	at COL
June **24, 25, 26, 27**	at SF
June 29, 30, July 1	HOU
July 2, 3, **4, 5**	PIT
July 6, **7, 8**	at CHI
July **9**, 10, 11	at PIT
July 15, 16, 17, **18**	FLA
July 19, 20, 21	CHI
July 22, 23, 24, 25	at FLA
July 26, 27, 28	at HOU
July 30, **31**, Aug. **1**	SD
Aug. 2, 3, 4	COL
Aug. 6, **7, 8**	at SD
Aug. **9, 10, 11**	at SF
Aug. 13, 14, 15	ATL
Aug. 16, 17, 18	NY
Aug. 20, 21, **22**	MON
Aug. 23, **24, 25**	at NY
Aug. 27, **28, 29**	at PHI
Aug. 30, 31, Sept. 1	at STL
Sept. 3, 4, **5**	PHI
Sept. 7, 8	STL
Sept. 10, 11, **12**	at MON
Sept. 13, 14, 15, **16**	at ATL
Sept. 17, 18, **19**	SF
Sept. 20, 21, 22, **23**	LA
Sept. 24, **25, 26**	at COL
Sept. 28, 29	at SD
Oct. 1, **2, 3**	HOU

Colorado

Apr. **5, 7**	at NY
Apr. **9, 10, 11**	MON
Apr. 12, 13, 14, **15**	NY
Apr. 16, **17, 18**	at MON
Apr. 20, 21, 22	at STL
Apr. 23, **24, 25**	FLA
Apr. 26, 27	CHI
Apr. 28, **29**	STL
Apr. 30, May 1, 2	at FLA
May 4, **5**	at CHI
May 6, 7, **8, 9**	ATL
May 14, 15, **16**	at CIN
May 17, 18, 19, 20	at SD
May 21, 22, **23**	at LA
May 25, 26, 27	at HOU
May 28, **29, 30**	PHI
May **31**, June 1, 2	PIT
June 4, 5, **6**	at PHI
June 8, 9	at PIT
June 11, 12, **13**	HOU
June 14, 15, 16	SD
June 18, 19, **20**	SD
June 21, 22, **23**	CIN
June **24, 25, 26, 27**	SF
June 29, 30, July 1	at ATL
July 2, 3, **4, 5**	CHI
July 6, **7, 8**	FLA
July **9**, 10, **11**	at STL
July 15, **16, 17, 18**	at CHI
July 19, 20, 21	at FLA
July 22, 23, 24, **25**	STL
July 26, 27, 28	ATL
July 30, 31, Aug. **1**	at SF
Aug. 2, 3, 4, **5**	at CIN
Aug. 6, **8**	at SD
Aug. 9, 10, 11, **12**	at LA
Aug. 13, **14, 15**, 16	HOU
Aug. 17, 18, **19**	PHI
Aug. 20, **22**	NY
Aug. 23, 24, 25	PHI
Aug. 26, 27, 28, **29**	at NY
Aug. 30, 31, Sept. 1	MON
Sept. 3, 4, **5**	PIT
Sept. **6, 7, 8**	at MON
Sept. 9, 10, 11, **12**	at PIT
Sept. 13, 14, 15, **16**	HOU
Sept. 17, 18, 19	LA
Sept. 20, 21, 22, **23**	SD
Sept. 24, 25, 26	CIN
Sept. 28, 29, 30	at SF
Oct. 1, 2, **3**	at ATL

Houston

Apr. 5, 6, 7	PHI
Apr. **9, 10, 11**	at NY
Apr. **13, 14, 15**	at MON
Apr. 16, 17, **18**	FLA
Apr. 20, 21, 22	at CHI
Apr. 23, 24, **25**	at PIT
Apr. 26, 27	STL
Apr. 28, **29**	CHI
Apr. 30, May 1, 2	PIT
May 4, 5	at STL
May 7, **8, 9**	at CIN
May 10, 11, 12	ATL
May **17**, 18, **19**	at SF
May 21, 22, **23**	at SD
May 25, 26, 27	COL
May **28, 29, 30**	at FLA
May **31**, June 1, 2	NY
June 4, 5, **6**	NY
June 7, 8, **9**	at PHI
June 11, 12, **13**	at COL
June 14, 15, 16	LA
June 18, 19, **20**	SF
June 21, 22, 23, **24**	at LA
June **24, 25, 26, 27**	at SF
June 29, 30, July 1	at CIN
July 2, 3, **4, 5**	STL
July 6, 7, 8	PIT
July **9**, 10, **11**	at STL
July 15, 16, **17, 18**	at STL
July 19, 20, 21	PIT
July 22, 23, **24, 25**	CHI
July 26, 27, 28	CIN
July 30, 31, Aug. **1**	at NY
Aug. 3, 4, **5**	LA
Aug. 6, 7, **8**	SF
Aug. 9, 10, 11, **12**	at SD
Aug. 13, 14, 15	at COL
Aug. 17, 18, 19	FLA
Aug. 20, 21	PHI
Aug. 24, 25, **26**	at FLA
Aug. 27, 28, 29	at MON
Aug. 30, 31, Sept. **1**	at NY
Sept. 3, 4, **5**	MON
Sept. 6, 7, 8	NY
Sept. 10, 11, **12**	at PHI
Sept. 13, 14, 15, **16**	at COL
Sept. 17, 18, **19**	SD
Sept. 20, 21, 22, 23	SF
Sept. 24, **25, 26**	at LA
Sept. 27, 28, 29	at ATL
Oct. 1, 2, **3**	at CIN

Los Angeles

Apr. **5, 6, 7**	at FLA
Apr. 8, 9, 10, **11**	at ATL
Apr. **13**, 14, 15	STL
Apr. 16, 17, **18**	PIT
Apr. 20, 21, 22	at MON
Apr. 23, 24, 25	at PHI
Apr. 26, **27**	at NY
Apr. 28, 29	MON
Apr. 30, May 1, 2	PHI
May 4, 5	NY
May **7, 8, 9**	at SF
May 10, **11, 12**	at CHI
May **14, 15, 16**	at HOU
May 17, 18, 19	CIN
May 21, 22, 23	COL
May 24, 25, 26	SD
May **28, 29, 30**	at PIT
May **31**, June 1, 2	at STL
June 4, 5, **6**	ATL
June 7, 8	FLA
June **10**, 11, 12, **13**	at SD
June 14, 15, 16	at HOU
June 18, 19, **20**	at CIN
June 21, 22, 23, **24**	HOU
June **24, 25, 26, 27**	CHI
June 28, 29, 30	SF
July 2, 3, **4**	at MON
July 5, 6, 7	at PHI
July 8, 9, **10, 11**	at NY
July 15, 16, 17, **18**	MON
July 19, 20, 21	PHI
July 22, 23, 24, **25**	NY
July 26, **27, 28**	at SF
July 30, 31, Aug. **1**	at CHI
Aug. 3, 4, **5**	at HOU
Aug. 6, 7, **8**	CIN
Aug. 9, 10, 11, **12**	COL
Aug. 13, 14, 15	SD
Aug. 17, 18, 19	at ATL
Aug. 20, 21, **22**	at STL
Aug. 23, 24, 25	PIT
Aug. 27, 28, 29	STL
Aug. 31, Sept. 1, 2	PIT
Sept. 3, 4, **5**	at FLA
Sept. 6, **7, 8**	ATL
Sept. 9, 10, 11, **12**	FLA
Sept. 14, 15, 16	at ATL
Sept. 17, 18, 19	at COL
Sept. 20, 21, 22, **23**	at CIN
Sept. 24, **25, 26**	HOU
Sept. 27, 28, 29	CHI
Sept. 30, Oct. 1, **2, 3**	SF

San Diego

Apr. 6, **8**	at PIT
Apr. 9, 10, **11**	at FLA
Apr. 12, 13, 14, **15**	PIT
Apr. 16, **17, 18**	STL
Apr. 20, 21, 22	at PHI
Apr. 23, **24, 25**	at NY
Apr. 26, **27**	MON
Apr. 28, **29**	PHI
Apr. 30, May 1, **2**	NY
May 4, 5	at MON
May **7, 8, 9**	at CHI
May 10, 11, 12	at CIN
May 14, 15, 16	SF
May 17, 18, 19, **20**	COL
May 21, 22, **23**	HOU
May 24, 25, 26	at LA
May **28, 29, 30**	at STL
May **31**, June 1, **2, 3**	at ATL
June 4, 5, **6**	FLA
June 7	FLA
June **10**, 11, 12, **13**	LA
June 15, 16, 17	at HOU
June 18, 19, **20**	at COL
June 21, 22, **23**	at SF
June 24, 25, 26, **27**	CIN
June 28, 29, 30	CHI
July 2, 3, **4, 5**	at PHI
July 5, 6, **7**	at NY
July 8, 9, **10, 11**	at MON
July **15**, 16, 17, **18**	MON
July 19, 20, **21**	NY
July 22, 23, 24, **25**	MON
July 26, **27, 28**	at CHI
July 30, **31**, Aug. **1**	at CIN
Aug. 3, 4, 5	SF
Aug. 6, **8**	COL
Aug. 9, 10, 11, **12**	HOU
Aug. 13, 14, **15**	at LA
Aug. 17, 18, **19**	at STL
Aug. 20, **22**	PIT
Aug. 23, 24, 25	STL
Aug. 27, 28, 29	at PIT
Aug. 31, Sept. 1, 2	at FLA
Sept. 3, 4, **5**	at ATL
Sept. 6, **7, 8**	FLA
Sept. 9, 10, 11, **12**	ATL
Sept. 14, 15	at SF
Sept. 17, 18, **19**	at HOU
Sept. 20, 21, 22, **23**	at COL
Sept. 24, **25, 26**, 27	SF
Sept. 28, 29	CIN
Sept. 30, Oct. 1, **2, 3**	SF

San Francisco

Apr. 6, 7, **8**	at STL
Apr. **9**, 10, **11**	at PIT
Apr. **12, 13, 14**	FLA
Apr. **15**, 16, **17, 18**	ATL
Apr. 20, 21, 22	at NY
Apr. 23, **24, 25**	at MON
Apr. 26, **27**	at PHI
Apr. 28, **29**	NY
Apr. 30, May 1, **2**	MON
May 4, **5**	PHI
May 7, **8, 9**	LA
May 10, 11, 12, **13**	at COL
May **17**, 18, 19	HOU
May **20**, 21, 22, **23**	CIN
May 24, 25, 26	at CHI
May **28, 29, 30**	at ATL
May **31**, June 1, 2	at FLA
June 3, 4, **5, 6**	PIT
June 7	STL
June 11, **12, 13**	CHI
June 15, 16, **17**	at CIN
June 18, 19, 20	at HOU
June **21**, 22, 23	SD
June **24, 25, 26, 27**	COL
June 29, 30	at LA
July 2, 3, **4**	at NY
July 5, 6, **7**	at MON
July 8, 9, **10, 11**	at PHI
July 15, 16, **17, 18**	NY
July **19, 20, 21**	MON
July 22, 23, 24, 25	PHI
July 26, **27, 28**	LA
July 30, 31, Aug. **1**	at SD
Aug. 3, 4, 5	at SD
Aug. 6, 7, **8**	at HOU
Aug. **9, 10, 11**	CIN
Aug. **13, 14, 15**	at CHI
Aug. 17, 18, **19**	at PIT
Aug. 20, 21, **22**	FLA
Aug. 23, **24, 25**	ATL
Aug. 27, 28, 29	at FLA
Aug. 31, Sept. 1, 2	at ATL
Sept. 3, 4, **5**	at STL
Sept. **6, 7**	PIT
Sept. 9, 10, **11, 12**	STL
Sept. 13, 14, **15**	CHI
Sept. 17, 18, **19**	at CIN
Sept. 20, 21, 22, 23	at HOU
Sept. 24, **25, 26**, 27	SD
Sept. **29**	COL
Sept. 30, Oct. 1, **2, 3** at LA